The Ultimate Lark

The Ultimate Lark

In Search of Epicurean Adventure

by Jim Lark
with Mary Lark

Illustrations by Doug Parrish

Momentum Books, Ltd.
Troy, Michigan

Edited by Frank DePirro

Manufactured in the United States of America

1999 1998 1997 1996   5 4 3 2 1

Momentum Books, Ltd.
6964 Crooks Road, Suite 1
Troy, Michigan 48098
USA

Lark, Jim, 1930–
    The ultimate Lark : in search of epicurean adventure / by Jim
Lark.
        p. cm.
    ISBN 1-879094-49-5 (alk. paper)
    1. Restaurateurs--United States--Biography. 2. Voyages and
travels. 3. Lark, Jim, 1930–   . 4. Lark (Restaurant) I. Title.
TX910.5.L365A3 1996
647.95' 092--dc20
    [B]   96-41204

"If a restaurant will be honest about a few things, it can outlive any rival with a long, pretentious menu."

—M. F. K. Fisher, the dean of American food writers

To Mary with love

Touring Guide

Contents

*T*his book would not have been written without the encouragement of Bill Haney and Bob Talbert for which I am more grateful than I can express. The Lark would not have survived and prospered without Bob's support over more than 15 years as well as that of Len Barnes, Evelyn Cairns, Sandra Silfven, Keely Wygonik, David E. Davis Jr., Jim Harrison and most especially the good patrons of The Lark who made all the work worthwhile. We have been blessed with one of the finest chefs in America and in the world—Marcus Haight—and I thank God that Marcus is The Lark's Chef de Cuisine. Thanks also to Kyle Scott and Frank DePirro for their help and to all the dedicated staff of The Lark. Finally, there would be no Lark and no book without Mary. Our children Adrian, Jarratt, Eric, Kurt and James II also helped The Lark in many ways, especially with quality control.

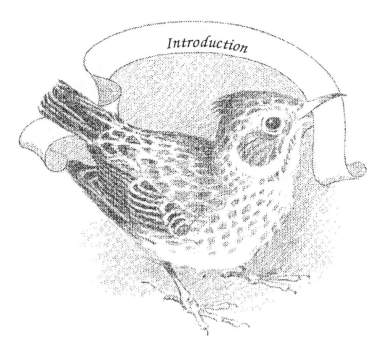

*M*ary and I opened The Lark, the restaurant of our dreams, fifteen years ago in West Bloomfield. Mary was an award-winning potter. I was an attorney and real estate developer. Neither of us had any experience in the restaurant business. In chatting with the more than two hundred thousand patrons who have since come to The Lark, we have been asked one question over and over: "Why did you decide to open your own restaurant?" The joking-but-almost-true response of many new restaurateurs to this query is "temporary insanity," but our guests are not satisfied with the evasion. Mary and I opened The Lark for what we believe were the right reasons: an overwhelming interest in food, a need to perform as perfect hosts, and a hope to create magic.

Eating out at a family restaurant or fast-food outlet is just that—eating. At a tablecloth establishment, the meal becomes dining. At a very few restaurants, ambience, service, and food form a magical event. We had shared this experience on rare occasions, at Rouxinol in the mountains of southern Portugal, at Hacienda east of Marbella,

Spain, at Castelets on St. Barts. Although many of our favorite restaurants are in cities, the magical settings were all country inns, and all were small. They were rustic in an elegant way, had wonderful food that was never fussy or elaborate, and perfect service by a cheerful wait-staff in black tie. Our goal became to bring all of these elements together in Michigan.

We hesitated, reluctant to take the plunge, but finally came to agree with the final words of Daniel Miller in his book, *Starting a Small Restaurant:* "There are no guarantees in the restaurant business or in life. The only true security is in doing your best at whatever you choose to do. This real adventure is always at a risk. Are you alive? Go on, open your restaurant. To say 'I once thought about opening a restaurant' doesn't count."

The early days were torture. While other restaurants opened to great applause and then faded, the acclaim that has come to The Lark is especially sweet because it was earned the hard way. By 1984 the readers of *Metropolitan Detroit* magazine had voted The Lark Detroit's best continental restaurant. Beginning in 1985, it was yearly voted the town's best restaurant overall. Several chefs came and left, but patrons discovered that The Lark just kept getting better, especially after the arrival of Chef de Cuisine Marcus Haight, Michigan's only fully French-trained chef. Founding America's first monthly restaurant newsletter and theme dinners, begun in October 1981, boosted sales and added more loyal fans. In a field where 99 percent merely copy or clone, innovation followed innovation. These efforts received increasing notice and appreciation from the dining public and imitation by other restaurants. A scroll in our vestibule summarizes some of the more important honors received by The Lark over the years. This was capped last year when The Lark was named the best restaurant in America in the Condé Nast *Traveler* magazine "Readers' Poll."

It is especially gratifying to be so honored by the readers of a prestigious travel magazine. Mary and I have found that whatever makes one explore the globe, also leads one to fine restaurants. Call it "lust for life." We love to fly away as often as our consciences permit. A catalyst who cranked up our globe trotting was Harris Machus, founder of the Machus group of restaurants.

While dining at The Lark one evening, Harris said to me, "Jim, you know by now this is a very demanding business, and you have to get away from it to refresh yourself. You and Mary should take at least one vacation each month." Astounded, I replied in disbelief, "Once a month?" Harris insisted, "Once a month." We didn't need much encouragement, and began trying to meet the goal set for us by Harris Machus. A few years later, I was at an industry wine tasting. Several Machus restaurant executives were present and I told them what their boss had recommended to me, and that Mary and I were attempting to comply. They responded, "Mr. Machus never did that. He hardly gets away at all." Nonetheless, we gladly follow Harris's good advice.

Mary and I are most grateful to patrons of The Lark for supporting our efforts to create a truly world-class restaurant. With us, fine dining, traveling, and improving The Lark are an unceasing, integrated adventure of love. I hope you will enjoy the adventure of reading *The Ultimate Lark*. The book takes you with us on some of our enjoyable dining and travel experiences around the world and shares our insights on wine, food, and the disciplines involved in running a fine restaurant. *Bon appétit et bon voyage!*

—Jim Lark

Europe, Africa, and Asia

Barcelona and the Costa Brava

*I*t's fun to be ahead of the crowd. We explored China when it reopened in 1978. We fished for marlin in the 1960s off Baja when the only access to Cabo San Lucas was by small plane to a dirt air strip. And we dined at San Domenico in Imola years before the opening of its New York branch. Mary and I thought of those adventures when we decided to make a fall 1991 trip to Barcelona, which was then preparing for the 1992 Olympic Games.

Barcelona is the capital of Catalonia and Spain's second-largest city. It was bursting with pride as host of the Twenty-fifth Olympiad. *European Travel & Life* proclaimed, "Barcelona is certain that its street life is friskier, its fashions gaudier, its girls prettier, its culture livelier, and its night life saucier than anywhere else in Europe."

Our base was the Hotel Ritz, which has a central location and impressive lounge, bar, and dining room. Also, the concierge and his assistant were especially helpful. But service, in general, and room furnishings were not on a par with Ritz Hotels in either Madrid or Lisbon. Our room (part of the Royal Suite) had no comfortable

3

chairs, and a morning paper and evening candy were provided only one day out of three.

Many major hotels in this largest of Mediterranean cities were renovated in preparation for the Olympics, and twelve new hotels were at various stages of construction. Most of the new hotels, such as the Hilton, are removed from the city's center and are closer to the Olympic facilities near Montjuic and the port.

The importance of Barcelona's Olympic selection is the renaissance it created, making the finest Mediterranean city even more enjoyable. Where once were slums are now Olympic villages. New roads and tunnels make travel much easier and old facades have been cleaned. The long-ignored waterfront has been rediscovered and restaurants burst with vitality.

After checking into the Ritz, we lost no time checking out the scene at Reno *(ray-no),* the long-established, clubby dean of local fine restaurants. Ensconced in leather booth number 1, we enjoyed a fine lunch whose highlights were a dish of seasonal wild mushrooms and *crema* Catalana *(crème brûlée),* which was done on a flat plate to increase surface area and deliver as much delicious crunch as possible. We confidently ordered the Marqués do Alella Chardonnay, as it also graces our own reserve wine list.

We had not been in Barcelona since 1963, so we treated it as a new destination and oriented ourselves the next morning with a limousine tour. Our driver, highly recommended by the Ritz's concierge, was Miguel Regol I Font of the International Limousine System. He has chauffeured presidents and was simply perfect, showing us this city's great variety of attractions as well as the Olympic facilities.

In addition to having been the most important of four sites for Olympic events, Montjuic (Mountain of Jews—the old Jewish quarter) has several other attractions including the Joán Miró Museum and the Archeological Museum. Unfortunately, our timing was unbelievably bad, because the Museum of Catalonian Art was closed for repairs.

The Ramblas is the most famous street in Barcelona, and one of our few memories from 1963, a zigzagging boulevard atop a former river bed bordering the Gothic Quarter. Both the Ramblas and Barrio Gótico have a host of shops, cafés, and restaurants in addition to buildings from the thirteenth to fifteenth century. Most impressive are the cathedral and Frederic Mares Museum.

When in Spain, we enjoy our principal meal as the Spaniards do, at what passes for midday, 3 P.M. in Madrid, 2 P.M. in Barcelona. Today's destination, Vio Veneto, is considered by many to be the city's top restaurant. It is classical, like Reno, but a bit more with-it despite a wonderful Art Deco ambience with huge oval wood-framed, leaded-glass interior windows.

Most guests were well-turned out, although as almost everywhere in Europe today, some wore Eurotrash. There is no longer a dress code on the Continent, but anyone dressed in blue jeans will be treated less graciously than well-dressed diners.

Our luncheon was uniformly excellent and included complimentary sweet and nutty air-cured ham, duck pâté in a plate of aspic, clams with thin potatoes in a Spanish green sauce, peppery pressed duck (shades of Tour d'Argent), veal sweetbreads and kidneys, tea sorbet with blackberry sauce, and a Grand Marnier soufflé. Wines were a 1985 Rioja and a Torres Gran Vina Sol.

After lunch, we enjoyed visiting some of the city's fine architectural sites and art museums. Barcelona has had a love affair with the arts since Roman times, and it is impossible to consider the city outside of this context. At the turn of the century, Barcelona fostered Modernismo, whose milder form became known as Art Nouveau. Picasso, Miró, Dali, and the architect Gaudi were all luminaries in Barcelona's art world.

Undoubtedly, the most famous building in Barcelona is the Church of the Sacred Family, begun by Gaudi in 1884 and incomplete when he was killed by a tram in 1924. Supported solely by private donations, construction recommenced in 1950 and continues. The 350-foot spires of the Twelve Apostles, bottle shaped and topped by pink ceramics, dominate the city.

Almost as amazing a sight is the block between the streets Aragon and Consejo de Ciento on the magnificent Paseo de Gracia Boulevard. Here are flamboyant buildings, not only by Gaudi, but also by his contemporaries, Domenech y Montaner and Puig y Cadafalch.

In addition to the museums mentioned previously, we enjoyed the Picasso Museum housed in the fourteenth-century Aguilar Palace. But perhaps the finest single local art collection is Baron Tyssen's, housed in the Museum of the Royal Monastery of St. Maria de Pedralbes where a few remaining cloistered nuns still reside.

Mary and I typically have our evening meal in Spain at tapa bars. Tapas, the small hot and cold dishes served in an informal atmosphere, are accompanied by either Fino Sherry, vino tinto (red wine), or small glasses of beer—never hard liquor. Food and travel writers imply that tapa bars are ubiquitous in Spain, but that is not true. We could not find even one in Galicia or Asturias in northwest Spain. Seville, and most especially Madrid, are blessed with wonderful tapas. Barcelona has some tapa bars, but not many.

We enjoyed La Flauta on Aribau between Diputacio and Consell de Cent. As implied by this restaurant's name, the specialties were long, thin, flute-shaped sandwiches on excellent French-style bread about two and one-half inches wide and sixteen inches long, for a full sandwich, or eight inches for a half. The best fillings are air-dried hams, salamis, and local cheeses on bread brushed with fresh Catalan tomato and olive oil spread. The next night we chose the more upscale José Luis at Diagonal 52, which offered a greater array of hot tapas including squid, oysters, and clams as well as small chicken, pork, and veal cutlets.

Mary and I are dedicated market freaks and revel in local markets whenever possible in our travels. Barcelona's La Bouqueria, adjacent to the Ramblas near the Gothic Quarter, is one of the world's greatest food markets, taking full advantage of the city's bountiful sea on one side and fields and forests on the other.

This 150-year-old, square-block, covered market is open from 8 A.M. to 3 P.M. and from 6 P.M. to 8 P.M., with early morning most exciting as elaborate and colorful displays are set up at hundreds of stands.

Produce includes a great variety of wild mushrooms from the nearby Pyrenees Mountains, dates and figs from Andalusia, local melons and artichokes, many different kinds of olives and grapes, and a much greater variety of other fruits and vegetables than can ever be seen in our country. Meats and poultry also include items rarely if ever found in the United States, such as suckling pigs, game birds, and many kinds of Catalan sausage.

The fish stalls, however, are the high point. The favorite fish of Iberia, bacalao, or dried salt cod, has its own area with an amazing variety of styles. In this fastidiously clean market, other seafood is artistically arranged on shaved ice: tuna, swordfish, hake, flounder, dorado, eels, red mullet, moray eel, sole, octopus, squid, shrimp, different kinds of lobster, crayfish, salt- and fresh-water crabs, clams, oysters, mussels, snails, and even jellyfish.

On the second aisle to the right after entering the market is Pinocho, a food stand with ten bar stools. Its proprietor is so outgoing that he has captured the attention of food and travel writers from all over the world who recommend enjoying a freshly cooked breakfast or snack here.

Respected food writer Patricia Wells says if she could only have two or three meals in Barcelona, one would be at Eldorado Petit, a mansion in a fashionable residential area north of the city. We chose it for our final midday meal in Barcelona. The original Eldorado Petit, still going strong at St. Feliu de Guíxols on the Costa Brava, is credited by some with beginning the trend to lightened and updated Catalan cuisine. In addition to these two locations, a third branch has now opened in Manhattan.

Because they are usually done so poorly, like most Nouvelle Cuisine, Mary and I are not partial to green salads that include seafood or meat. But here, we had the best salad of our lives, impeccably fresh lobster and very thin orange slices over mache and other perfect greens with a citrus essence.

Next came a classic of Catalan cuisine—*fedeus*—a unique pasta dish composed of two-inch lengths of vermicelli, fried golden crisp, then simmered in fish stock until less than al dente and finished with olive oil and garlic. As lovers of garlic and seafood, Mary and I devoured this creation.

Our main course was the famous local fish preparation, dorado, or *daurada à la sal*. Our closest equivalent to this firm, white-fleshed fish is probably red snapper. A whole fish of a bit more than a pound was baked under a salt crust to serve two, the fish presented, the salt crust and the skin removed, and the fish divided for two and served warm, not hot, with a light sauce. The result was similar to but better than oriental steamed fish, every bit as delicate, but firmer and not soft and overly moist.

The Penedes wine region near Barcelona is the source of almost all of Spain's *cavas* or *espumoso*, sparkling or Champagne-style wines. Many other table wines are also produced, the best of which are from Bodegas Torres, which picked us up by car for a visit after our last lunch in Barcelona. Torres is most famous for its flowery, part-Chardonnay Vina Sol and Gran Vina Sol and its reds, Coronas, Gran Coronas, and Coronas Black Label (Cabernet), which is always found on our reserve list. In addition to its pre-eminent position in Spain, Torres now has wineries in California and Chile. Marimar Torres, who lives in California, has produced a fine cookbook, *Exceptional Recipes from the Torres Family.*

Those visiting Barcelona should set aside some time to enjoy the nearby Costa Brava, which although not totally unspoiled, is less congested than the Costa del Sol. Brava means wild and this is a rugged, rocky coast with many inlets as well as broad beaches.

Highlights of the Costa Brava, in addition to beach resorts themselves, include good restaurants such as Sa Punta at Platja de Pals, Big Rock at Palamos, the aforementioned original Eldorado Petit at St. Feliu de Guíxols, Can Toni at the same town, and Els Tinars at Llagostera. Other attractions are ceramics at La Bisbal (where we purchased dinner favors for a Barcelona dinner at the Lark), archaeological sites at Empures and Ullastret, and the largest collection of Salvador Dali art in Spain at the Muséo Dali in Figueres. Dali laid out the museum himself, and it is tremendous fun. Of the many charming seaside towns, the art colony of Cadaqués was most favored by Dali and is an action town, often called the St. Tropez of Spain.

Having had more than enough action, we stayed not at Cadaqués but at the most impressive resort hotel of the Costa Brava, the five-star Hostel de la Gavina at S'Agaro. We had been reading rave reviews of this extraordinary establishment for years and long looked forward to our stay. King Juan Carlos, Liz Taylor, Frank Sinatra, and Sylvester Stallone are but a few of its famous guests.

La Gavina (Seagull) has two beaches, tennis, nearby golf, and a fine swimming pool. The whitewashed exterior is dramatic and elegant. Interiors are unrivaled with marble, parquet, tile, oak, walnut, silk walls, and antique furniture and furnishings. Perfection.

La Gavina has as many staff as there are guests and seems more like a luxurious private estate than a hotel or resort. Such attitudes come from the top, in this case the regal owners, Josep and Carmona Ensesa. Señor Ensesa was gracious enough to join us as host at dinner where we especially enjoyed the house foie gras and Atlantic salmon.

We neglected to learn why Big Rock restaurant on the Costa Brava is so named, but the concierge of Hotel Ritz and our limousine driver both recommended it strongly. Shortly after being seated for lunch, we met the gregarious chef-proprietor, Carles Camos, who bought us an apéritif before having his own meal in an adjoining room. Afterwards, he toured the dining room again, finally joining one table of patrons. Seafood was the specialty, and all of our choices were excellent: grilled scampi (lobster, not shrimp), mixed-seafood-stuffed red peppers with a Catalan sauce, clams marinara, and codfish with a garlic sauce. Big Rock, located in a five-hundred-year-old farmhouse with distant views of the sea, is only a fifteen-minute drive from La Gavina.

At Señor Ensesa's suggestion, our other luncheon on the Costa Brava was at Els Tinars, also just a short drive from La Gavina. It was big, bustling, very busy—the decor, rustic Spanish roadhouse. Service here was a problem since only the host took orders, and he was far behind. The food, when it finally arrived, was hearty and good. Mary declared her calamari in a sauce of its own ink the best ever. My starter of twenty small "dry" snails were well seasoned with garlic, paprika, salt, pepper, and oil and were served with toothpicks rather than a small fork. A fine Vina Ardanza Rioja Alta '82 accompanied our main course of oxtails for me and a veal shank with wild mushrooms for Mary.

Spain was the first European country Mary and I visited, and it has been a favorite ever since. Catalonia is unique in that it combines the cosmopolitan attractions of Barcelona, Spain's second-largest city and the most attractive metropolis on the Mediterranean, with the outdoor pleasures of the Costa Brava. Hotel reservations in Barcelona and at La Gavina or other resorts should be made as far in advance as possible.

How to Get the Best Out of a Restaurant

We were interviewed by the restaurant editor of *Food & Wine* magazine for inclusion in his column. In "Dining Advice from Four Insiders," I and three other restaurateurs offered tips on how to get the best out of a restaurant. My comments were as follows:

"I research restaurants. I keep folders organized by city and country. My customers recommend restaurants from their travels, and I put their recommendations in my files, along with newspaper and magazine clippings. I seek out detailed information on the best tables, the best sections of restaurants, specific dishes, and house specialties.

"I have my secretary make the reservation. She can establish a rapport with the person taking the reservation, and she can say things that I can't say. She's wonderful. She might say something like, 'Please give him a good table. Otherwise, he'll be a terrible grouch.'

"In order to be treated well in a restaurant where you're not known, you need a strong take-charge person in the party. When you walk in the door, quickly figure out where the bad tables are, and request the section of the dining room that you want. It's important to do that before you get to an undesirable table. Otherwise, the maître d' has a problem. If you refuse his choice, he loses face. Make it easier for him by requesting the section you want.

"Don't ask a waiter, 'What should I order?' What's he going to say? He's looking for his tip, and he'll likely recommend the most expensive dishes. Instead, I ask the waiter to recommend one of my two choices. 'Should I have this or that?' My wife does the same, and so does everyone in the party. Then we have something to go on.

"I would avoid anything that's not typical of the restaurant. If you're in a restaurant that's noted for a special cuisine, don't order something outside that cuisine. All chefs get bored. They experiment. I don't want to order too many chefs' experiments.

"If you can establish a rapport with your waiter, he or she will guide you. If you can kibitz with the service staff, if you can get a little humor into the situation, they'll become your allies. They know what's good. They know what's bad. If they like you, they won't let you make a mistake. Even in three-star restaurants in France, we found that if you use a little humor with the waiters, captains and maître d's, they'll take your side, not the restaurant's. But if you sit there with a stone face, what can they do to help you?

"There's nothing inherently different between a restaurant situation and any other situation in life. The way you interact with people will determine what you get back. You'll get the best or the worst from the staff, depending upon your attitude. Being objectionable is not going to work.

"I was also a real estate developer. The rule I lived by in real estate is that you can never purchase anything at the right price if you *have* to buy it. If I'm going to a restaurant I don't know, I am always prepared to leave. This happens very rarely. But if it becomes apparent when you walk into a restaurant that they're not going to treat you right, it's better to leave."

11

The Lark's Chocolate Truffles

These truffles are a special favorite of the staff of *Gourmet* magazine who have had a number of private dinners at the Lark.

> *2 pounds very good quality semi-sweet chocolate (do not use chocolate chips)*
>
> *1 cup whipping cream (preferably Guernsey)*
>
> *3 tablespoons liqueur of your choice (raspberry, hazelnut, etc.)*

To make the ganache:

Melt over hot water 1 pound semi-sweet chocolate. As the chocolate melts, scald the whipping cream. Pour hot cream over chocolate and stir until melted and smooth. Add the 3 tablespoons of liqueur. Put the mixture in the refrigerator to chill 3 hours or overnight.

To assemble and dip chocolate truffles:

Melt slowly over hot water the remaining 1 pound of semi-sweet chocolate. While it is melting, roll chocolate ganache into 1 inch balls. Set on cookie sheet lined with waxed paper or parchment paper. When all are formed, set tray in freezer for 10-15 minutes. Dip each candy in melted chocolate. Keep refrigerated in covered container. Makes 3 dozen 1" candies.

Southwest France

*O*ur sojourn in Spain was but a prelude. Mary and I next crossed into France driving a midsized Ford Orion rental car, capable of the 100-mph-plus European expressway speeds. Our journey stretched from late September to mid-October, as we avoid Europe in the summer.

As mentioned in the previous chapter, Cadaqués on the Costa Brava is often compared to St. Tropez before Bridget Bardot made it overly popular. The same is said of Collioure, a Mediterranean seaside town, not far from the Spanish border in that part of France known as Roussillon or the Coast of Languedoc. Although it was now off-season, we detoured to Collioure to have a look and lunch, our first French meal of this trip.

Collioure looks better than St. Tropez. Not only does the town itself have more attractive buildings, it also has the spectacular backdrop of the Pyrenees Mountains as they fall to the sea.

El Bodega, owned by Collioure's ex-mayor and the most recommended restaurant, had closed—not for the season, but forever.

However, we had read a rave article that La Balette, a restaurant and hotel, served the best fish on the coast and offered a wonderful *menu homard*, featuring grilled lobster.

Located at the west end of Collioure, La Balette drops two stories down from the road toward its typically unappealing European beach, with views of the harbor and town to the left. Mary ordered the *menu homard*. I had something I prefer to forget. It was the worst food we have ever had in France—an example of Nouvelle Cuisine in the hands of a chef who does not know how to cook. A mackerel first course not only smelled bad, but was raw. The lobster was half raw, and every dish was poorly seasoned. Either the food writer who recommended this spot has defective taste, or there had been a change of chefs. The only decent part of the meal, which we paid for and left halfway through, was a pleasant white Ch. Cap de Fouste, Côtes de Roussillon '88.

Back on the autoroute, we plunged through a furious rainstorm to Le Domaine d'Auriac near the much-photographed medieval walled city of Carcassonne. D'Auriac is a period country house of twenty-three rooms set in a three-century-old park and features a golf course, swimming pool, tennis court, and billiards. It is the top-rated hotel and restaurant in the area.

On this, our first visit to southwest France, we planned to see as much as possible, principally in the valleys of the Lot and Dordogne rivers, staying at members of the exclusive Relais & Châteaux group of rural hostelries. Fortunately, the weather was good except for rain during our drive to Carcassonne and for two days near the end of the trip. May or September would be a better choice, not only because of more reliable weather but because many establishments close on October 16. On the other hand, preferred hotels and inns would have to be booked in advance. We made reservations as we went along.

At d'Auriac, we again accomplished our goal of obtaining accommodations whose photo was featured in its brochure, as we had at Hotel Ritz in Barcelona and at La Gavina on the Costa Brava. Dinner at d'Auriac, our first true taste of southwest France, featured mellow duck foie gras with aspic, a tasty but overly salty *cassoulet,* and an excellent partridge, complete with head. Most of the staff at d'Auriac were charming and efficient young ladies who, for example, delivered requested ice to our room in ninety seconds. This country hotel is comfortable and pleasant, but not deluxe or elegant.

The rain having abated by morning, we strolled about medieval Carcassonne. Everyone has seen photos of its walls, which embrace an ancient town of stone buildings and cobbled streets, with châteaux, castle, church, agreeable small hotels, restaurants, and shops. At one shop, Mary purchased a Santos doll of a rustic hunter.

It was Saturday and off-season and we had foolishly not made reservations at our intended luncheon destination, Les Loges de l'Aubergade, to the west in Puymirol. On arrival after bypassing southwest France's metropolis of Toulouse, we had forebodings of rejection. There were so many cars, I had to park a block away after dropping Mary at the door. But, while awaiting my arrival, Mary charmed the maître d' into giving her the well-placed and only vacant table, which he had been saving for a party now a half-hour late who never did show. This was the finest meal of our trip, and remember you heard it here first. Highlights included a *ballottine* of rabbit with herbs, duck foie gras, and salmon in sorrel cream sauce. The greatest dish, however, was *croustillant aux poires,* paper-thin, crystallized, light-green slices of pear, artfully arranged above a hemisphere of sorbet.

I doubt many diners experience *Michelin* six-star days, but we were in the midst of one and hesitate to recommend it. After breakfast at one-star d'Auriac and lunch at two-star Le Loges de l'Aubergade, we continued our detour west to Les Près d'Eugénie at Eugénie-les-Baines, dubbed "The most sophisticated fitness club in the world." Chef-Proprietor Michel Guerard is the inventor of Cuisine Minceur, and rooms in his "white colonial palace" are top rated.

Given its reputation, Près d'Eugénie can only be described as the emperor's new clothes. Like Père Bise on Lake Annency, which had three stars when we felt it should have none, it is now nothing but a tawdry tourist trap. The hotel was obviously laid out and decorated on a whim by someone who knew nothing of the subject, presumably Chef Guerard or his wife. Carpeting was white, so impractical that ugly pseudo-leather runners were tacked down the center of the hallways to cover the worst stained and spoiled areas. In rooms, the condition of white carpeting in bathrooms, particularly around toilets, was gross beyond description. There was no place to read in one's room. Furthermore, there were no pen or paper, hair dryer, minibar, menu, or any information on the hotel or its operation whatsoever except a *blah-blah* book.

Guests were forced to sit in a cocktail area before dinner and wait a half-hour to be seated at a table, whether they wished an apéritif or not. We did not. Hordes of diners were herded about. After finally being seated, I ordered a 260-franc ($47.50) bottle of plonk (cheap wine), which would have been overpriced at $10. Ravioli of morels and truffles were good, as was salmon with salt and herbs. But veal kidneys were drenched in tarragon, thinly sliced fried potatoes were soggy, and rolls were hard as rocks. We were served more rocks when we requested fresh ones. Service was very poor. There did not seem to be a maître d' or anyone else in charge, merely young ladies rushing about to serve the masses. After our magnificent lunch, the contrast was stark.

Regretting our visit to Près d'Eugénie, which was definitely not "worth a detour," we drove north with anticipation to the Valley of the Lot, arriving for a two-day stay at Château de Mercuès. Situated on a high bluff overlooking the valley some eleven kilometers northwest of Cahors, Mercuès has seven apartments (suites) and twenty-five chambers (rooms). This former residence of bishop-counts since the twelfth century is known variously as the finest castle hotel in France or one of the best château hotels in Europe.

Not surprisingly, the best suite in this former home of the Bishops of Cahors is the Bishop's Bedroom with a sundial parquet floor, marble fireplace, and a bed resembling an altar. It was here that Charles de Gaulle wrote his memoirs. Although the Bishop's suite was spoken for, we had our choice of the two next finest. The one in the tower was two stories high, with bath below and bedroom-sitting area above. That in turn had a huge ceiling that tilted up dramatically by electric controls to reveal vast roof beams. We chose instead number 17, La Cour d'Honneur, which was very large and elegant with a high ceiling, views over the valley, and a magnificent bath with rock and stone walls. Although we had arrived rather late for lunch, we were graciously served our daily ration of foie gras, codfish, duck with figs, cheese, and fondant of chocolate, accompanied by host Georges Vigouroux's own wine, an excellent Ch. de Mercuès, Cahors '88. (The identical wine is on The Lark's reserve wine list.)

After a relaxing afternoon, our light dinner of oyster soup, two truffle dishes, and a prune liqueur soufflé was accompanied by Ch. Bicoty, Bergerac '88, which was pleasant but not nearly as fine as the Ch. Mercuès at lunch.

Descriptions of southwest France are often confusing. No writer has taken the trouble to point out that any area there may be identified in at least three different ways: ancient names, like Périgord, Gascony, Armagnac, or Quercy; geographical locales, like the Valley of the Lot or Dordogne rivers; or the official name of that department of modern France. Rather than drive the reader to distraction by shifting references among all three, suffice it to say that Mary and I rambled about the Valley of the Lot, which runs generally east and west, then the Valley of the Dordogne River to the north, which also runs mostly east and west, finally driving farther west to Bordeaux on the Atlantic from where we flew home. In our travels near the Lot and Dordogne, we were variously in Périgord, Gascony, Armagnac, and Quercy, collectively famous for duck and goose foie gras, cèpes and morel mushrooms, *confit* of duck and goose, *cassoulet*, truffles, game dishes, cheeses, prunes, walnuts, rustic red wines, and Armagnac brandy, which is older in origin and often preferred over Cognac. This cuisine is enjoying a renaissance in France because of the reaction against Nouvelle Cuisine and a renewed appreciation for simpler and more rustic fare.

If the Alps of Haute-Savoie are the most impressive part of France, the Lot and Dordogne are the most beautiful. And they are not yet overdeveloped. Rather, as in Alsace, gentrification has tidied up the appearance of many areas. In addition to the beauty of nature and the atmospheric ambience of ancient buildings in scores of charming villages and towns, the principal attractions are appealing lodgings in country inns, châteaux, castles, and small hotels; France's most magnificent rustic cuisine; and a rich cultural heritage that includes the art of Cro-Magnon man, as seen in numerous rediscovered cave paintings.

On a perfect October morning, we drove out of the courtyard of Mercuès, turning east toward and then past Cahors to explore the Valley of the Lot. The Lot is France's most winding river and the forty miles from Cahors east to Capdenac is known as the most stunning stretch of river in the country. The principal trees were oak, chestnut, walnut, poplar, and pine. Chestnuts littered the ground, free for the taking, thus few stores bothered to sell them. Walnuts were more eagerly gathered. Buildings, walls, and bridges are all made of the local limestone, which often towers in cliffs above one bank of the river or the other, so that structures seem organic, and nature and the works of man blend.

Each side of the river has a two-lane road, most often close to the river and separated from it by a low stone wall. But at times the road climbs one of the cliffs, affording fine views.

Following advice from a travel guide and articles, we meandered up the river, crossing over stone bridges from bank to bank to search out the best sights. These included the old fortress town of St. Cirq-Lapopie, La Mounine's Leap with an intriguing legend and great view, and a succession of picturesque villages.

We had hoped for lunch at La Pescalerie, the Relais & Châteaux member in the area in addition to Mercuès, but this was the day of the week its dining room was closed. Disappointment turned out to be a stroke of luck for we would not otherwise have discovered and lunched at La Ferme de Montbrun, about one mile east of the cliffside village of Montbrun. Some restaurant proprietors and their establishments are so charming that all of the food and wine seem improved and enhanced. Here, Chef Michel Josyane produces simple but excellent dishes to order in his open kitchen, while wife Josyane is hostess, sommelier, and waitress at this old stone farm building with eight tables inside and a few outdoor tables with views looking over and across the valley.

Our first course of salad with scallops and duck foie gras was followed by guinea fowl in a red wine and vinegar sauce, and a *confit* of duck. Desserts were chocolate and Armagnac crêpes and *pastis,* which is an apple and pear tart with an ultra flaky and buttery pastry top. We devoured every delicious morsel.

Heading back toward Cahors after lunch, we stopped at Pech-Merle Cave, used by prehistoric man and rediscovered in 1922 after twenty thousand years. In addition to paintings of mammoths, bison, horses, and a pike, there are petrified footprints of a woman and her child.

Cahors was an important university and commercial town in the Middle Ages and continues today as the principal town of the Lot. There are fine ancient churches, museums and other buildings, but the most famous structure is the Valentré Bridge with its three towers, "a remarkable example of French medieval military architecture." Cahors is bustling and very attractive, but the best lodging and restaurants, such as Mercuès, La Pescalerie, and La Ferme de Montbrun, are found in the countryside.

Back at Mercuès, we visited its wine and tasting room. Wine is a very important part of its total operation. In addition to Ch. Mercuès, it produces the equally well-known Ch. Haute-Serre. Both are red Cahors, the best wine of the region.

Our dinner destination was Gindreau, twenty-five minutes northwest of Mercuès in the little village of St. Medard-Catus. We drove at night, but if one goes for lunch, the road affords great views of the valley as it climbs into the hills. This atmospheric country inn has very reasonable prices. Our comforting dinner featured huge cèpe mushrooms, the best pigeon (not underdone) of our lives, and a duck *confit* even better than that of La Ferme de Montbrun.

Driving north the next morning, we climbed out of the Valley of the Lot in Quercy and then dropped down into the Valley of the Dordogne in Périgord. Our hostelry for the next two nights was Hôtel du Centenaire in Les Eyzies de Tayac, one of the few lodgings during our travels through Spain and France that was not in the countryside.

Rooms at Centenaire, although lacking the romantic ambience of country inns or châteaux, are almost perfectly laid out and appointed and are extremely well maintained. Unlike Près d'Eugénie, every detail has been intelligently thought out. On the other hand, the hotel's restaurant is overrated. Excessively creative dishes, which *Michelin* as well as *Gault Millau* now favor, are poorly executed. Ambience and service are pleasant and soothing, as is everything at Centenaire.

The touristic but pretty village of Les Eyzies is located at the juncture of the rivers Vézère and Beune, two tributaries of the Dordogne, and is surrounded by forested cliffs. It is known as the capital of prehistory, as it is in this area that Cro-Magnon remains were first found. Les Eyzies is the site of the important National Museum of Prehistory in a thirteenth-century castle located halfway up one of the limestone cliffs that surround the village. In addition to its rich display of prehistoric art and objects, diagrams and displays explain the chronology of prehistory.

Cro-Magnon man lived at the front of caves up in limestone cliffs facing small rivers. Their artists, however, went deep into caves, where no one lived, to paint by the light of stone lamps fueled by animal fat. Materials used were charcoal for black, calcite for white, plus oxidized iron and ocher. Escorted tours through these caves are a principal tourist attraction of the Dordogne. They must be reserved in advance. Groups of visitors are led by their guide through dimly lit underground passages leading to spine-tingling drawings of animals that seem magical.

We continued our exploration of the Lot in the morning, that river being only a short drive from Les Eyzies. Our first stop was the village of Domme, perched on a rocky crag overlooking the valley and offering a spectacular view. This old walled-fortress town was the site of a gruesome massacre by Heugenots during the battles of the Reformation. During our visit, it was the site of a lively open-air market. The few stores here, as everywhere in the region, featured canned foie gras, *confit,* and other comestibles in addition to pottery and other tourist wares. From Domme, we wandered west along the river to Beynac, which has a thirteenth-century castle perched high on a rock commanding the Dordogne as it winds between hills topped with other castles. Beynac Castle was captured by Richard the Lion Heart, who pillaged the countryside. A series of small towns decorated our way as we returned to Les Eyzies for a well-earned lunch.

At the opposite end of the village from Centenaire lies the other principal hotel in Les Eyzies, Jacques and Christiane Leyssales's Cro-Magnon. While Centenaire featured expensive and ill-conceived Nouvelle offerings, Cro-Magnon presented a luscious and broad medley of traditional Périgord cuisine complimented by carefully chosen modern dishes. Ensconced in a country dining room with a large fireplace, I began with a superb presentation of salad greens, quail, foie gras, and artichoke hearts. Tiring of finding only elaborate dishes on menus, we often asked if we couldn't begin with a simple bowl of soup. Cro-Magnon was the only spot capable of meeting that simple request, and Mary enjoyed an off-menu vegetable soup, the best.

Also excellent were our main courses of lamb stew with noodles, and snails, mushrooms, and walnuts in a mushroom cream sauce. Half-bottles of Ch. Gloria Bordeaux '86 and a Faiveley Rully white Burgundy '89 were reasonably priced, a great rarity as the majority of restaurants visited used unconscionable markups. Wines identical to those on the wine list of The Lark were priced at two to three times our prices, even though they had surely cost the restaurant much less than we pay with added transportation and middlemen.

That afternoon we explored the cave of Font-de-Gaume, conveniently located on the edge of Les Eyzies. This is a 130-yard-long passage whose drawings of horses, bison, mammoths, and deer are considered second only to Lascaux as the finest polychrome prehistoric paintings in France.

Dinner that evening at Centenaire was disappointing. We searched the menu in vain for dishes that were not overelaborate. The need in France to impress *Michelin* and *Gault Millau* has led to menus at most upscale restaurants with never a simple soup or salad, never a simple roast, braise or grill. Nouvelle Cuisine was billed as a reaction against overrich and overly elaborate dishes, but it spawned a crazy collection of food that is not only tiresomely complicated—it rarely tastes very good. Lest the reader consider me a misanthrope, the three most respected chefs in France voiced similar views, quoted in *Nations Restaurant News*.

Alain Ducasse of Louix XV says, "For many years, French cuisine has been tasteless." Joel Robuchon also feels dishes will become simpler as the public becomes more sophisticated and learns to appreciate a perfectly roasted chicken or a well-made salad. "The more complicated dishes may dazzle, but they are not the hardest to prepare.... For a long time, taste was lost as everyone went in for presentation." Paul Bocuse believes regional cuisines, such as that of southwest France, are the wave of the future.

Checking out of Centenaire, we drove north along the Vézère River, which is famous for its beauty and its prehistoric sites. Almost all buildings are of limestone with either slate or tile roofs. Of the small villages. St. Leon-sur-Vézère was especially charming with a fine Romanesque church, a castle, and a château. Of more interest is St. Christophe Cliff, about 250 feet high and a half mile long, facing the nearby Vézère. Some twenty thousand years ago, scores of caves housing two hundred to three hundred Cro-Magnons were hollowed out of the limestone rock at five different heights or stories.

Our Relais & Châteaux home for the night was Château du Puy Robert, two kilometers outside Montignac. The rooms in the château itself seemed pleasant, but we selected a larger suite in a separate building. Part of our supplies, unloaded at every stay, was bottled water. We purchased this in stores, using about two liters per day. It would not be practical or cost-sensible to obtain this quantity from minibars or room service. Of the two common brands, Evian was much better than Vittel, and Badoit was even better.

Luncheon first courses at Puy Robert were a trio of duck foie gras preparations for me, and fresh black truffles, egg, and truffle juice in a topless egg shell for Mary. It was very elegant, and also tasty. *Confit* of duck was not the usual presentation of a crisp thigh and leg, but rather a sack of thin, flaky pastry enclosing pieces of duck nestled above julienned vegetables. This was surrounded by potatoes *à la sarladaise* topped with cèpes, chanterelles, and other mushrooms in a light sauce. Frankly, the classical *confit* preparation is better than this adaptation, as much of the appeal of *confit* is the crisp skin.

Our wonderful desserts were black and red raspberries in pastry with two sauces, and a hot apple tart with ice cream and caramel sauce, a favorite in this region. Puy Robert, like Cro-Magnon, was the rare establishment with fair wine prices, so we enjoyed a half-bottle of Ch. Smith Haut Lafite '86 and one of Chablis, Misserey '89. In other restaurants, a knowledge of wine enabled us to find offbeat good wines at rational prices. Also, every sommelier or waitperson rose to the challenge and made excellent recommendations when requested to suggest a good wine at a reasonable price.

We had but a one-kilometer drive from Puy Robert to Lascaux, the finest prehistoric site in Europe. Discovered in 1940, damage from the carbon dioxide and humidity of more than one million visitors caused its closing in 1963. An unbelievably exact replica, Lascaux II, opened to the public in 1983. It is fantastic—one of the most memorable experiences of a well-traveled life. Although only 492 feet long, there are more than 1,500 paintings or engravings created seventeen thousand years ago. The effect is so overwhelming that Lascaux should be one's last cave of any visit, or the other fine caves will not be properly appreciated.

In Montignac, which is a small town rather than a village, we visited a bakery, *charcuterie*, pastry shop, and wine store, collecting the makings of a picnic, which we enjoyed that evening while relaxing in our very spacious suite.

Our next morning's drive, past fields of honking geese being fattened for foie gras, led south again to the Dordogne, then west a short distance to Tremolat, an especially picturesque village with many fine stone buildings and a twelfth-century Romanesque church.

We had reserved a garden-front suite at Le Vieux Logis et ses Logis des Champs, a sprawling Périgord inn of eight apartments and fourteen chambers. The dining room and various lounges are well decorated in the country style. All of its public rooms and many of its guest rooms and suites open onto or overlook well-tended gardens and a swimming pool.

Dogs were *"oui, bienvenus,"* as in most of France; in fact, one with a nearby table at lunch was served his own elegant meal. I offered him a glass of wine, which he declined. Mary and I savored cold potato and leek soup with black truffles, and a miniature cèpe tart prepared like a *tarte Tatin*. But a filet steak was served rather than the beef ribs we had ordered, and a *tarte Tatin* was burned. Vieux Logis must have been decorated at the same time as Près d'Eugénie, as the same impractical white carpeting was found, even in the bathrooms. We hope experience has killed this ridiculous idea.

Obviously, our journey through the Dordogne was not a logical progression, but rather was dictated by the availability of reservations as we accomplished our goal of staying at every Relais & Châteaux in the Lot and Dordogne, save only Le Pescalerie. The most difficult booking to obtain was Château de Roumegouse near Gramat, where we stayed the next two nights.

Driving toward Roumegouse, we came to the village of St. Caprien where an outdoor Sunday-morning market was in full swing. The main street was lined for about six hundred feet with stalls offering *charcuterie*, fruit, vegetables, mushrooms, wines, and clothing. We bought provisions for another picnic supper. Many dogs enjoyed the festivities as did twenty-four bicyclists from the United States, the Dordogne being a favored area for their tours. In fact, long-standing reservations by bicyclists were one reason it was so hard to book Roumegouse. The other reason for that château's popularity is its location convenient to the most beautiful stretch of the Dordogne Valley and to Rocamadour, the second-most impressive site in France.

Roumegouse, an old château in a thirteen-acre park, has four suites and twelve rooms, of which we were given the worst—quite a comedown after snagging so many suites featured in brochures. The proprietress spoke no English, but the château was managed by her multilingual niece, a rather snippy but efficient young lady.

Both of the formal dining rooms having been reserved for a private luncheon, Mary and I were banished to the breakfast room, which had inspiring views over the tableland of Rocamadour. We enjoyed a fine repast that began with local garlic and egg soup for Mary and a mixed salad with walnuts and walnut oil for me. Then, *confit* duck with wild mushrooms and thin potatoes, and veal over pasta with truffles and wild mushrooms in a fine sauce. The best *tarte Tatin* of the trip was accompanied by cinnamon ice cream. A *crème brûlée* was done on a flat plate to maximize the area of crunchy top. Half-bottles of a red Ch. de Chambert, Cahors '85 and a white Ch. de la Jaubertie '90 were both very good. I even began to like the young lady manager.

A tour of not-distant Padirac Chasm was our afternoon excursion. Admittance was by luck, since this was its last open day this season. The chasm, 247 feet across and 325 feet deep, terrorized the local population in olden days as they thought it Satan's path back to hell after an encounter with St. Martin. Today, two lifts and a staircase bring visitors to the lowest level, where they explore passages on foot and by way of a half-mile boat journey on an underground river. The guides are very agreeable and amusing.

Rocamadour, a site we explored the next morning, comprises a castle, churches, other old buildings of all sorts, and fortifications perched on a rock 492 feet above the Alzou River. Its appearance when first seen is so striking as to be almost unbelievable. It is called the second-most impressive site in France—the first being Mont-Saint-Michel in Normandy.

Rocamadour has a rich history. Legend has it that the body discovered there in 1166 was that of Zaccheus, a disciple of Jesus. Reports of the many miracles that followed made Rocamadour a famous pilgrim destination, with thirty thousand penitents arriving on some days. Money poured in, and impressive chapels and other buildings were built as Rocamadour reached its zenith in the thirteenth century. Recovering from the bad times of the French Revolution, it is once more a pilgrim destination as well as a not-to-miss tourist site. Visitors should park in the top parking lot and walk downward, viewing the various attractions, rather than walking up. Completing one's visit, an elevator is available to ascend again to the parking area.

The town of Gramat near Château Roumegouse is not worth a visit except to eat at the restaurant of the hotel Le Lion d'Or, which should be awarded a *Michelin* star. Our pleasant luncheon included an excellent galantine of chicken breast and duck liver with aspic, a mixed salad with walnuts, and a superb *cassoulet* of duck *confit*, sausage, ham, lamb, and white beans. Dessert was a black currant tart.

After lunch, following a map provided by Roumegouse, we toured the Valley of the Dordogne to the northwest, seeing Carennac, Magnagues, La Poujade, Loubressac, Castelnau, Bretenoux, St. Ceré, and Montal. This was the scenic climax of our trip since this part of the Dordogne is, as far as we know, the most beautiful area in France. From atop hills, there are views of fifteen to twenty miles across, up, and down the valley. Castles perch on hills, stone towns and villages also crown hills, while small villages are sprinkled about the valley, which is a mixture of fields and forests with the Dordogne a curving silver ribbon. The towns and villages themselves, with their stone buildings and cobbled streets, are achingly atmospheric, as well as clean, tidy, and untouristic.

The morning of our thirty-first wedding anniversary was spent in a rather long and uneventful drive, passing through Périgueux to arrive at Le Moulin de l'Abbaye at Brantôme in Périgord. This small town is a gourmet's mecca with three one-star restaurants: Moulin de l'Abbaye, Chabrol, and Moulin du Roc.

Moulin de l'Abbaye, a former mill on a small river, has been exquisitely converted to an elegant restaurant and hostelry of three suites and nine rooms. Our suite, number 18 in an annex across the river by bridge, was the finest accommodation of our trip; in fact, one of the best of our lives. Some of its features were a stone fireplace and a balcony with views of the river and mill.

For lunch, we selected two cold foie gras, one plain and one marbled with duck gizzards, an elaborate salmon preparation, roasted and grilled rabbit, breaded and sautéed pork *confit,* and a hot praline soufflé. Outstanding food in a magnificent riverside dining room.

Our next and last day in France was to have been spent visiting Bordeaux wine châteaux with a luncheon at one of them, leaving no time to see the city of Bordeaux itself. Deciding to save wine touring for some future trip, we canceled château visits and were free to enjoy Bordeaux.

Although travel literature spoke highly of Bordeaux, we were still surprised at the attractions of France's fifth-largest metropolis, a great walking city with fine boulevards, impressive buildings, and excellent shopping. In fact, the "triangle" from Place de la Comédie up the Allée de Tourney, Cours Clemenceau, and Cours de l'Intendance is the finest shopping area we have seen anywhere.

At Chez Phillipe, reputedly the best seafood restaurant in town, snails, lobster salad, broiled mussels, scallops, and oysters were all fine. A Ch. Fieuzal white Bordeaux, here in its native city, cost twice as much as the identical wine at The Lark.

Our last night in France was spent at the Relais de Margaux, north of Bordeaux in the wine commune of Margaux. This newly constructed relais is too elegant to call an inn, and our suite was especially grand. The magnificent accommodations and perfectly served dinner of foie gras, salmon and veal, accompanied by fine wines, were a memorable final note to our almost epic odyssey.

Most of our European trips are driving tours, and most of our accommodations are at Relais & Châteaux, which are very rarely less than good and are often excellent.

Take Foie Gras to Heart

Mary and I returned from southwest France laden with guilt over our almost daily ration of irresistible foie gras, one of the region's culinary triumphs. But foie gras, made from the specially fattened livers of ducks and geese, is, alas, 87 percent fat. Residents of Gascony, where foie gras is produced, have a diet higher in saturated fat than any other group in the world except Eskimos.

But *voila! The New York Times* reported that the same foie gras eaters of the Lot Valley and surrounding areas have the lowest death rate from cardiovascular disease in France. And, the difference was remarkable: 80 deaths per 100,000 middle-aged men in southwest France, compared with 145 for that country as a whole and 315 in the United States. The unimpeachable source was a study by the National Institute of Health and Medical Research in Lyon.

What does this mean? How does it tie in, if at all, to studies of the beneficial effects of a "Mediterranean" diet and the revelation that red wine lowers cholesterol and that moderate daily drinking reduces the risk of heart attack? Obviously, the subject is more complicated than the U.S. medical establishment has led us to believe. The high-fat U.S. diet is obviously unhealthy, as attested by our death rate for middle-aged men from cardiovascular disease. Perhaps an old-fashioned, fun-loving, hearty diet is healthy and a modern snack- and fast-food regimen kills. That is what I have always suspected.

Champagne

I've never tasted a French champagne that I didn't like, although they do vary from merely good to excellent. On the other hand, I've never had a bubbly from another country that I liked as much as the least-good French champagne.

Our patrons seem to have the same feelings, since (other than at special ethnic dinners) California, Spanish and other non-French sparkling wines just don't sell, even at half the price of champagnes. Norm Roby of *Wine Spectator* put it bluntly:

"Let's be honest, with the exception of Maison Deutz, Chandon Reserve in magnums, Mumm Reserve, a cuvée or two from Schramsberg (the '85 Blanc de Blanc L. D. is outstanding), and Iron Horse Vineyards, most California sparkling wines are far from exciting. Good, pleasant and well-made in the tutti-frutti style describes the majority."

Congratulations Received

The Lark's designation as the best restaurant in the United States by the *Condé Nast Traveler* "Reader's Poll" brought a deluge of congratulatory letters. Two had Parisian content.

The first was from Jean-Claude Vrinat, proprietor of Taillevent, the premier restaurant of Paris:

"Cher James,

"I congratulate you for the *Condé Nast Traveler* recognition of your efforts and talent.

"Many mutual customers share the same opinion: you have risen to the top....

"I am proud Champagne Taillevent is present in the number one of the 'top ten'—I wish you go on being in the same position for years.

"I hope to visit you one day....

"J. C. Vrinat"

Jim Harrison, novelist, essayist, screenwriter (e.g., *Legends of the Fall*), wrote from Patagonia, Arizona, where he winters:

"Dear Jim,

"Trust you're pleased with the *Condé Nast* poll results. Please accept my congratulations and pass them on to [Chef] Marcus.

"Lousy winter quail season—drought and vast overgrazing. (Only bury ranchers six inches deep so they can keep a hand out.)

"Have to go to Paris again in May. If you get there my new favorite bistro is Le Brin de Zinc in Les Halles area—simple (relatively) hearty stuff, splendid break from haute cuisine assaults.

"Yours,

"Jim Harrison"

Middle European Adventure

$\mathcal{W}$e're obsessed by travel, having learned that we live life to the fullest when nudged from the routine of everyday existence by new surroundings and experiences. Hunting and fishing excursions can be the best trips, because they lead to especially different, hence more stimulating, places and activities. Thus, Mary and I travel the world, sometimes just exploring, but often hunting or fishing. We used to always be on our own, but now we sometimes travel with a few others.

One such group is men only, but I'm urging them to include wives as it's more fun—like a traveling house party. Such was the case on a hunting jaunt by six couples to Hungary, followed by R & R in Vienna, Austria. We chose Hungary for driven-pheasant and wild boar hunting because the combination of two different types of shooting appealed to us; the price was more reasonable than driven-pheasant shooting in England and Wales; we'd never been to Hungary; and we'd had only good reports of this trip led by Jack Jansma of Wingshooting Adventures.

Other than dining at a fine restaurant, the best buy in the world is taking a limousine to and from the airport, avoiding driving, bag handling, and shuttle busing. We had our limo also pick up one of the other couples. I was dressed sensibly for the overnight flight in a designer jogging suit. The other chap was arrayed in the full business attire of an old codger.

We really liked the service and efficiency of our flight to Budapest via Amsterdam, which began and ended with the usual formalities and inspections encountered when bringing firearms to a foreign country. All of our group, some of whom were on other flights, now came together at the Budapest airport. Fellow travelers from prior adventures in England, Wales, Africa and Argentina, they were David E. Davis Jr. and Jeannie Davis, Ham Schirmer and Weezie Schirmer, Joe Frey and Karen Frey, Charles Eisendrath and Julia Eisendrath, and Jim Ramsey and Marnie Ramsey. Also awaiting us were the outfitter from Grand Rapids, Jack Jansma, as well as Aggie, his Hungarian cohort who was our guide, arranger, and interpreter in her country. Also present was John, our very capable and safe bus driver, who whisked us off to Hotel Hegyessy Nyerges in Monor, less than an hour south of Budapest.

This two-year-old hotel of thirty-four rooms and suites boasts that it is the largest thatched-roof hotel in Central Europe. After checking in to tiny rooms, we gathered in the hotel restaurant for a dinner of a meat-filled crêpe, followed by a copious platter of veal, chicken, large mushroom caps, corn, and french-fried potatoes. Red wine was good, the white undrinkable. The two musicians accompanying our feast reminded Ham of a polka hall.

After a night's sleep under a duvet (there are no tucked-in sheets in Hungary), we arose the next morning for the first of three days spent shooting driven pheasant at two private middle-class clubs. Hunting clubs lease their land from the state and sell hunts to a few "big shooters" from abroad, like us, supplementing their income and making their shooting clubs economically feasible.

Our hunting was in Hungary's beautiful countryside of mixed

fields and woods, which resembled northern Michigan. As in much of Europe, the terrain is pristine, free not only of billboards, but of all but a few houses, since the populace is concentrated in villages and small towns.

Our first day's hunt was at the nearby Dabas Club, where we were met by the club members, who were to be our beaters and loaders. They might be doctors, lawyers or businessmen, but all turned out to help, since the income from our hunt made their own hunting possible. Some were in stylish hunting loden; others in rougher outfits. All were hearty, friendly outdoor types.

After an exchange of greeting and a short lecture on safety, each of our "guns," or hunters, was paired with a loader and led to a "stand" for the first drive of the day. We had seven guns—the six men plus Jeannie Davis. The other five wives accompanied their husbands. So, other than David and Jeannie, each stand consisted of a gun (husband), his wife, and a loader. The loader's job, when the shooting was hot and heavy, was to quickly insert two new shells in the over-and-under or side-by-side shotgun as soon as spent shells were ejected. His other unstated but important task was to make certain we didn't do anything stupid. As all of our guns were experienced, the club members soon relaxed.

In driven shooting the beaters form a line abreast at the far side of some type of cover, such as brush, woods or heavy grass, which has a natural attraction for pheasants. The stands for the hunters are located in a line abreast on the near side of the cover. The beaters proceed through the cover, hooting and hollering and beating the underbrush with staffs. Obviously, the pheasants, at some point, will stop running in front of the beaters and fly toward the hunters. If there is only a short distance between the end of the cover and the location of the stands, there may only be two or three seconds to locate a bird, aim, and fire. The next most important factor in determining difficulty is the height of the birds. The English, in particular, love drives that result in very high birds because of the added challenge.

Whether in Britain or in Hungary, each day's shooting has a definite number of birds that may be shot, and that number has been factored into the cost of that hunt. A hunt may be a 300-bird hunt or a 350-bird hunt. Birds killed above that number are an added cost. In Britain the additional charge was about $32.50 per bird, in Hungary $13.

An obvious question is why the five nonshooting wives accompanied their husbands in the field, rather than going sight-seeing or shopping. A wife could answer better than I, but I know it is exciting and interesting to watch, and that the total ritualized event with beaters, loaders, hunting horns, and ceremonies in a beautiful outdoor setting is a wondrous and totally unique experience for shooter and nonshooter alike. The fact that the law of supply and demand has made such hunting so expensive, even in Hungary, attests to its appeal.

The shooting in Hungary was spectacular, not every drive for every hunter, but on the average and in total. At times, every hunter repeatedly had birds overhead at the same time, which is as good as it gets.

We had six drives that first morning, and I bagged some seventy-five birds; Charles and I drew applause from the beaters for our shooting. We saw roebuck on the fifth drive.

The luncheon break added to the charm of the hunt. Arriving at the simple farmhouse that served as clubhouse, we found two big iron pots of beef goulash (stew) bubbling over an open fire. Served family style at a long table, it tasted as good as it looked and smelled, accompanied by vegetables, crusty breads, and local wine and beer. Dessert was too many homemade doughnuts, which we spread with apricot jam.

Following the afternoon drives, we were mesmerized by our first Hungarian after-hunt ritual, based on and confirming the great respect felt for the game. The pheasants were carefully laid out, cocks alternating with hens in rows of sixteen, the whole tableau surrounded by a rectangle of freshly cut pine boughs with a bonfire at two corners. Since there were 254 birds, the display was quite large. Beaters, loaders, and dog handlers stood on one side with the hunters opposite. A spokesman from each side made a short but fulsome speech, complimenting the other side: in our case saying how much we enjoyed the hunt and how great it was; the representative of the club saying that Jeannie Davis "shoots just like a man."

After more thanks and good wishes all around, we rushed back to our hotel, flung our gear in duffels, and drove on to our next hotel, the not greatly distant Fenyoharaszti Kastelyszallo, meaning the Hotel Kastely in Fenyoharaszti, a short distance east of Budapest. It is luxurious: eighteen rooms in a nobleman's mansion built in 1806, situated in a thirteen-hectare park. The staff said that this was the spot where the Communist bosses brought their girlfriends. The rooms were huge and there were lots of amenities: a sauna, bowling alley, and an off-beat bar.

Hungarians love crêpes, and our hotel dinner that night began with one of meat and peas and ended with one with chocolate sauce. Our main course was another mixed platter presentation. This one featured roebuck, veal, and salt pork. The other guys stayed up late smoking Cuban cigars with their booze. Being vice-free, I turned in early.

The next morning, John drove us and our gear to our second club, Hatvan. Our arrival was obviously quite an event for the town. Women and children as well as beaters and loaders turned out to greet us. The terrain was open, not mixed woods and fields. Our stands were in large fields, with the drive coming across a large cornfield to our north. We were widely spread to cover the width of the birds' possible flight paths. It was a great drive—one of the best ever. High birds came over every gun in waves.

Lunch was a different goulash, this one of roebuck. I regret to say that all goulash begins by melting a block of lard in the bottom of the iron kettle, but each one tasted wonderful.

The post-hunt ceremony after the afternoon drives was even more impressive than the first day's. The birds were arranged in alternating rows of cocks or hens, 25 birds to a row, 356 birds in all. A fox that was taken by Charles was placed in a position of honor at the top. A nearby table was stocked with glasses and bottles of sparkling wine, and the bonfires were lit. Following a trumpet salute, there were speeches and thanks by both sides. David E. Davis Jr. was our spokesman and said that we were honored to be with our hosts this day, the anniversary of their ill-fated 1956 revolution. We later learned that we had goofed by walking through the game tableau, which has an almost religious significance.

Dinner that evening featured chicken, salt pork, and dumplings. The red wine was Cabernet and the white a Tokay, not the very sweet dessert style, but a lighter table wine. Dinner table conversation that night was not fit for reporting in this family book.

The highlight of the next morning's shoot was the last drive, which found us stationed along a road bordered on both sides by high trees. That created ultra-challenging shots as the pheasants burst from the trees in front and dove into or over those to the rear, offering only an instant to shoot. A humbling but fun experience.

Our clubhouse field lunch this day featured a hearty and filling bean soup, of which we had seconds and thirds. A bad idea, since it was only a prelude to a cheese pasta dish. We learned that this is a Hungarian custom, and that the pasta is supposed to counteract the effect of the beans.

Our final pheasant tableau totaled 378 birds. Ham Schirmer, our spokesman of the day, apologized for our previous day's transgression of the tableau, which made both sides feel better. Our three-day bag totaled 988 pheasants, an average of 141 for each of seven guns. What happened to all these birds? With the exception of a few given to beaters and loaders, they were shipped to market at cities in western Europe. They are, after all, a crop, which we have paid for the privilege of harvesting.

In what seemed like a comedy skit, Jeannie coveted one of the beater's green knit hats. She tried to trade hers, but the beater insisted on Ham's brand new Barbour hat, which Ham said was so new it didn't even have dog hair on it. Well, Mrs. Davis ended up with the beater's hat, the beater with Ham's, and Ham with the hat no one wanted.

After cocktails in one of the former Communist salons, it was off to dinner and early bedtime, since tomorrow was the big boar hunt.

Tomorrow, however, turned out not to be the big boar hunt. Arriving at Nagyborzsony, just off the Danube near the Czech border, we learned that the local hunting club had it scheduled for the next day. Executing plan B, we returned to our hotel, packed quickly, checked out of Kastelyszallo, and bused to Budapest a day early to check into the Atrium Hyatt. This is a very nice hotel, except for the hookers in the lobby, one of whom apparently snagged Mrs. Davis's wallet in an unguarded moment. Ham, our on-board comedian, promised Jeannie he would strip every hooker in Budapest until he found her wallet.

Budapest is a beautiful city, rising on hills on both sides of the Danube. We toured about that afternoon and the next morning. Must-see spots include the castle district, Heroes' Square, Parliament, and St. Stephen's Basilica.

I insisted that our one dinner in Budapest be at Gundel's, Hungary's grand old restaurant, which dates from 1910 and was as famous as Sacher in Vienna, Horcher in Madrid, and Kempinski in Berlin. American gastronome Joseph Wechesberg compared founder Karoly Gundel to Escoffier and Fernand Point. Naturally, Gundel's had gone to seed under the Communists. But in 1991, it was purchased by George Lang, food writer and consultant and proprietor of New York's Café des Artistes, with the help of Mr. Estée Lauder. After a couple of million dollars in restoration and kitchen upgrading, Gundel's has returned to its former glory.

Gundel's baroque, turn-of-the-century opulence befits its position as the "Maxim's of Budapest." China, crystal and other appointments were admirable, and a fair-sized ensemble provided a melodic and soothing background. Although not a terribly large restaurant, fifty chefs and cooks labor in its kitchen.

Karoly Gundel's approach, still followed today, was to sort out the great Hungarian specialties of the past and combine them with the best of the present. A large menu in Hungarian, English, German, and French began with "The Gundel Story" and a page of suggested before-dinner drinks. There was a separate, extensive dessert menu as well as specials of the day. Our favorites included venison pâté, goose liver with sliced potatoes, pheasant stuffed with goose liver, tournedos Franz Liszt with goose liver, wild boar, a platter of boiled meats with condiments, goose with cabbage, and an apricot crêpe. Wines were the ubiquitous but very good Tokay white and an excellent Cabernet from Villany.

Some of our troops spent the balance of the evening in the hotel's Las Vegas Casino, but most retired in preparation for try two at the great boar hunt. Departing the hotel at 6 A.M., we arrived at Nagyborzony at 7:20 to be greeted by coffee, hard biscuits, and a well-armed (rifles) group of what looked like Hungarian Freedom Fighters. After greetings from the club president, a doctor of forensic medicine, everyone piled into former Russian military trucks and took to the hills.

After thirty minutes on terrible, rutted and muddy two-tracks, we arrived at the hunting grounds—wooded and hilly but with little brush or ground cover. We were spread in a long line, out of sight of each other with a guide for each of our seven hunters. We were armed with our same shotguns, now loaded with slugs and buckshot.

The guides had rifles with scopes, to be used if the boars were too far for shotguns or to save our skins if a boar objected to being wounded. As with the pheasant shooting, our guides and beaters were club members. This club has forty-seven members and leases about sixteen thousand acres.

Boar hunting consists of waiting in the woods while successive drives proceed. We saw numerous deer, which we could have easily bagged. Then two large wild pigs appeared within range, but running between them were a row of piglets. Not wanting to make them orphans, I hesitated until they were out of range, then fired a deliberately wild shot at the guide's urging. Ham missed a monster wild boar, Charles nailed a seventy-kilo sow, and then Ham wounded, trailed, and killed an eighty-kilo sow.

Our club lunch this day was outdoors on a long table near an old Russian field-command trailer used by the club. The main course was the usual boiling pot of goulash, the best bread of the trip, various accompaniments, and the typical assortment of wine, beer, vodka, and brandy. As in Britain, there is no nonsense about alcohol and gunpowder not mixing, and deaths from gunshot by hunters are far lower than ours, the difference being the lack of amateur or poorly trained hunters (and drinkers).

In the final drive of the day, David E. used his guide's rifle to kill a ninety-kilo boar, the only boar of the hunt.

Most European hunters have a great tradition of respect for game, which is often evidenced in ceremonies. In the after-hunt tableau, the boar was at the point of a triangle and the two sows on either side, all surrounded by the usual pine boughs and bonfires. Foliage was placed in the dead pigs' mouths, signifying their last meal. Then another sprig of leaves was smeared with blood and presented to the hunter to place in his hat to denote a kill. Because it was their first boar, Charles and Ham were part of a special ceremony. As they lay across their animals, they were struck three times with a bough—once for St. Huburtus (patron saint of hunters), once for the animal, and once for the club. In the glow of the bonfires twilight arrived as sparkling wine was opened and the day relived in exaggerated remembrance.

Dinner that evening at our hotel is best forgotten. A better memory is a scenic boat trip that night along the Danube with night-lit views of Buda and Pest on opposite banks of the river.

The next morning, the Davises departed for London and David's induction as a Knight of St. Huburtus, the knighthood of hunters; Charles sped off to the Czech Republic to research cherry trees; and Julia Eisendrath and Jack Jansma left for the United States. The Freys, Larks, Ramseys, and Schirmers left for Vienna at 1 P.M. by our bus. A better idea would have been to proceed up the Danube by boat, but we were told that none was available this late in the year.

After a little shopping that morning and before taking off for Vienna, Mary and I had a very good lunch of simple Hungarian food at Menes Csarda Restaurant near the hotel. Following a red cabbage salad wrapped in a red cabbage leaf, we enjoyed a goose leg and liver with peppers, vegetables, and onions for Mary and a veal chop with calf's liver for me.

Our drive to Vienna was broken by a stop at a roadside gypsy marketplace near Gyor. Five hundred thousand gypsies are the significant minority in Hungary's 8.5 million population, a continuing economic and social problem with 42 percent unemployment and a disinclination by all parties to absorption.

Mary and I would have liked to put up at the old Imperial Hotel, but going along with the group resulted in a stay at the probably better Intercontinental.

Two separate Viennese patrons of The Lark recommended to Mary and me that we dine at Restaurant Drei Husaren, which we had read about many times. So, imposing my will on the unruly group, we dined there our first night.

Drei Husaren (Three Hussars or Cavalrymen) has much in common with Gundel's in that it is the long-established elite restaurant of a capital city—in Hungary, in one case, and Austria, in the other. Like Gundel's, Drei Husaren had an elegant and spacious ambience, fine appointments, and was well staffed. The food was excellent, the service less so.

While The Lark has one hors d'oeuvre trolley, Drei Husaren had three. Our only problem was obtaining service from them. After a half-hour wait, a party of six was seated and immediately all three trolleys were wheeled to their table. I blew a fuse and cornered the maître d'. While apologizing, he explained the strange goings-on by informing me that Madame Fauchon of the famous Paris food establishment was at the other table. I replied that I didn't care who it was, and wanted immediate service. A waiter other than ours then snatched the trolleys for his table, evidence that the maître d' had little if any control over this restaurant.

When finally sampled, the hors d'oeuvres were very fine, including everything from *prosciutto*, eel and prawns, to an elaborate, wonderful preparation of calf's brains. Unlike The Lark, there is a separate charge for every item selected. To soothe our ire, the kitchen produced a complimentary course. Main courses included Viennese classics such as *tafelspitz* (boiled beef), *schnitzel*, and venison. A great dessert was vanilla ice cream with diced candied chestnuts in a circle of very thin cookies on a bed of chocolate sauce.

While the food was superb, service continued poorly and we had to request more water and nag for more rolls. The table was never crumbed, and one of the two lights on our table was out. To top this off, the charge record when it arrived had emphasis marks inked in at "tip." I added none, but made a point of overtipping the piano player. Vienna is very expensive, the bill totaling close to $250 per couple, making The Lark seem a great bargain.

We learned the next morning that our Intercontinental Hotel had a fabulous buffet breakfast, $24 per person for the rest of the group, but free to Mary and me as we booked through American Express Platinum Card Travel Service. Furthermore, although our room was the same as the rest of the gang's, it was about $100 less per night because of our platinum card booking, for a total savings per day for Mary and me of $150 or $600 for four days.

Vienna was the imperial seat of the Hapsburgs for over six hundred years, the capital of the Austro-Hungarian Empire, which included not only Austria and Hungary, but all or parts of Poland, Czechoslovakia, Yugoslavia, Italy, and Romania. While its power has faded, its appeal remains in architecture, art, music, and a charming and nostalgic life style. Like all great cities, there was more than we could explore in years, let alone days, but we did try to hit the highlights, while avoiding any feelings of duty or compulsion.

Many of the most important of Vienna's imposing structures are located along the famous Ringstrasse or Ring Road. The Emperor Franz Joseph ripped down whole sections of the city to build the State Opera House, Museum of Fine Arts, Museum of Natural History, the Hofburg, the Parliament, City Hall, Burgtheatre, and Votive Church. We also saw the giant Ferris wheel at the Prater and, finally, the Danube.

While the Danube flows through the center of Budapest and is central to its ambience, it is on the outskirts of Vienna, with only the mostly dried-up Danube Canal near the city's center. We especially enjoyed Schonbrunn, the emperor's summer palace with its extensive park and gardens. Grand in size, it is nevertheless smaller than the Hofburg, which has 2,600 rooms and was the favorite imperial palace as well as the site of the Spanish Riding School with its great Lippizaner horses.

The *In World Guide* (Fifth Edition, 1988–1989) says, "More than the Waltz, even more than the imperturbable blue Danube, the café epitomizes the Viennese approach to life's ups and downs. They are Vienna's sitting rooms, where the most important activities in a singularly somnambulant life are conducted; sitting, talking, reading and sharing that indefinable atmosphere of tristesse, the aura of faded grandeur. Sometimes alone but never lonely, you can sit by the hour in quiet contemplation and appreciation of possibly the finest cup (or glass) of coffee in Europe."

So, to recover from our explorations, we lunched at Demel, one of Vienna's most famous cafés. It was so popular that the only way we got a table was to be given one reserved for a group, which was late. Demel's method of ordering solved any language problem. The patron goes to a display counter and selects one or more items, which are brought to the table by a waitress. Our selections included smoked trout with cold green beans and tomato, veal pâté *en croûte*, vegetable strudel, ham and noodle pie, and noodles with sauerkraut. Drinks included great coffee, beer, and mineral water. Then it was back to a separate dessert display to choose desserts such as Sachertorte (dry), strudel (great), chocolate nougat cake (the best), and a fine chestnut, coffee and almond cake. These could further be slathered with rich whipped cream. Lunch totaled eighty-two dollars per couple, causing an uprising from my frugal troops and my loss of the position of restaurant selector.

A stroll through pedestrian-only old town after lunch brought us to St. Stephen's Cathedral, where a fine choir was practicing. Only a fine choir could survive in this city in love with music. We spent hours browsing this area of charming old buildings and fine shops.

That evening, while my rebellious minions ate sausage and drank beer at the Schwartzenberg Konsert Café, Mary and I dined at the palace of the famous family after which our friends' café was named—the Palais Schwartzenberg. One writer describes the Palais as a nostalgic treasure chest whose views into the palace's park evoke sentiments of a bygone era, as did its service and menu. After a small surprise of veal forcemeat and kidney pâté, Mary enjoyed smoked trout with a white wine sauce and horseradish, followed by perch filets with small potato cubes and tiny green beans. I began with a lasagna of salmon and wild mushrooms with both white and green asparagus. My main course was rabbit loin and leg with the liver and kidneys on a bed of fresh noodles. Desserts were a plum soufflé and a blackberry sorbet.

The next morning was spent with Rembrandt, Bruegel, Rubens, and some other guys at the magnificent Kunsthisorisches Museum. With the guidance of the concierge (whom Ham called my "evil co-conspirator"), I had selected the great Café Gestener for lunch. When the group saw white tablecloths and otherwise fine ambience, they again rebelled and attacked me for "trying to trick us again into a financial vortex." Wandering around searching for a reasonable (i.e., cheap) alternate, they stumbled on Café-Restaurant Halali, where I had the old Viennese standard, boiled beef, and others had game. It was at least half as good as Gestener and only a little more expensive.

At cocktails that evening, we bid fond *adieu* to the Freys and Schirmers, who were off to the airport and home. Still under Ham's waning influence, we and the Ramseys dined modestly, but well, near the hotel at Dubrovnik, which didn't look good from the outside, but which was quite nice with piano and violin music and Balkan specialties emphasizing pork, onions, and peppers.

Saturday was flea-market day, within a fair walk of our hotel. Scores, maybe hundreds, of booths sold anything and everything. As is general in Austria, there were no great buys, but Mary snagged an antique Italian mosaic glass pin and an antique woodworking tool for number-four son. Mary and I lunched at Café Gestener, a classic Viennese café with magnificent ambience, fun people-watching, and excellent food and service. We talked our way into a previously reserved table by telling the manager we would be done by the time noted on the reserved card. Mary had a Greek salad complete with sections of stuffed grape leaves, followed by a quiche. I enjoyed an artichoke salad and a smoked trout plate. For dessert we tucked into a Dobos torte and a chestnut-shaped chocolate shell filled with chestnut purée.

After lunch, we visited the Sacher Hotel. Its café was more elegant than the hotel. Later, we stopped by the world-famous Imperial Hotel. We were tempted to dine there that night, but instead reserved at the dining room of the Bristol Hotel, which is affiliated with the Imperial and with Goldener Hirsch in Salzburg. The dining room was pleasant with poor service and good food, the best of which was roast guinea hen.

Sunday mass was otherworldly in the Imperial Chapel of the Hofburg with the old traditional singing of the Vienna Boys'

Choir—some of the most beautiful singing in the world in one of the most perfect settings in the world.

Following mass, we meandered through the Sunday crowds in the old city, finally arriving at Café-Restaurant Landtmann, which was even more elegant than Demel, Sacher or Gestener, with high ceilings, terrazo floors, paneled walls, fine curtains, and comfortable booths. Lunch included the best *tafelspitz* ever with football-shaped potatoes, cubed vegetables, horseradish cream, apple sauce, and cabbage in a light butter sauce. This superb café was the best of our trip and, we suspect, the finest in Vienna.

Pouilly-Fuissé

The most popular single wine at The Lark is Bollinger Special Cuvée champagne. Second in demand is a dead heat between Chalk Hill Chardonnay '93 and Château Beauregard Pouilly-Fuissé, Burgundy, Louis Latour '94. All three are house wines, available by either the glass or bottle, which increases their sales. Pouilly-Fuissé is so favored in the United States that in France it has been called the American wine.

In his *New Encyclopedia of Wine and Spirits,* the late Alex Lichine said of Pouilly-Fuissé, "The finest dry white wine of southern Burgundy and one that has for some years received the renown which it deserves in England and the United States."

Hugh Johnson in his *Pocket Encyclopedia of Wine* was unhappy that demand drove up prices. "The best white wine of the Mâcon area. At its best (e.g., Ch. Fuissé, Vieilles Vignes) excellent, but almost always overpriced."

The Vieilles Vignes appended by Johnson to Ch. Fuissé means "old vines," a reference that Ch. Fuissé's top offering is just that, made from grapes from the château's oldest vines. *The New York*

Times wine writer Frank Prial wrote in an article, "Mr. Vincent, at the Château de Fuissé, makes a Pouilly-Fuissé from very old vines that ... I've never seen in this country."

Pouilly-Fuissé varies widely in quality; very little is from a single estate or domaine bottled. Our approach, as usual, is "Why not the best?" Hence our selection of Château Beauregard as our house Pouilly-Fuissé. As to the finest wine of the appellation, Ch. Fuissé, Vieilles Vignes 1992 may be found on our reserve list. Visit Detroit, Mr. Prial, and try a bottle.

Attitudes

It is quite common for reviewers to praise a restaurant's food but knock the dining room staff's attitude. This could indicate the owner has an attitude problem, but more frequently it means he or she is not present. It seems an almost universal rule: When the owner is absent, restaurants are run for the convenience of the staff rather than to please the paying customers.

Aegean Odyssey

*O*ne of the hottest travel trends is the burgeoning popularity of small luxury cruise ships. To quote Andrew Harper's *Hideaways Report:*

"Sea Goddess started the revolution. Windstar followed with some new twists, and slowly, the discerning traveler discovered the attractions of cruising small yachtlike ships that emphasized unregimented lifestyles, personal space and service, and cruised to exotic off-the-beaten-path destinations.

"Then, all of a sudden, there were more of these ships being launched—eight by Renaissance; one by Seven Seas; the Royal Viking Queen [now Royal Cruise Line's Queen Odyssey]; and most recently, Silversea.... It's almost more than you can keep track of."

Seabourne must be added to the list and, perhaps, the Radisson Diamond, although its 350 passengers make it larger than the other ships listed. As price wars flared, choice of destinations proliferated, and glowing reports poured in, Mary and I were increasingly tempted to climb aboard. Usually, we lead the way in travel, but we'd avoided cruises because Mary was seasick on our only prior cruise twenty-some years ago. We were finally hooked by a Renaissance advertisement of a cruise to Greece and Turkey at a savings of $4,000, with upgrade to business-class flights to and fro at only $495 additional.

Thus, after a blessedly uneventful flight, a sunny autumn morning found us checking into the Athenaeum Inter-Continental Athens for our two days in the city of Pericles, Sophocles, Aristotle, and Plato. Despite our well-traveled lives, neither Mary nor I had previously visited Greece—mostly because of the anti-American rhetoric of left-wing Greek politicians. That virus seems to have run its course, with rabble-rousing abated and the natives friendly. Our hotel was also agreeable, well-run and reliable, if unexceptional. Although there are no grand hotels in Athens or all of Greece, acceptable choices are the handsome Hilton and Le Grande Bretagne, known as the Claridge's of Athens because the government uses it as a guest house for visiting heads of state.

By request, our room had a splendid view of the Acropolis—important because it is the dominant presence, tourist site, and historical fact of Athens. After a bountiful buffet lunch at the Intercontinental, which included everything from prawns and smoked salmon to a Greek salad, we enjoyed touring the city. Its highlight is the Parthenon, the culmination of Greek architecture and sculpture. Also on the Acropolis are the Propylea, Temple of Wingless Victory, Athena Nike Temple, and the Erechtheum Temple with its famous Porch of Maidens. Other sights include the Ancient Agora (market), Tower of the Winds, Herod Atticus Theatre, Temple of Zeus, the 1896 Modern Olympic Stadium, and the House of Parliament and its guards with funny-looking, up-curving, pompon-toed shoes. Despite the tremendous ancient booty carried off to the British Museum and to other museums throughout the world, the National Archeological Museum is a treasure trove of Greek art and, after the Acropolis, the principal reward for any visit. The great Mycenaean finds of Heinrich Schliemann are but one example.

On this first evening in Greece, we naturally dined at one of the most popular and typical Greek tavernas, Myrtia. It boasts a charming rustic decor and a Zorba trio playing to a packed house of both Athenians and visitors. No need to order. The very practiced waiters brought a series of a dozen authentic Greek dishes, including the traditional taramossalata fish roe appetizer, fried calamari, mussels in an herb-laced tomato sauce, grilled prawns, pork, lamb, and more. This veritable feast with bottled water and simple but good white and red wines cost about forty-five dollars per person including service. (Throughout our journey we eschewed retsina wines which contain Alep pine resin and are unpleasantly pungent.) It was already apparent that Greece is a nation with good taste buds, since every dish at our buffet luncheon and at Myrtia was perfectly seasoned.

Other than its ancient buildings, Athens is largely an unplanned urban sprawl of banal low-rise apartment and commercial buildings—the result of a great influx of Greeks driven from Turkey in the 1920s and a more recent migration to the capital from the countryside and the islands of the Aegean. Thus, except for archeological sites, museums, tavernas, and nightlife, Athens has little to attract the visitor besides the Plaka and Piraeus. Plaka is Athen's old town, the oldest continually inhabited village in Europe and the site of many small shops and a wide variety of restaurants. Mary enjoyed shopping there, finding appealing favors for The Lark's Aegean theme dinner. Unfortunately, while we bargained for the favors with the shop owner, a gypsy family of father, mother, and child created a diversion and stole the shop owner's purse. This so upset us that we gave her a hundred-dollar bill over and above the price of our purchases.

Highly recommended Gerofinikas, where we enjoyed a luncheon of authentic Greek cuisine, had a better ambience than Myrtia, was less touristic, had finer food, and was also reasonably priced. We ordered after viewing a display of prepared cold selections and the raw ingredients, such as fish and prawns, for hot dishes. Octopus salad, stuffed mussels, grilled sea bass, grilled red mullet, and lamb with artichoke hearts were all very good.

The other must-see area of Athens is its port of Piraeus, famous for seafood restaurants. Our choice for dinner, 42 Koxyvia, was spacious, simple, and clean with a view of the harbor. As at Gerofinikas, the staff was extremely friendly as well as helpful in taking our order. Tzatziki cucumber and yogurt dip, fried calamari, grilled prawns, sautéed sea bass, and baklavas were all excellent. The prawns were especially sweet and flavorful. Dinner for four totaled only about one hundred dollars including wine, tax, and service.

The next day, our last in Athens, found us driving along the coast of the Saronic Gulf past the fine beaches of Glyfada, Vougliagmeni, and Varkiza, the nearest of which were residential suburbs of Athens as well as summer beach resorts. We soon arrived at Cape Sounion where King Aegeus awaited the return of his son Theseus from Crete. Theseus flew black sails in error and King Aegeus, believing his son had been killed, leapt to his death in the sea. Hence, this part of the Mediterranean is called the Aegean Sea. Windswept Cape Sounion, with an inspiring view of the Saronic Gulf and its islands, was an obvious choice for a temple to Poseidon, god of the sea. The remains of his fifth-century temple are a dramatic combination of the austere Doric and the graceful Ionic styles. Lord Byron and other famous visitors have carved their names into the remaining columns.

Having now "done" as much of Athens as possible in two days, we eagerly reported aboard Renaissance IV (RIV), our floating home for the next week. RIV is the smallest of the new breed of yachtlike cruise ships, accommodating a maximum one hundred passengers in fifty cabins.

RIV is 290 feet long with a 50-foot beam and six decks, a hundred-seat lounge, hundred-seat restaurant, piano bar, library, pool, casino, Jacuzzi, beauty salon, and hospital. Since the restaurant has a seat for every passenger, there were no sittings, and one could come to dinner at will; a couple could request a private table or share a table with one, two, or three other couples. The only amenity we missed was an exercise facility with a NordicTrack for our daily workout.

Our Renaissance Suite was one of only four on the top deck and had a king-sized bed; seating area with sofa, two easy chairs, and cocktail table; vanity with chair; adequate closet and storage; bath with shower; and sliding-glass doors opening onto a private veranda. This last pleased Mary most of all, since the openness avoided any sense of claustrophobia contributing to seasickness.

Polls bear out that the best points of the Renaissance ships are their cabins and their appealing itineraries. To this add an eager-to-please, almost gung-ho staff, and relatively low pricing if one takes advantage of special offers. Renaissance has no really weak point other than a lack of grand luxury, and food that varies from mediocre to good. It is not for those who prefer black-tie dinners with caviar and foie gras. Although gentlemen were requested to wear ties and jackets at dinner, some did not.

After our first night at sea, we approached the fabled Greek island of Santorini in the Cyclades. Friends who had traveled the Aegean advised us to arise early to experience the ship's entry into the great bay enfolded by the high cliffs of this crescent-shaped island. Venetian-named Santorini, known as Thera by the Greeks, was a round island 3,500 years ago, when a tremendous volcanic eruption blew out its center and created its present shape. The bay is the volcano's collapsed core, the largest caldera on earth. Our solitary view from the rarely used sun deck in front of the four Renaissance suites was unforgettable and included the island's capital of Fira, perched on the edge of cliffs nine hundred feet above the bay.

We enjoyed a light breakfast, selected from a buffet on the pool deck and carried back to our cabin. Other choices would have been an outdoor table near the buffet, breakfast served in our cabin, or a more elaborate meal in the dining room. Thus fortified, we began our first shore excursion. The land behind the cliff's edge, outside the town of Fira, proved to be rolling hills and vineyards overlooking black beaches. Crowded by artists and tourists in the summer, in autumn we had the roads and sights largely to ourselves. Our goal was the ancient Minoan town of Akrotiri, buried under light volcanic ash and pumice by an eruption around 1500 B.C. Rumored to be the lost Atlantis, excavation of the wonderfully preserved ruins did not begin until 1967. They compose an almost complete ancient town 1,625 years older than Pompeii. Unlike Pompeii, however, the inhabitants must have had warning, since no human remains nor jewelry have been found. The force of the blast is unimaginable, and some scientists believe that the resulting tidal wave destroyed the Minoan civilization on Crete.

Fira, the capital, called the most splendidly situated town in all of the Greek islands, is also very picturesque with twisting streets and alleys and houses perched on the cliff's edge. It is once again a bustling town, the tourist boom having lured back Santorini's population of twenty thousand, which fled after an earthquake in 1957 destroyed 80 percent of the buildings on the island. Our fine lunch on the terrace of Ari's had a perfect view over the great bay. The tasty fare included warm stuffed vine leaves of lamb and rice with lemon sauce, spinach pie, puréed fava beans with onions, fried calamari, and grilled fresh fish. Santorini by itself would be worth a trip to Greece.

The Greek islands are, of course, very chic. As an example, on our return to the ship we were treated to a strange tableau from our cabin's veranda; a helicopter with a photographer hanging out its side made swooping pass after pass toward a woman on a high isolated cliff, who pirouetted and danced each time the helicopter approached. We saw another photo shoot the next day on Mikonos and learned from its director that his shoot was for an upscale catalog, and that the woman on the cliff of Santorini was performing for a TV commercial.

Having now acquired a taste for Greek islands, we eagerly invaded Mikonos the next morning, following the overnight voyage from Santorini. Mikonos is probably the most cosmopolitan and well-known of the Cyclades, in contrast to its obscure past before the tourist boom of the 1950s. Most famed for picture-perfect windmills and 365 white-domed churches, Mikonos actually has 400 churches, almost all Greek Orthodox, but at least one a Roman Catholic reminder that the island was once a province of Venice.

Mikonos's unique architecture combines native traditions with

Byzantine and Western influences. Local law requires that even recently built hotels follow the traditional architectural style. Winding and twisting streets and alleys, captivating in effect, were originally laid out to cut the wind and to provide places to ambush and fight invading pirates. Arches and vaults over the alleys combined with hibiscus and bougainvillea spilling over whitewashed garden walls add to an almost overpowering charm.

Both Santorini and Mikonos are shoppers' paradises. Cotton fishermen's sweaters, pottery, and tourist items are offered, but the real attraction is gold jewelry. The more expensive pieces, some of antique design, have exquisite workmanship, much superior to that available in Istanbul. Precious stones are also incorporated into rings, bracelets, and necklaces. Bargaining is expected and necessary. I knocked the price of a stunning Burmese ruby necklace down from $13,000 to $8,500 before I decided Mary did not really need it. I think she still disagrees.

Lunch at a taverna in Mikonos town followed the path of least resistance and most enjoyment—stuffed vine leaves, octopus salad, Greek salad of tomatoes, olives and feta cheese, and fresh prawns and fish. By now, we had found the inexpensive red and white Greek wines to be simple, adequate, and enjoyable. Mikonos has some of the best beaches to be found in Greece or the Aegean islands, adding to its appeal to summer tourists. Another attraction is the "Little Venice" quarter of town, where balconied houses have been built at water's edge. Mary and I and the other three couples occupying Renaissance Suites were invited to dinner that evening by ship's Captain Bruno Malatesta. He impressed us as a competent professional sailor and a boyishly charming host. We learned he was a motorcycle-driving bachelor from Genoa, and that he would soon be taking his ship RIV on a "transitional" cruise from the Med to Southeast Asia, stopping by India and other points en route. Early 1995 would find RIV a participant in the increasingly popular cruises through the Indonesian islands and environs, a trip we took in January 1996. A Barolo from the great 1989 vintage added to the festive evening.

Breakfast time the next morning found RIV docking at the capital city of Rhodes, the largest of the Greek Dodecanese Islands, close to the southwest Turkish coast. Rhodes's history includes settlement by the ancient Achaeans and the later arrival of the commercially and artistically active Dorians. Their culture peaked in the fourth century B.C., when Chares of Lindhos built one of the seven wonders of the ancient world—the Colossus of Rhodes, which was destroyed by an earthquake in 22 B.C. After the passing of the Roman Empire, Rhodes was governed by a succession of Arabs, Saracens, and Crusaders. The Knights of St. John of Jerusalem ruled from 1306 until ousted by the Turks in 1552. The Knights removed themselves to Malta, and after that island was seized by Napoleon, they gave up their role as warriors and became an exclusively charitable order of the Catholic Church.

A drive through vineyards, barley fields, and fig and citrus groves brought us to Lindhos, which has the island's only natural harbor and was important to the Byzantines and medieval Greeks as well as the ancient Dorians. Today its population is only seven hundred compared with seventeen thousand in ancient times. Highlights included the fifteenth-century Byzantine Church of St. Mary with fine frescoes and, more importantly, the Acropolis of Lindhos with the fourth-century-B.C. Temple of Athena on the edge of a precipitous cliff. There are also ruins of a Byzantine fortress and a Commander's Palace of the Knights of St. John.

Returning to the capital, we visited the fourteenth-century Palace of the Grand Master of the Knights of St. John, converted to a prison by the Turks and now a museum. It lies at the heart of old town in a maze of narrow streets and quaint houses. Most impressive is Knights Street, with its "inns," where each national group of Knights had its own quarters. The Inn of France was the largest and most beautiful. It must be remembered that all of the Knights were also noblemen. The Knights Hospital was built on Roman ruins and was the reason for the Knights' existence. Unfortunately, most of the patients were Knights wounded defending the island.

Next day's island du jour was Patmos, one of the northernmost of the Dodecanese and one of the smallest of the inhabited islands of the Aegean. Like all of the Dodecanese, Patmos was ruled by Italy from the time of the Turkish defeat in 1912 until the end of World War II, when it was reunited with Greece. Here we saw the cave, now a shrine, where St. John the Divine wrote the Book of Revelations, the last book of the New Testament, in 95–97 A.D. Next we proceeded to St. John's Monastery, crowning the peak of Chora, founded in 1088. The monastery amassed riches from commercial shipping and acquired treasures now on display, including ancient icons, early Christian and Byzantine manuscripts, silverwork, amulets, and gold medallions. Just as impressive is the view from the monastery of the Aegean Sea as far away as Mikonos.

Leaving the Aegean Greek islands behind, our next morning's port of call was Kusadasi, a port and tourist center on a peninsula of the Turkish mainland. Disembarkation was delayed until Turkish officials cleared the ship and its passengers and collected their Scotch and cigarettes. Kusadasi itself is unremarkable, its principal attractions being the ancient Mehmet Pasa Caravanserai (now a hotel and restaurant), seafood restaurants, and a Turkish bazaar and shops catering to visitors. Drawn by the challenge, I again plunged into a round of haggling—this time for a handsome silk carpet with hundreds of knots per square inch. After bargaining its price down from $4,000 to $2,200, I again decided this was something Mary could do without. It became apparent that I should abandon this practice. God, however, was watching over me as the "Ombudsman" feature in Conde Nast's *Traveler* magazine subsequently reported that a reader purchasing a "silk" carpet at this very store was actually given a cotton rip-off.

Every prior traveler we had spoken to of our impending trip had insisted that we see the ruins of Ephesus, and this was the principal reason for the stop at Kusadasi, the nearest port and jumping off place for tours of Ephesus. The not-distant ruins of Ephesus are one of the largest and best-preserved ancient cities. The estuary on which it was located is now silted up, but it was an important Greek and Roman port of two hundred thousand inhabitants, a magnificent center of trade between the West, whose goods came by ship, and the East, whose trade was by camel caravans. Ephesus was also the center of Anatolian Christendom. St. Paul taught here, and the Apostle John brought the Virgin Mary here after the crucifixion. Mary died in a house outside the city, and St. John's tomb is here in the Basilica of St. John.

Destroyed by an earthquake in 17 A.D., Ephesus was rebuilt by the Emperor Tiberius, so its ruins are largely Roman. One highlight is the Arcadian Way, named after the Emperor Arcadius (395–408 A.D.), stretching from the harbor to the theatre and bordered by the Harbor Thermal Baths and Gymnasium and a host of other buildings. The theatre was the most spectacular building and is well preserved. Others include the Library of Celsus (connected to a house of ill repute by a tunnel), the Temple of Serapis for eastern merchants, the Marble Way, Hadrian's Temple, and the Baths of Scolastica. Many of the temples, public buildings, and finer houses have been partially reconstructed. The grandeur of Ephesus drew Anthony and Cleopatra, who trod its Marble Way, and the number, variety, and quality of its buildings almost demands a trip here by everyone who can possibly arrange it.

Renting a small boat with crew has been a popular way for three or four couples to explore the islands of the Aegean. Now, similar cruising along the Turkish coast is also growing in popularity. Certainly, Kusadasi and Ephesus would be one of their stops. Another not-to-be-missed stop would be our next day's adventure—the port of Çanakkale and the nearby ruins of Troy. Readers will recall the graphic detail of its story in Homer's *Iliad*, including the abduction of Helen and the siege that culminated in the ruse of the Trojan horse.

At Troy, we viewed the excavated ruins of its nine successive cities—the oldest that of 3,000 B.C. and the last, the Roman city of 400 A.D. It remains uncertain whether King Priam's Troy was Troy VI or Troy VII. I climbed up and inside a huge replica of the wooden

Trojan horse. Sticking my head through an opening to look down at Mary, someone apparently wishing a photo of the horse without my presence yelled, "Get your head back in a————," which doubled me over with laughter.

Not having been seasick the entire voyage, Mary decided to forego the scheduled replacement of her behind-the-ear anti-seasickness patch. Bad decision. This, our last night at sea before reaching Istanbul, brought a full gale, sinking a ship in our vicinity. Spume from the huge waves reached even the veranda of our top sixth-level cabin. I was thrown about the cabin as I packed, our luggage being required outside our door before we retired for the night. Fortunately, a shot from the ship's doctor cured what ailed Mary.

RIV and other cruise ships sail from Istanbul along the Turkish coast and through the Aegean islands to Athens, as well as the reverse itinerary that we experienced. We were fortunate, as Istanbul is a truly fitting grand finale, making Athens (other than the Acropolis) seem a mere town. Istanbul is wonderful, which is understandable for a city that was a capital of the Roman, Byzantine, and Ottoman empires. Occupying both the Asian and European shores of the Bosporus, Istanbul rises dramatically up seven hills, its European sky-line dominated by the huge dome of Justinian's sixth-century Haghia Sophia, or Church of Holy Wisdom.

The new American-owned-and-managed Conrad Hotel was our base for the next two days as we explored the city. Istanbul has enough treasures to occupy one for weeks, but highlights include the afore-mentioned Haghia Sophia, the Blue Mosque with its blue-green Iznik decorative tiles, the Hippodrome, and the huge Topkapi Palace with its harem. The Hippodrome was the site of Roman chariot races and gladiatorial contests. The Topkapi Palace was the official residence of the Turkish sultans until deemed too old-fashioned by Sultan Abdulmecit I, who around 1850 built the present-day Dolmabache Palace, well located on the European shore of the Bosporus. After the post-World War I collapse of the Ottoman Empire, Attaturk, founder of modern Turkey, stayed at the palace when in Istanbul and died there in 1923 at age fifty-seven. I suspect the palace was a case of keeping up with the Hapsburgs. It has 295 rooms, forty-three halls, six balconies, and six elaborate Turkish baths. The contents include 280 vases, 156 clocks, fifty-eight crystal candlesticks, and thirty-six chandeliers of Bohemian, Venetian, French, and English crystal. Basically sound, it does lack proper housekeeping. Mary longed to attack it with bottles of Pledge and Windex. Fourteen tons of gold and forty tons of silver are said to have been used in its construction.

Istanbul's Grand Bazaar, with its hundreds-of-years-old history, must be the ultimate shopping experience with over four thousand shops, some narrow and some large, lining a labyrinth of passageways. Everything is for sale—especially carpets, woodwork, copper, and jewelry. Bargaining is, of course, essential. Mary was either so charming or so poor a bargainer, or both, that the shopkeeper from whom she bought small tapestries gave her a present.

After so much sight-seeing and shopping, we felt entitled to dinner at "S" restaurant, reputed to be Istanbul's most elegant. In addition to a rich but subdued ambience, "S" has sophisticated dinner music and a good view of the night-lit Bosporus. Our meal included bargain-priced fresh caviar with warm blinis, an excellent rack of lamb, and a mellow chocolate soufflé. As usual, we were especially well tended when it was learned we were "in the trade," and bar supervisor H. Murat Ortac chose a good Turkish wine to accompany our dinner.

The next day we taxied to the ferry terminal for the traditional and essential boat trip up the Bosporus, stopping alternately on the European and Asian sides. Both shores were lined with old palaces, hotels, wooden cottages, seaside restaurants, and small villages. Thus inspired, we had the Conrad's staff reserve a table that evening at Korfez, one of the waterfront restaurants we had passed on the Asian side. At the prearranged time, Korfez's boat met our taxi at a landing on the European side and carried us across the Bosporus to the restaurant. That passage was the high point of the evening and a romantic and final memory of our Aegean odyssey.

Now That's Feta

I've always liked feta, even the American-made version of this Balkan cheese. Lately, however, imported Bulgarian feta has been available at some stores. It is fabulous! Ersatz U.S. feta is made from cows' milk while the real thing is a product of goats' milk. Another important consideration is that feta loses its flavor if not kept in the original brine, which includes goats' milk. Look for feta labeled Bulgarian or Greek and sealed in heavy plastic, not packed in a round plastic tub.

Grape Leaves

Stuffed grape leaves are an essential part of the cuisine of most countries of the Balkans and Middle East such as Greece, Bulgaria, Turkey, and Lebanon. Collecting and using wild grape leaves for this purpose is an easy and fun activity, well suited to the current interest in foraging for mushrooms, berries, ramps, and other wild foods. In West Bloomfield, Michigan, in the early summer, Mary Lark, Julie Jonna of the Merchant of Vino, and other savants may be seen collecting the new leaves from fallow fields and hedgerows. Grape leaves should not be taken from vines that have been sprayed, nor from those close to a road, as they may have absorbed pollutants from engine exhaust.

Choose tender leaves of the desired size, free of insect damage. Shaded leaves will be most tender and flexible. Make a neat pile of leaves, roll them, and secure each pile with a rubber band. To prepare the leaves for stuffing, remove the rubber band, grasp six leaves firmly with kitchen tongs, and immerse them in heavily salted boiling water for ninety seconds. Drain the leaves in a colander and let them cool. Discard any torn or tough ones. Separate the leaves and dry them in one layer, dull side down, on paper towels. Trim the tough end of the middle stems with kitchen shears. Grape leaves are stuffed with the dull side up. Stuffing will vary from one teaspoon of filling if it contains rice, which will expand, to a scant tablespoon of fillings that do not contain rice. The filling is placed at the stem end, the sides folded in, and the leaf rolled up tightly. Many excellent recipes are readily available. For best results, use fresh herbs of the season.

Paris to the Riviera

*O*ur Sunday evening departure from Detroit was very much in the fast lane as we had hosted the annual Michigan Chili Cookoff at The Lark that afternoon. The juxtaposition of a chili cookoff with a trip to the starred restaurants of France reveals an omnivorous approach to food.

Our journeys to Europe typically feature an inauspicious start, and this one was no exception. Having sat on a runway for close to two hours with computer boarding problems, the flight was so late reaching London that our luggage did not make the connecting plane to Paris.

Arriving at the Hotel Crillon, we were assigned a very small room. Forewarned by a good customer, we rejected it and were then given room number 101—a romantic jewel adjacent to a large salon fronting on the Place de la Concorde, siding toward the U.S. Embassy and used for midday receptions. Returning each night after dinner, we closed the door from our inner hallway to the main hallway and opened the door from the inner hallway to the salon. *Voila!* A free two-thousand-square-foot living room with balconies overlooking the Place de la Concorde! Under the influence of apéritifs, fine food, wine and Armagnac, it seemed appropriate to address the crowds below from the balcony. *"Mes amis!"*

Taillevent, universally described as the city's finest restaurant, was our dining highlight in Paris. We had written in advance for reservations, enclosing a copy of our own menu, and the way had further been prepared by Cannan and Wasserman, wine negotiants and friends of Jean-Claude Vrinat, Taillevent's charming and tireless proprietor. Our repast included a seafood sausage with truffles and pistachios, salmis of pigeon, duck breast with peach sauce, cheese, pear soufflé, and *marquise au chocolat*. I chose a 1976 Clos de Vougeot when the sommelier, obviously an accomplished liar, told me he would not recommend a wine as I was "an expert." It is difficult to be objective when flattered with special service and complimentary offerings, but Mary and I thought the meal perfect. Over the years Jean-Claude Vrinat has become a good friend.

Not so perfect was dinner at Hotel Crillon's two-star restaurant. Duck foie gras and truffle ravioli were excellent, but untrimmed veal kidneys were tough, and rare medallions of lamb layered between filled ravioli were overpowered by fennel, which should be forbidden to some chefs.

It soon became apparent that we could not enjoy both lunch and dinner at two- and three-star restaurants, so we asked M. Vrinat of Taillevent for bistro and brasserie suggestions. Julien in Faubourg St. Denis, which our cab driver thought *"très chic,"* was crowded, noisy and fun. As at all but three-star restaurants, dress ranged from punk rock to elegant. The maître d' was the only person in France to question our lack of fluency in the language. I gave him my pre-prepared response. *"Je parle français très mal. Parlez vous chinois? Non? Parlez vous japonais? Non? Portugais?"* At which point he cracked up, and we got along fine. With the exception of two grouches who were equally rude to the French, we were treated well everywhere. A happy attitude and attempts at humor were especially appreciated and always brought a smile and a lively response. Julien's serving of mussels was gigantic, and three lobster halves were only 108 francs. Our bone-dry wine was a modest Muscadet sur Lie.

One of Jean-Claude's other recommendations, Brasserie Lipp on Boulevard St. Germain, was already on our must list. It is not a practical choice for a must list since James Villas, the noted food writer, described it as "the most exclusive public club in the world. Getting into The Connaught Grill in London, Taillevent in Paris, or Le Cirque in New York is mere child's play compared to landing a table at Brasserie Lipp.... Monsieur Cazes stands like Cerberus every day and night, inspecting all who arrive, jotting down notes on strange round cards, and deciding who gets seated, when, and where.... For years I was rejected by Monsieur Cazes with the cold proclamation that there would be no table available at eight, nine ... midnight."

I had forgotten those observations of Mr. Villas, and arrived with Mary at 8:15 P.M., the height of the dinner hour. Bright with expectancy, I missed the significance of the stream of would-be customers who spoke to M. Cazes, turned, and sulked out. When I naively requested a table for two, the dour host said, "10:15." I thought he said ten or fifteen minutes and replied, "Fine." Having been set straight, I shamelessly dropped Mr. Villas's name and also tried the old ploy, "We have a restaurant also." Something worked, probably Mary's charm, and after a brief wait in the café area, we were shown to a fine banquette. At that, a Frenchwoman who was part of a waiting party screamed her rage at M. Cazes to no avail. Feeling guilty, we assuaged those pangs with luscious herring, *choucroute garnie,* and what Mr. Villas describes as "the best *boeuf gros sel* on earth." In keeping with the Alsatian theme, our wine was a fine Gewurztraminer.

At M. Vrinat's third suggestion, the bistro Chez Georges, we enjoyed sausage Lyonnais, turbot, sole, and a foot-long caramel eclair. Nearby diners ate, among other things, a pig's ear and a four-inch-thick grilled roast beef for two. A Chablis le Forêt, although not overpriced, cost more than our food.

Hating to leave the Crillon, where Mary had been invited to join a reception in "our salon" by a confused president of Angola, we departed by bullet train from the Gare de Lyon. This bullet train, although amazingly comfortable and clean, was not properly pro-pelled since we arrived in Lyon quite late and missed our luncheon reservation at Alain Chapel's three-star bastion of Nouvelle Cuisine. Trouble coming in sets, our rental car broke down shortly after we became lost in Lyon. A take-charge, multilingual tourist from the Netherlands made the necessary phone calls and dispatched us back to Hertz by taxi. I never met a Dutchman I didn't like.

Now equipped with a Volkswagen Golf and set on the right road, we arrived at the Ostellerie du Vieux Pérouges in the perfectly preserved medieval town of Pérouges, thirty-five kilometers northeast of Lyon. Our host, M. Thibaut (who is also mayor of the town), greeted us as "dear colleagues" and assigned us the "Noble" bedroom. Complete with four-poster bed and fireplace, it appeared special, and this was con-firmed when we discovered the chamber featured on color post cards for sale in various gift shops.

Our fixed-price dinner in the Ostellerie's one-star dining room was hearty, yet grand. Some of our dishes were fresh local crayfish, a huge serving of black morels in cream sauce, chicken from Bresse, the best Roquefort ever, *cassis* sorbet, raspberries with *crème fraîche,* and panache Pérougienne—the pizza-shaped, cookielike, special dessert of the village. The house wine, a sparkling Seyssel, proved excellent. The room was full with diners, the mood enhanced by country musi-cians in wooden shoes and an ancient hunting dog who lay quietly at our feet. Mary rewarded her with a scrap of chicken, saved for the purpose, when we took our sated bodies off to bed.

The walled town of Pérouges, which sits on a hill enthroned like a queen, is convenient in size (about eight hundred by four hundred feet) and charming beyond description. All buildings are of stone with tiled roofs; the narrow streets are cobblestone. It could not fail to attract film producers, and numerous movies have been shot there including *The Three Musketeers* and *Monsieur Vincent.* The morning spent exploring Pérouges sparked our appetite for our rebooked luncheon at Alain Chapel. The setting was an impossibly elegant country inn. The menu we selected speaks volumes:

Image de Mionnay

salade fraîche de tout jeunes légumes,
du cerfeuil et un oeuf de caille "mimosa"

des cuisses de grenouilles à la crème et ciboulette,
des haricots blanc et des truffes

rouelle de grosse langouste rouge à la vapeur de
verveine, aux giroflles et chicorée

des gousses d'ails rôties, des petits oignons nouveaux,
une rognonade de lapin de "cabane"

quelques fromages fermiers

granité de chocolat amer et des meringues
moelleuses, mignardises

amandine au kirsch "d'anne-marie"
et des abricots en compote

If one could pick a highlight from such a meal, it would be the main course of rabbit loin, boned and rolled around rabbit kidney, accompanied by the tender leg, all beautifully garnished and sauced.

The service was formal but friendly and the details of presentation the finest. The welcoming tidbit of good, salty, deep-fried whitebait and parsley was presented on a pedestal in an elaborately folded napkin. Another course was served on grape leaves. Baguette bread was rolled in linen, twisted at each end. Vegetables were miniature. The lobster pieces were wrapped in cooked cabbage. Cigars served to French gentlemen at a neighboring table were offered from a huge antique box, trimmed with a silver cutter, and lit with long wooden tapers. Detail followed detail.

Our wines were the house champagne and Puligny-Montrachet. Armagnac was "sweet for Madame" and "strong for Monsieur." Dinner was out of the question that evening, and we nibbled on bread and cheese with the local wine. The next morning found us rushing southward on the A-6 Autopéage at the "normal" speed of 80 mph with German cars passing us at well over 100 mph. Any "slow" car in the fast lane risked God knows what fate. Our route paralleled the Rhône River through fine countryside, and thoughtful roadside signs told us of local sights, vegetation, and activities.

Arriving at lunchtime in the walled city of Avignon, former home of the Popes, our restaurant guidebook led us to the two-star Restaurant Hiely where we were fortunate to find an unbooked table. Our meal included fresh duck foie gras from Lalande, mussels, and guinea fowl. Banoh was the best goat cheese we had ever had. We noticed that the French asked more questions about cheese and deliberated more in its selection than over any other course. Cheese was eaten with a knife and fork and bread or crackers were omitted. After exploring historic Avignon, we drove thirteen more kilometers south to the wonderful country inn, Auberge de Noves, which has been rightly described as an elegant hostelry in an ancient manor with beautiful views. Presided over by witty and sardonic M. Lalleman, it boasts a one-starred restaurant, an appealing terrace, tennis courts, and a pool. The staff were especially solicitous.

Obviously slow learners, we now faced a serious dinner at Noves after a two-star luncheon at Hiely. Nevertheless, we enjoyed an abbreviated dinner whose best course was oysters on the shell that had been gently poached, napped with a sauce of cream and white Châteauneuf du Pape, garnished with tiny slivers of carrots and scallions, and run briefly under the broiler. A magnificent wooden sorbet trolley held eight choices in elaborate pewter tankards, including a smooth and rich chocolate sorbet. We fled from the dining room before dessert, a separate course after the sorbets and before the inevitable miniature pastries. Our host, not realizing how full we were, thought we had departed early because dessert service was slow. To make amends, a note of apology and a bowl of fresh raspberries were delivered to us the next morning as we breakfasted on the terrace.

Auberge de Noves is perfectly located as a base for short drives to nearby Avignon, Arles, Nîmes, and Les Baux—so off we went after breakfast to the eagle's-nest fortress town of Les Baux. Noted for its awesome views and buildings dating to Roman times, Les Baux is equally famous for the Oustau de Baumaniere, a resort whose restaurant has been awarded three stars and five pink knives and forks by *Michelin*. We were warmly received when we stopped to look about, but were in no mood for a three-star lunch, contenting ourselves with a snack at Lou Roucas, an excellent café in the village of Noves.

Dinner at the Auberge de Noves that evening included more of its wonderful oysters and a lobster fresh from an outdoor tank, finished at the table in a copper pot. The *petite pâtisserie* included sugared currants on their stem. An ugly American upset M. Lalleman by demanding to know what on the menu was fresh and what was not—an especially stupid question at an establishment with its own tanks for crayfish and trout as well as lobster.

A short two-and-one-half-hour drive the next day, broken by a *pique-nique* at a scenic outlook, brought us to the Mediterranean coast at St. Jean-Cap-Ferrat and the luxurious but relaxed Hôtel Voile d'Or. Cap-Ferrat, east of Nice, has been called the quietest, most unspoiled, and possibly most beautiful corner of the Riviera. We were fortunate to have a top, fourth-floor room with a magnificent view of the tiny picturesque port. Dinner at the hotel's one-star dining room was good with an embarrassment of Alpine strawberries for dessert.

Our luncheon reservation the next day was at Roger Verge's famous three-star Moulin de Mougins in the almost excessively pretty village of Mougins in the hills above Cannes. Home to six other fine restaurants and a number of tiny shops, Mougins is where it's at and where a good patron of The Lark had recently purchased a villa. Verge's restaurant in a converted mill was the catalyst that brought three-star dining to the Côte d'Azur and made Mougins.

An opening surprise, an olive and anchovy paste, whetted Mary's appetite for the day's fixed-price luncheon, which featured a salad of a full, half lobster and a pâté-stuffed chicken breast with sauce

Bordelaise plus other courses. I fasted on a starter of wild wood mushrooms, followed by a main course of two whole but trimmed veal kidneys in a mustard-chive sauce. A special refresher course consisted of a melon sorbet in red wine with pepper, which tasted much better than it sounds. The white Hermitage served was one of The Lark's own wines, Chante-Alouette (Song of the Lark). Although food and service were very good, Moulin de Mougins appeared very touristy and the waiter looked down his nose at 22 percent gratuity. Absentee ownership!

We dined lightly that evening at Voile d'Or with Ed and Elaine Perkins of Bloomfield Hills, Michigan, who were also staying at the hotel. Small world. We had also run into customers of The Lark in Paris.

Feeling it might be tacky, but what the hell, we took the short drive along the Lower Corniche to Monaco the next morning and were glad we did. The shopping was great, and a lunch of salad Niçoise and charcoal-grilled rib steak for two at the grill of Hôtel de Paris accompanied by a simple Bordeaux was a refreshing change of pace. The view over Monte Carlo's yacht harbor was romantic enough, but midway through our meal the painted wooden ceiling opened like a fan and sunbeams danced among the tables. Loaded with treasures, including six bonus gifts from the friendly salesgirl at a perfume shop, we returned to Cap-Ferrat. As usual, we enjoyed the lively driving including the sight of a German who leapt from his Mercedes to scream invectives at a gendarme.

We retired early after a dinner at the one-star Le Provençal in the port of St. Jean-Cap-Ferrat featuring mussels and the local white Bellet wine. Our trip home the next day via Air France was flawless, good food and service accompanying complimentary champagne, wine and Armagnac.

Our dominant impressions of France were of the warmth of its people, the sophisticated yet charming life style, and the beauty found everywhere. After being treated as odd for most of my life because of an undue devotion to food and wine, a country where such interest is the norm was like discovering home at last.

The Battle for Perfection

Running a very fine restaurant is a never-ending battle, fought anew each day, to alter human nature—to make a perfectionist of every staff member.

Pre-Dinner Parisian Drinks

The French typically drink whisky or gin and tonic when not at table—almost never a glass of white wine. *Wine Spectator* reported on what Parisians order in restaurants before dinner: 70 percent opt for champagne, either plain or with a fruit extract or liqueur added, such as *cassis* (black currant), *framboise* (raspberry), or even peach or strawberry.

Port is a traditional pre-dinner wine in France, but modern restaurants suggest obscure French fortified wines called *vins doux naturels,* naturally sweet wines. According to *Wine Spectator,* the most fashionable of these is Muscat de Beaumes de Venise from the southern Rhône, which it describes as having "a heady scent of Muscat grape and a hint of peaches and apricots." Although rarely found in the U.S., Muscat de Beaumes de Venise was a house wine of The Lark for years, offered as a dessert wine. This was recently replaced by the 1994 Muscat de Rivesaltes of Ch. de Lau for two reasons. Robert Parker rated it an astounding 94 points, calling it an "enormously endowed …knockout wine." Equally important, I love saying "Muscat de

Rivesaltes."

Innovative Parisian wine lists offer light dry sherries, especially Tio Pepe, as does The Lark. Sauternes, almost invariably enjoyed after dinner in the United States, continues to be popular as an apéritif in France. Finally, as here, there is a trend to begin with a wine that is also appropriate for the first course, perhaps a white Burgundy such as Meursault or Chassagne or Puligny Montrachet.

Bistros and Brasseries

A true bistro is a small inexpensive restaurant with wooden floors where waiters offer meals of traditional cuisine and modest regional wines. Bistros are never carpeted and are antithetical to Nouvelle or other experimental cuisine.

In a *Town & Country* magazine article, after noting that typical Parisian visitors dine at overpriced Nouvelle temples, food writer James Villas continued, "Ask, on the other hand, French natives (including most chefs from the famous three-star restaurants) or serious American gastronomes to cite the places in Paris where they truly love to eat, and rest assured that the vast majority will say bistros (many of which are not listed in the guide much less bestowed with stars and toques)."

An authentic brasserie has Art Deco, Art Nouveau, or Belle Époque decor, offers snacks as well as meals, features draft beer, and serves Cuisine Bourgeoise. The name means "beer joint." Like bistros, brasseries shun innovative cuisine.

Jean-Paul Bucher, known to Parisians as "King of the Brasseries," states that "restaurants with faddish themes … are here today and gone tomorrow.... Brasseries will never be outmoded."

Cape, Kalahari, and Okavango

*I*t was about 11 A.M. All ten of our party had returned to the safari camp, having spent the morning viewing African game from seats mounted above and behind the cabs of flatbed Land Rovers and Land Cruisers. Our rehash of fabulous sightings was interrupted by Patrick, our host, pointing and shouting, "Two elephant! There! Who wants to go see them?"

Mary, sportswriter Tom Opre, and I clambered back up to the Land Rover's exposed seat and sped toward the huge beasts browsing some four hundred yards distant, just to the right of the dirt track leading out of camp.

Slowing as we approached, Patrick edged closer for a good photo opportunity. The nearest elephant turned to face us, flapping his ears in a threat display. Not to worry, since he had neither raised his trunk nor trumpeted. Mary took photos and Tom ran his Sony mini-camcorder as our Rover crept even closer. Big mistake! The elephant threw up his trunk and bellowed his rage. Tom, on my left, forgot about his camcorder and yelled to Patrick, "Back up! Back up!" Mary, on my right, kept snapping away while trying to crawl onto my lap. Obviously, however, the elephant did not carry through his charge.

This happened at James Camp in the Okavango Delta of northern Botswana, just across the Kwando River from Namibia's Caprivi Strip. The Okavango was the third and final locale of an African bird-hunting and game-viewing safari that began ten days earlier at Mountain Shadows, a luxurious South African country inn.

Our party consisted of *Automobile* magazine's David E. Davis Jr., and Jeannie Davis; Masco advertising executive Ham Schirmer, and Weezy Schirmer; Texas ophthalmologist Joe Frey, and Karen Frey; Mary and I; and the safari outfitter, former *Detroit Free Press* outdoor writer Tom Opre and his friend Sally Stevens of Maritz, a corporate booking agency. The Davises, Schirmers, Freys, Mary and I had enjoyed previous shooting trips together in England and Wales as well as shoots closer to home.

Mountain Shadows nestles among vineyards in the Klein Drakenstein Valley near Paarl, a mere forty-five kilometers from Cape Town. The Dutch-style stucco manor house, owned by Basie and Sandra Maartens, dates to 1823 and has been declared a national monument. Accommodations in separate guest buildings were simple but charming, the wines excellent, and the cuisine beyond any reasonable expectation.

Our hosts joined us each evening for dinner at a long table in the manor's dining room with views through French doors of the terrace, swimming pool, and fields sprinkled with browsing guinea fowl. First courses included avocado mousse wrapped in smoked salmon, cèpe mushrooms with hollandaise sauce, cornets of trout with chervil *beurre blanc,* and butternut and celery soup. Elegant main courses were guinea fowl packets with branberry sauce, roast leg of bontebok antelope in red wine sauce, and leg of lamb with herb stuffing. An outdoor barbecue on the pool-side terrace included antelope, pork filet, chicken, pork ribs, sausage, and much more. Desserts at four dinners were ice cream in brandy-snap baskets with chocolate sauce, trifle, fruit with Cointreau and Chantilly cream, and malva pudding.

Nothing we had read prepared us for the reality of the Cape area. Almost all of the city and countryside is more attractive than the States, being neat, clean, and free of billboards. The Cape of Good Hope itself is barely above sea level and unremarkable. Nearby Cape Point, on the other hand, is towering and dramatic with seas crashing at its base and grand vistas along the coast.

Inland from the Cape were more surprises. Framed by nearby mountains, the countryside was divided between vineyards, fruit, vegetable and grain farms, and arid red-rock areas reminiscent of the high desert of the western United States.

We knew South Africa produced wine, but were surprised at the vast acreage devoted to grapes, accented by wine routes and tasting rooms comparable to those in France, Germany, and California. Cabernet, Syrah, and Riesling are especially popular, but except for the best wines, the blending of different varieties is much favored and the aggravating labels fail to reveal what grapes have been used. South Africa only consumes a small portion of its wine production.

City and country are served by an excellent infrastructure of expressways, paved roads, railroads, and coal and nuclear power plants that will soon be supplemented by oil and gas from newly found off-shore fields. The country is the economic giant of the continent, producing more goods and services than the rest of sub-Saharan Africa combined, with many of the other countries relying on South Africa for everything from toothpaste to cars and trucks. South Africa also has the only competent, reasonably uncorrupt government in Africa with the possible exception of Botswana and newly independent Namibia.

Contrasting with the beauty and prosperity of much of the country are poverty-stricken black townships and squatter camps. Faster than the government can build housing, flimsy huts are thrown up by blacks from the interior seeking a better life. Shacks are liable to be anywhere, even next to mansions and villas. We saw no signs of the civic unrest or violence, which at its worst is minor compared with what occurs daily in the United States on a per capita basis.

But such considerations were far from our minds on the morning of our first full day in South Africa as we motored in the early dawn to a not-too-distant farm. There we hunted, crouched behind bales of straw near irrigation ponds. Our waterfowl bag included Ham Schirmer's Egyptian goose. After lunch and a siesta back at Mountain Shadows, the late afternoon was given to pass shooting for doves and pigeons from pit blinds in open countryside. I was lucky enough to add a passing shelldrake duck to the tally.

One of the most popular eating birds in France is guinea fowl, and they were our quarry the next morning. Driven birds and those "walked up" served to restock our inn's larder, which we had depleted of guinea fowl at dinner our first evening. The morning will be best remembered, however, as that on which Mary bagged her first bird, a dove.

Both big game hunting and bird hunting in South Africa are pursued almost exclusively on private farms or private game preserves. Since good management means good profits from hunting fees, big game hunting is superb. Bird hunting is top drawer because hardly anyone does it. Macho Americans, Europeans, and South Africans do not get the desired buzz from shooting anything as small as a bird. Bird dogs are a rarity, and even professionals lack some basic knowledge, such as proper shot sizes.

Mountain Shadows is an anomaly, providing superior bed and board only forty-five minutes from Cape Town, yet serving as a base for excellent bird shooting, big game hunting, fresh-water fishing for trout and bass, and deep-sea fishing for tuna. A hunter from New York, who claimed to have sixty-five entries in big game record books, left with a professional hunter each morning and returned only hours later with magnificent antelope trophies of various species, the meat of which was featured on the inn's menus.

Our last day in the Cape area was devoted to sight-seeing, which included southern right whales, spotted while skirting the sand and rock coast on the way to Cape Point and the Cape of Good Hope. We also explored Cape Town's university, attended by black, "colored," and white students. Our guide, who became lost at one point, emphasized that blacks and coloreds have very different cultures, life styles, and political views, and we were not to lump them together. A festive lunch at The Wharfside Grill included steamed mussels, grilled lobster, and South Africa's famous fish, kingclip. The next day found us lodged at the very modern Sandton Sun Hotel in suburban Johannesburg, or "Joburg," a stopover on our way to Botswana. Joburg, the largest city in South Africa, owes its existence to the nearby diamond mines. Cape Town is the second-largest city, followed by Durban on the Indian Ocean, and the capital, Pretoria. Buildings in downtown Joburg are ripped down after fifteen or twenty years and replaced by new ones, almost all of which are ugly.

Joburg was our shopping stop. Mary bought a perfectly designed and executed ostrich purse for less than 40 percent of what it would cost in Europe or the United States. One couple purchased a magnificent statue of a warthog carved from serpentine with actual warthog tusks for thousands of dollars less than the wholesale U.S. price. Diamonds were also a very good value.

The best shopping was conveniently grouped at two locations: a large mall of elegant shops connected to our hotel, and a similar mall appending the Carlton Hotel in downtown Joburg. The mall at the Carlton included Roland Ward's, famous since early in the century for the best Africana—art, crafts, rare books, and so forth.

Ham Schirmer purchased a Stewart Granger-type white hunter's hat with zebra hatband, of which the salesgirl said, "Very nice. Only tourists buy them." I later asked our host in the Okavango, who had a similar hat, why his hatband was missing. He said it was "a stupid zebra band," so he had thrown it away. Flocks of tourists sporting this ubiquitous chapeau decorate the departure area of Joburg's airport.

Dinner in Joburg was at the most recommended restaurant, Gatrell's, and featured very good duck and cherry pie, braised oxtails, and the seemingly inevitable kingclip fish. Mary and I are no longer surprised at whom we run into at remote locales. Here, Mary's ex-classmate Julie Powers and husband J. D. Powers, publisher of the like-named automotive reports, were part of a group at a nearby table.

Botswana, the former British protectorate of Bechuanaland, which celebrated its twenty-fourth anniversary of independence during our stay, is a landlocked country the size of France, bordered on the west and north by Namibia, the east by Zimbabwe, and the south by South Africa. Some 80 percent of the land is waterless grassland and Kalahari Desert, but in the north the Okavango, Kwando, and Chobe rivers bring the desert to life in an annual flood, creating the Okavango Delta or Swamp, an ecosystem that has become Africa's most sought-after wilderness.

Air Botswana took us from Joburg to Botswana's capital of Gaborone and then to dusty, shabby Maun on the edge of the Kalahari Desert, the jumping-off point for hunting and photographic safaris in the Kalahari and Okavango. We lunched, surrounded by the flotsam and jetsam of Africa, at Maun's popular Duck Inn, enjoying dishes as diverse as curried lamb, cheeseburgers, chicken pie, and authentic Italian pizza. Botswana's newspaper, *The Guardian*, revealed more of the local culinary scene, including the existence of a restaurant named The Lark, featuring pizza, and the Gaamangwe, with chicken necks and gizzards for the equivalent of twenty-five cents.

After lunch in Maun, we motored seventy-two dusty kilometers south to Bird Safaris, a tent camp near Lake Ngami, which is dry except for an annual influx flowing south after the rainy season in the north. Our camp consisted of a primitive cane-walled dining area with one long table, a bar and eight lounge chairs off to one side, plus five separate tents, one for each couple in our party. These tents had canvas floors, zipper-opening screened entrances front and rear, and three-screened window openings on each side. A canvas-enclosed rear area was open to the sky and boasted a flush toilet, sink with running water, and a gravity shower—a large metal can that was filled with warm water by bucket on request.

Perhaps two dozen similar camps are widely scattered in the vast Okavango Delta and Chobe National Park to the east. Most serve as a base for big-game hunting as well as some bird shooting, but there is tremendous growth in photo and game-viewing safaris. Our host, forty-five-year-old Mark Kryiacou, is a professional hunter of Greek descent, a second-generation citizen of Botswana who actively uses his influence to promote conservation and stricter standards for professional hunters. Prior to our visit, a neophyte professional hunter permitted an unqualified native helper to carry a gun. When a lioness roared, a panic-induced shot went through the client-hunter before tearing off the arm of the professional hunter, killing them both.

We saw little game except birds in Mark's eight-hundred-square-mile hunting concession, leased from the local tribe with government approval. Cattle, burros, horses, goats, and ostrich were common, as were pigeon, dove, guinea fowl, francolin partridge, sand grouse, double-banded grouse, and some waterfowl. Nongame birds included African fish eagles, huge tawny eagles, owls, and marsh harrier.

Shooting was "hot barrel." I blasted over five hundred shells from my 12-gauge Browning over-and-under shotgun and that was fewer than any of the other four men in our group. Not having touched a gun in a year, my shooting had been mediocre in South Africa, but now improved markedly, culminating in numerous doubles on dove and pigeon, including a "Scotch double"—two with one shot. Following a normal two-shot double on francolin, I surprised myself with a quadruple on sand grouse, three with the first barrel and one with the second.

The Lake Ngami region was very hot, dry and dusty, but thankfully almost insect-free. Shooting was done in the early morning and late afternoon, as we lay up in our tents to escape the midday sun. An excellent cooling trick recommended by Tom Opre was to place one towel on a bed, then soak and wring out another towel and lie down with the wet towel spread on top of one's body.

The countryside consisted of dusty soil with dry-brown grass, thorny trees, thorny bushes, and spreading acacia trees. Dove and pigeon were hunted standing under trees near a water hole or some form of moisture. There were very few natural water holes at this time of year, so the natives created them by pumping water for their cattle into depressions in dry river beds. That created pass shooting for sand grouse and double-banded grouse flying to the water.

Obviously, bird hunters had no effect on the bird population of so vast a concession. Birds were safe from natives as they were not worth the cost of a shell. All birds shot throughout our trip were eaten, either by our group or by the camp staff and their families. Birds were retrieved by natives, not dogs, and very few were lost. There were one or two bushmen, the original inhabitants, among the staff, but most were black and all were good-natured and helpful.

Food at Bird Safaris camp was simple and good. And the entire group was composed of old friends, creating a continuing jovial party, especially notable for the charm of the ladies, the raconteurship of David E. Davis Jr., the wit of Ham Schirmer, and the unfailing good nature of Joe Frey. I felt like Johnson's Boswell.

Eager to hunt francolin partridge, we drove twenty kilometers south one hot midafternoon, crossing the dry lake bed of Lake Ngami past herds of livestock and ostrich to reach strips of brush and trees on the far shore. Hunters were positioned at breaks in these strips, and the shooting was quick and tricky when beaters flushed francolin and guinea fowl toward the guns. Great owls, small antelope, and an African wildcat were also flushed but not harmed.

All agreed that the hunting at Bird Safaris was better than any previous experience—better than Mexico, Britain, Wales, Scotland, or wherever. We were now ready for more exotic sights, however, and flew from the edge of the Kalahari north by small plane to the Okavango.

Some of the ladies had problems with James Camp, our home in the Okavango. The tents were smaller and, instead of flush toilets, there were "long drops"—outhouses out back with canvas sides and no top. The shared showers were also some distance from our tents. There was no running water, but a table in front of each tent with a bucket of water, basin, and mirror. Game wandered through the camp, especially after dark, as was obvious from giant elephant droppings scattered about. A favorite prank on safaris is to chocolate frost one of these and present it as a birthday cake to the unsuspecting victim.

We came to James Camp strictly for game viewing and photography, and ours was only the second nonhunting party to do so. A group of bird watchers, who just preceded us, identified 215 species. Professional hunter and owner Terry Palmer had recently sold a part interest in the camp to Patrick and Heather Petstone, our hosts, who ran the camp for photo safaris in the off-hunting season.

Terry Palmer is famous for having survived an awful bout with a leopard. He was driving a Land Rover with the hunting client atop, outside on the viewing seat, when a leopard dropped from a tree onto the client. Terry jumped out and pulled the leopard by the tail. It turned, ripped off his scalp and slashed him to the bone several times. This occurred about 5 P.M., too late for an emergency medical flight. Thus, it was fortunate the client was a doctor, who lay Terry out on the dinner table, closed his wounds, and sewed his scalp back on. He was flown out the next morning to intensive care in Joburg. Terry's scars are a reminder that danger is ever-present in this wilderness.

We canvassed hundreds of square miles surrounding James Camp for game, perched on open seats mounted above and behind the cabs of Land Rovers and Land Cruisers, as described previously. Antelope were most common—a litany of species ranging from tiny springbok to great waterbuck and all kinds in between.

Giraffe here are wisely protected, as who could shoot such an unsuspecting, cowlike, gentle creature? Surely their opposite must be wild dog, unrelated to dogs as we know them and even more loathsome than jackal and hyena, the most feared predator with a 98 percent kill rate. Success comes from running down every quarry with individual wild dogs alternating as chase animal while the pack cuts the corners to substitute fresh chasers.

Lions were seen by finding the carcass being fed upon—either young elephant killed from eating toxic plants, or other game killed by the lioness. Discovery was by odor from the carcass or by sight beneath circling, carrion-eating storks and vultures.

Hippos seem gentle and cute, but kill more humans than any other African animal. Surprisingly, most of their food is consumed by grazing inland at night, often miles from their watery homes. Whoever unsuspectingly comes between them and water is viewed as a threat. A hippo runs faster than a human, and all threats are killed. Disputes between male hippos are commonly settled by a fight to the death. We saw remains of the losers as well as scores of hippos in open water—every snout turned toward us.

One afternoon we pontoon-boated down the Kwando River, on the Namibia-Botswana border, angling for tiger fish and hoping to sight sitatunga, a very rare swamp-dwelling antelope. Sitatunga are hunted by searching from a platform erected above and between two log boats. When alarmed, they submerge with only their nostrils above water.

Cape Buffalo are often nominated as the most dangerous of the big four, especially when wounded. We were fortunate to find groups of up to one thousand animals, which we herded in stampedes back and forth between Land Rover and Land Cruiser. The feeling as they passed within one hundred feet is indescribable.

The terrain at James Camp was a mixture of acacia, savannah, bush veld, and swamp. Acacia were especially dramatic viewed against the rising or setting sun. It was home to tsetse flies, which induce sleeping sickness and displayed a special fondness for Mary. Malaria-carrying mosquitos prompted our use of preventive larium pills. We had also been inoculated for tetanus, typhoid, and hepatitis A.

Thanks to Heather, food at James Camp was excellent. Various antelope made toothsome rump roasts, but the best was roast loin of warthog, cute critters that scurry through the bush or explode from holes at the base of giant termite hills.

Ignoring warnings from our son the doctor against blinding snail-borne Bilharzia, we swam in a swift-flowing rivulet whose bottom was marked by crocodile tails. Thankfully, both crocodile and the leeches of which we had heard so much were absent.

Mary hoped that elephant would see us off and was not disappointed as two lumbered to the end of the dirt runway on our departure. Our itinerary home consisted of flights from James Camp to Maun, Maun to Gaborone, Gaborone to Joburg, Joburg to Lisbon, Lisbon to Paris, Paris to Raleigh-Durham, North Carolina, and Raleigh-Durham to Detroit. We can't wait to return to South Africa and Botswana and would add Namibia plus the shore of the Indian Ocean.

Syrah—Beyond Cabernet

The great majority of our red wine sales are California Cabernet Sauvignon and Merlot, followed by red Bordeaux, most of which also contain some Cabernet Sauvignon and Merlot. Pinot Noir, either from California or in the form of red Burgundy, is a distant third, while other reds are rarely ordered.

This is a plug for Syrah, also known as Shiraz, the best red grape variety of the Rhône. It is also widely planted in Australia and South Africa and is increasingly popular in California where its exponents, such as Randall Graham of Bonny Doon Vineyard, are known as "Rhône Rangers."

Hermitage is one of the finest wines made from Syrah; one of the single-best reds I have ever tasted was a 1966 Hermitage, Côtes du Rhône of Delas. At one time a great Hermitage was costlier than a top red Bordeaux or red Burgundy. Now, as grape-nut Robert M. Parker Jr. points out, they are greatly undervalued. He also says that at least 20 percent of the best fifty wines he has ever tasted were Hermitage.

Unlike Hermitage, which is underappreciated, the most fashionable wines in France today, harder to find than even Ch. Pétrus or Domaine de la Romanée-Conti, are the Côte Rôties of Ettiene and Marcel Guigal from the northern Côtes du Rhône. Bottles from their three small vineyards, La Landonne, La Mouline, and La Turque, fetch up to five hundred dollars per bottle. Parker has stated that La Mouline may be the finest red wine in the world, but this was said before the release of the even more highly acclaimed La Turque. The Lark has a great collection from all three vineyards.

The most sought-after and expensive Australian red wine is also a Syrah, or Shiraz as it is known down under, namely the Penfolds Grange. Parker gives the 1982 a rating of 98 and calls it the finest wine made south of the equator. Hugh Johnson calls it brilliant. Frank J. Prial reports it is one of the most sought-after wines in the world. *Wine Spectator* named the 1989 vintage its 1995 Wine of the Year.

Mirroring our frantic flight to France one year earlier, our flight to London was delayed five hours and the next available plane from London to Munich put us in that city nearly eight hours behind schedule. Our blacklist of airlines grew apace.

Previously, we had avoided Munich because of the tacky connotations of Oktoberfest, but so many friends sang the city's praises that we chose it as our jumping-off point. This capital of Bavaria is an Alpine bastion of Baroque culture blending German, Italian, and French influences. We learned that its architecture and parks, shopping, festivals, unique cultural attractions, fine hotels and restaurants have made it the favorite city of Germany and, perhaps, of Europe. We also learned that Oktoberfest is held during the two weeks preceding the first Sunday in October in huge prefabricated beer halls erected each year in a fair grounds at the city's center. Since the principal activity apparently consists only of listening to brass bands while eating chicken, wurst and the like, washed down with vast quantities of beer, we were not disappointed to miss it.

The little-known Splendid on fashionable Maximilianstrasse was our hotel in Munich for three nights. Awakening refreshed the morning after our arrival, we had what was to be the first of a long string of seemingly unavoidable Teutonic breakfasts consisting invariably of coffee, bread, rolls, cheese, and cold cuts. Throughout the Germanic Alps, whether we ordered bacon, sausage, or ham, we were always served cold cuts. "You vil eat cold cuts!"

While Munich is charming, the surrounding countryside is fabulous, so after breakfast we roared off in a rented Mercedes with driver to King Ludwig II's fairy-tale castle at Neuschwanstein. I say roared off because our speed exceeded 110 mph at times as driver Otto Mayer regaled us with tales of twice being stripped to the buff and searched by the U.S. Secret Service while driving President Reagan in Normandy. As in all German-speaking Alpine areas, the landscape was neat and tidy and the homes awash in what appeared to be a perpetual flower-growing contest. Neuschwanstein, where King Ludwig lived only briefly before his apparent murder, was properly romantic. His descendants, now gentlemen farmers, still reside in a nearby castle.

We broke our day trip for a rustic lunch at the simple Plotzbrau at Peissenberg, trading tastes of liver dumpling soup, braised lung with steinpilz mushrooms, pig's neck woodchopper style, and salad. Adventuresome eating for Americans, but Mary and I rarely resist ordering new dishes. All the food was very good as was the house beer. We seldom drink beer at home, but loved Bavaria's brews, especially the Aying brand. At Rottenbuch, we viewed a festive horse auction where Clydesdale-type yearlings fetched $1,500. Here, as throughout the countryside, we were surprised and pleased that men actually wore knee-length britches with suspenders and women dirndls, blouses, and vests.

Dinner that evening was at the small and intimate Boettner. Starters were fresh goose liver with black truffles, and smoked salmon with a miniature potato pancake. Mary followed with venison in a dried-cranberry sauce accompanied by morels and tiny spinach noodles. I enjoyed fresh goose liver with string beans. Dessert, which had been cooked on the serving plate, consisted of poached, thinly sliced apples topped with a whisper-thin crêpe, crystallized syrup, and calvados brandy. Count Matuschka-Greiffenclau, proprietor of the renowned Schloss Vollrads, has patronized The Lark, so here and throughout our stay in Bavaria we enjoyed his Halbtrocken Gourmet Dinner Wine.

We toured Munich the next morning by hired car and driver. Being market freaks, we especially enjoyed its Viktualien market with perfect and sometimes unusual fruit and vegetables, flowers, wild mushrooms, meats, sausages, and game. Here, we joined our driver in Bavaria's traditional "second breakfast," hot sausage with mustard, normally eaten at 11 A.M. Highlights other than palaces and museums were the Oktoberfest grounds, whose buildings were being rushed to completion, and the Nymphenburg china works, whose wares are far more expensive and respected than Rosenthal. Maximilianstrasse, the site of our hotel, is considered the most important artistic and couture-fashion boulevard in Germany.

Aubergine, our choice for lunch, is one of Germany's rare three-star restaurants. The decor is modern and sophisticated—the cuisine excellent Nouvelle. One starter included cold rabbit in aspic, and hot rabbit liver and tenderloin in a Nouvelle salad, while another salad featured warm sweetbreads and marinated steinpilz mushrooms. A main course of crayfish in butter sauce with miniature vegetables was good, but did not compare with a pigeon whose medium-rare breast in a rich wine sauce was accompanied by the braised ham-stuffed legs and baked apple slices. Sautéed goose liver apparently was added as a professional courtesy. Fresh goose liver has become a cliché in Europe, and we began plotting ways to avoid this too-rich treat.

Checking out of the Splendid the next morning, we picked up our VW Jetta. It proved a perfect car for mountain driving with power equal to the steepest inclines and a five-speed transmission to facilitate both ascents and descents. As we took the highway east toward Salzburg, Austria, the weather was clear and bright and remained so throughout our journey. Prior to our arrival it had rained for at least part of nineteen straight days.

An obvious stop was Berchtesgaden where we had a simple lunch of *Weiner schnitzel,* boiled beef, potato cakes, and beer at the Posthotel, dating from 1645. As at most country inns, the proprietor was complete with beer belly, knee socks, leather knickers, suspenders, and full white shirt. He "worked the floor," greeting his patrons with beery amiability.

What little remains of Hitler's Eagle's Nest, on the Kehlstein high above Berchtesgaden, is unimpressive, but the drive up the incredible road, climbing 2,330 feet, and the awesome view from the summit are unforgettable. Afterwards, it was only a fifteen-mile drive on the Obersalzburg mountain road to the Austrian border and Salzburg, dear to lovers of Mozart, Karajan, and *The Sound of Music*—home to the grandest music festival in the world.

Salzburg is beautiful and gives the impression of a huge village. It is also touristy, but not as bad at our visit as during the height of the summer season. We stayed at its premier hotel, the eight-hundred-year-old Goldener Hirsch, whose sixty rooms could be a set for a Trapp family film. We dined well that evening at the nearby Alt-Salzburg, beginning with what was described as a green Salzburger *nockerl,* not the dessert soufflé, but miniature tortellini with Gruyère cheese, cream, and bacon. One component of a salad was tiny watercress, common throughout our trip. A main course of salmon with fresh-water crayfish was overpowered by huge salty capers, but boiled beef with carrots, turnips, leeks, potato pancake, and apple-horseradish sauce was wonderfully soothing. Since The Lark is one of only a few restaurants in America offering Salzburger *nockerl,* we had to have it for dessert at its birthplace. We concluded that our revised soufflé was tastier, but theirs was made elegant by an accompaniment of warm raspberries. The chef had given us champagne as a complimentary apéritif, and we bought him a bottle of wine. Our waiter selected a dry Austrian Riesling to accompany our meal. Here, as throughout Austria, they were embarrassed by the Austrian wine-additive scandal and wanted to know if it had been publicized in the United States.

Driving west the next morning, we stopped for lunch at Goldener Adler (Golden Eagle) in quaint and touristic Innsbruck, Austria. Here, as elsewhere at this season, game was featured and we were served excellent chamois with *spatzle* and wild duck in a light cream sauce.

Quality of lodgings is very important to us, so it is always a close decision whether to book an entire trip in advance and be assured first choice of inns and hotels, or to wing it for the sake of adventure and flexibility. We had compromised, reserving our first and last three days and leaving the rest to chance. As a result, we were unable to obtain a room at the Schlosshotel Igls above Innsbruck and found ourselves driving instead to Seefeld. Here, two aspects of the Alpine region became apparent that no travel article we read had bothered to mention. First, to have a ski resort requires only a mountain slope, chair lift, village, and nearby hospital. As a result, though we hear only of St. Moritz, Gstaad, Zermatt, Kosters, Davos, Cortina, and a few other famous spots, there are literally hundreds that receive little or no publicity. Furthermore, every ski resort is also a warm-weather tourist resort. Such was Seefeld, a compact village with several dozen hotels and large guest houses, and an active area of shops and restaurants.

The next day we stopped in the village of St. Anton at the pass of the same name for a simple lunch of Austrian-style chicken with sauerkraut, potatoes, and Kaiser beer. From there it was but a short drive to Gasthof Post in Lech, a long-established inn and member of the Relais & Chateaux as well as the Romantic Hotel group. As experienced travelers will attest, the individually owned inns and hotels of both associations are rarely a disappointment. The Gasthof Post was magnificent and perfectly managed by the host Moosbrugger family. Our suite number 22 was both spotless and charming with pine walls and colorful flower-painted furniture. The bathroom had a heated floor and huge triangular bathtub. Our windows overlooked the village street, river, and the mountains beyond. Lech remains a true village and not a commercial resort like Seefeld.

Dinner that evening included jellied calf's head on salad greens with a warm vinaigrette, boiled beef with the typical apple-horseradish sauce, julienne carrots, onions, and inappropriate puréed spinach. A Salzburger *nockerl* for two at a nearby table would easily have served eight.

Any trip with Mary is a fun-filled adventure, and we loved all our Alpine travels. The next day, Sunday, was magical. As we breakfasted in our room, picking on the obligatory cold cuts, the music of a brass band came through an open window. Marching down the village street below were about twenty-five young musicians in native dress led by an aged flag bearer. Descending to the lobby, we were told they were headed for the small square next to the church for a concert after Sunday mass. Off we went, intending to listen for a few minutes. The cheerful band, wonderful costumes, romantic music, sunny day, and mountain backdrop were such that we stayed the full hour.

Wishing a different place than our inn for lunch, our host first suggested a long drive to some elaborate restaurant. When Herr Moosbrugger learned we were not adverse to walking, he advised a hike to Gasthof Rott Wand (Red Wall) in the Village of Zug (not the city of the same name). Our path paralleled the small river through cow pastures and forests. Zug (pronounced *zouk*) was very small and, although the Gasthof was wonderfully charming, we anticipated modest fare in this out-of-the-way setting. Wrong!

Our host, Josef u. Burgi Walch, was so jovial as to be almost a caricature and would easily have won an all-Alpine beer belly contest. The food? We predict this restaurant will become famous thanks to the talent of Frau Burgi Walch and her obviously well-trained daughter. Our game luncheon began with a *velouté* of steinpilz (cepes or porcini mushrooms) soup garnished with tiny chives for Mary and whole steinpilz arranged around noodles in a creamy sauce for me. Mary's main course of medium-rare roe deer medallions in wine sauce with cherries, cranberries, and small potato balls containing sour cream, then rolled in almonds and fried, was magnificent. I thought my tenderloin of hare, ten small medium-rare medallions in a blackberry and cranberry sauce accompanied by broccoli, was, if possible, even better. Both dishes somehow tasted like game without being gamey and were far better than any game we have ever had, including that at three-star restaurants. All the fare going by to other tables looked fantastic. Our hot crêpe with farmer's cheese and walnut filling, hot chocolate sauce, ice cream, and whipped cream disappeared in an instant.

The three small dining rooms were full (as well they should have been) with the usual well-behaved dog or two in evidence. Our windowside table looked out on the by-now normal, too-perfect mountain view. We topped this memorable experience by meeting the charming host family, taking their photo, touring the kitchen, and snagging a menu. Mary remembered she had left valuable jewelry sitting in plain view back at our lodgings—not to worry, I said, and we found it undisturbed on our return.

A dusting of snow topped the mountains as we sped off in our Jetta the next morning. As suggested by our hosts, we broke our trip for lunch at the Real in Vaduz, capital of Liechtenstein. It appeared the right choice as the food was fine and a dowager of the ruling family was at the next table. The town itself is small and, other than the castle and a few hotels and restaurants, appears to consist of banks, stamp shops, and duty-free stores.

Mary had a consommé with marrow dumplings followed by a lobster salad. I began with a terrine of foie gras, which I much preferred to the Nouvelle sautés. It was accompanied by a small salad and two aspics: one clear and one of port wine and cranberry juice. My medium-rare pheasant breast in a wine sauce was served with simple but delicious sauerkraut and mashed potatoes.

Passing at last into Switzerland, our country inn that evening was Waldhaus Hotel and Restaurant, which had a magnificent setting overlooking Lake Lucerne, a popular restaurant, and very modest rooms for a Relais & Châteaux. At dinner, as at most fine European restaurants, we were served a small complimentary starter, and cubed veal head with a fine sauce in puff pastry was splendid. I continued with fresh Beluga caviar, and over-smoked salmon and sour cream on a large, flat pancake, which seemed a good idea except there was far too much sour cream and the pancake was not buckwheat. Mary's fresh-water crayfish, chanterelles, and artichoke leaves was overseasoned, but she raved over her curried beef tournedos with marrow slices and rice. My thick, pink, veal steak with marrow, chanterelles, and noodles was also excellent. Believing in the wine of the country, we switched from our previous Austrian Rieslings to Clos des Mognes Dezaley of Lausanne.

Our drive the next sunny morning led along the north shore of the Brienzersee to the resort of Interlaken with its chestnut-lined streets and long-established hotels. We had a light lunch of *raclette* and whitefish from the lake at Schul before proceeding high into the Bernese Oberland to Kanderstag and the Royal Hotel Bellevue. The Bellevue is a member of the Leading Hotels of the World and the Relais & Chateaux. It is elegant and set in a small valley surrounded by towering peaks. We were fortunate to be assigned the "residence," a separate house of many rooms with exceptional furnishings. Members of the owning Rickli family staffed the front desk and were very helpful. The dining room situation, however, was pure comedy. Dinner was at 7:30 P.M., but none of the guests, most of whom were obviously old customers, wanted to enter first. When Mary and I strolled in, we were almost trampled by the following crowd. The staff then toiled mightily to cope with an entire sitting that had arrived within thirty seconds of each other. The cuisine here was continental of the old school—adequate and good. Dinner ended with a dessert buffet. Once again, no one would be first, but once someone made a move, watch out!

There are enough activities at Kanderstag to occupy a visitor for weeks. The hotel has a pool, tennis court, and a riding stable with what is described as "a resolute instructress" ("You vil ride vel!"). Hiking, however, was where it was at, so the next morning Mary and I were off—first by foot, then chair lift, and once more by foot through a beautiful forest full of mushrooms to a mile-high lake, Oeschinen. This was the most beautiful area we visited in Switzerland. So beautiful that we changed our plans and stayed two days, having canceled a reservation at Montreux, "the Riviera of Switzerland," on the east shore of Lac Léman (Lake Geneva).

We drove by Montreux as we continued our journey and were surprised to find it ringed by industrial fumes from the surrounding industry. Lac Léman, source of the Rhône River, is Switzerland's largest lake, and we enjoyed the drive down its shore before passing into France to arrive at the renowned inn and restaurant of Père Bise on Lake Annency.

Père Bise is idyllic. Its restaurant windows open directly on the romantic lake and a perfect sycamore-shaded outdoor dining terrace. Breakfast and lunch are served on the terrace and dinner in the dining room. Throughout our trip, in city and country, most people ate their meals outdoors whenever possible. At lunch, Mary found her crayfish salad with artichoke slices the best ever, while I enjoyed duck liver and truffles in pastry with an accompanying salad. The maître d' was very helpful, leading me to a Meursault and stating the Puligny-Montrachet was too heavy at midday and more appropriate in the evening.

The lakeside village of Talliores, site of Père Bise, is small and quaint, but several construction cranes erecting large condominiums loomed over it. Père Bise had a variety of rooms in its several clustered buildings. Ours was described as a chamber with mezzanine in the Villa des Roses and was of an elegant and sophisticated country-inn style. Highlights at dinner, other than the deferred Puligny-Montrachet, included a frogs' legs salad with walnuts and noisettes of lamb with marrow. All guests preceded dinner with a cocktail or apéritif on the unbelievable terrace, and both dinner and wine orders were taken there before going indoors to the dining room.

Restaurant Girardet in Crissier near Lausanne, Switzerland, is frequently described as the world's best restaurant, and we found the cuisine nearly flawless at lunch the next day. Unlike the chef-proprietor of many three-star establishments, Fredy Girardet minds the store rather than chasing dollars as a consultant in foreign lands. It makes a difference. On the other hand, as at so many chef-owned restaurants, dining room service was erratic and uncontrolled, albeit cordial and earnest.

Located in a period building named Hôtel de Ville, the square dining room of only twelve tables had unfortunately been redone in nondescript contemporary. Mud-colored paintings, singularly inappropriate in a restaurant, were so bad that we assumed they had been perpetrated by Fredy Girardet or a dear friend. Two tables were occupied by Japanese and four or five by Americans. When researching other restaurants, Mary usually is the only diner making notes. Here, pads and pens were in evidence everywhere. We were served a tiny crock of rabbit in aspic with chives with our apéritif. Mary opted for the menu of the day:

> *La crème de cerfeuil à la fricassée de grenouilles*
>
> *La paupiette de rouget et son sauté d'aubergines*
> *et de courgettes tomatées*
>
> *Le homard de Bretagne au beurre de poivre*
> *et d'aneth*
>
> *Le filet de veau poêle en persillade citronnée*
>
> *Brocoli et céleri glaces*
>
> *Les fromages du pays*
>
> *Les sorbets et les glaces à la crème*
>
> *Les desserts et pâtisseries du chariot*

The small servings of frogs' legs soup, a thin-rolled slice of red mullet, and lobster of Brittany were perfect. Sliced veal loin was very tender, but too garlicky for even a garlic lover. As promised, Mary permitted me to taste all of her courses, freeing me to order different dishes. Our wine was a Bâtard Montrachet. I began with an off-menu wonderment of thirty-two small, plump, impeccably fresh mussels from Brittany in a mellow sauce of wine, stock, butter, and herbs. My superb main course of veal kidneys in a light red-wine sauce was accompanied by a tiny cabbage roll stuffed with cheese and onions, carrots, turnips and, regrettably, a zucchini boat. Cheese and sorbets were skipped to save room for a Napoleon, lemon tart, floating island, and macaroon cake. Except for the dry macaroon, all were exceptional. Visiting the kitchen afterwards, we found Fredy Girardet (who had earlier visited every table) attired in shorts, T-shirt, and running shoes. His departure, leaping out an open window and jogging off, was a dramatic ending to a wonderful experience.

Continuing our drive southwest around Lac Léman, we were greeted warmly at Le Beau Rivage in Geneva by owner-manager Jacques Mayer. He flattered us with a front-corner room with a balcony and perfect view of Lac Léman, Mount Blanc, and the harbor with its famous four-hundred-fifty-foot fountain—Le Jet d'Eau. Proving once more what a small world it is, we ran into the Randy Aglees, fellow Detroiters, in our hotel lobby. Geneva is sophisticated and French with a well-dressed and obviously affluent population. By hired car and driver, we visited its old town, international institutions, and shopping areas, but were especially intrigued by the wealthy residential suburbs.

After Père Bise and Girardet we longed for simple food. Passing up the town's many grander restaurants, we wound down by dining *al fresco* at bistros recommended by Monsieur Mayer—Quay 13, Chez Bouby, and Wildemann, enjoying a variety of simple dishes as bacon salad, chanterelles, perch from the lake, and even a wonderful club sandwich.

In sharp contrast to our persecution by our airline coming to Europe, the return flight on Lufthansa was marked by punctuality and excellent service with good food and wine. Our impressions from our journey through the Alps mirrored the opinion expressed by Monique Burns in *Travel & Leisure* magazine:

"In fall, there are a number of splendid spots to alight in Europe. But if this autumn bird had to choose just one locale, she'd opt for the Alps, with its crisp air and alternating days of steel and sun. Within this region ... is virtually every attraction for which the Old World is renowned: sophisticated cities and sleepy hamlets, historic castles and monuments, craggy mountains and crystalline lakes, and fine wining and dining."

Caviar

We believe every fine restaurant should offer fresh caviar if at all possible. This has become difficult because a shrinking supply and rising demand have increased wholesale prices. As a result, a small restaurant applying normal restaurant markups would probably sell so little caviar that it could not be fresh, and caviar could no longer be offered.

Our solution has been to abandon normal restaurant markups in the case of caviar. Our price for a thirty-gram serving of fresh Petrossian ossetra molossol caviar with toasted-onion brioche and *crème fraîche* is forty dollars. This is a great bargain, especially since Petrossian of Paris has the best caviar and ossetra is the connoisseur's favorite.

Châteauneuf du Pape

Some wines are popular, not only because they taste good, but because they're also fun to say. The most famous example is Pouilly-Fuissé *(poo-yee-fwee-say)*. Another is Châteauneuf du Pape, meaning new castle of the Pope and pronounced *shah-toe-nuff doo pahp*. These thoughts spring to mind because of the great recent vintages in the southern Rhône River Valley where this wine is made from a blend of Grenach, Syrah, Mourvèdre, Cinsault, and other grapes.

To quote one authority: "It is a foregone conclusion now that 1989 and 1990 were the finest pair of vintages in Châteauneuf du Pape's long history. It was as if someone had cloned all the greatest wines of such legendary years as 1947, 1961 and 1978, and re-made them in the space of two glorious southern Rhône summers."

The pre-eminent CNDP is Ch. Beaucastel, rated outstanding by wine guru Robert M. Parker Jr., who writes, "The fact that Beaucastel produces the longest-lived red wine of the southern Rhône is irrefutable. However, the estate also produces one of the Rhône Valley's greatest and most distinctive wines. The wine is one of the few made totally by organic methods.... The results are stunning. The red wine is usually a black-ruby or purple color, loaded with layers of fruit, tannin, and a multitude of fascinating scents and aromas ... it is rarely a wine to be drunk young."

The 1989 Beaucastel received a 97 rating from Parker and was described as the greatest young wine he had ever tasted. Quite a compliment from the man who is also considered the greatest authority on red Bordeaux. *Wine Spectator* also rated the 1989 a 97. Both the 1988 and 1990 received rare 94s from Parker.

As might be expected, The Lark was quick to corral a supply of the now-impossible-to-find 1989. The fame of the 1989 is such that the entire allotment of an upscale Southfield, Michigan, restaurant was scarfed up by eager wine buffs within weeks of its arrival. Our supply is "hidden" on our reserve list. This writer was exasperated to learn that, while I was out of town, a patron at The Lark not only ordered a bottle of the 1989, but returned it as bad with the comment that he was surprised I had such a poor wine on my list. What a sad fate for "the greatest young wine ever." Grrrr! As you would assume, our waiters had the good taste to love finishing that treasured bottle.

Salzburger Nockerl
(Austrian Soufflé)

The Lark's first chef, Heinz Menguser, a native of Vienna, Austria, prepared this Austrian soufflé for special occasions. In 1985, after Heinz's departure, it was added to our regular menu and must be ordered at the beginning of the meal to give time for preparation. It differs from a French soufflé in that it is cooked on the china platter it is served on and is lighter and less filling.

> 2 cups egg yolks
> ¼ cup Grand Marnier
> ¼ teaspoon almond extract
> ½ teaspoon vanilla extract
> ¼ teaspoon orange extract
> 1 cup sugar
> ¾ cup flour
> 2 cups egg whites (from 16 eggs)
> 1 pinch cream of tartar
> 2 tablespoons cream

Mix first five ingredients and ¼ cup of the sugar together in a medium stainless steel bowl. Add flour, mix well and set aside.

In a separate stainless steel bowl whip egg whites with cream of tartar until mixture starts to thicken. While continuing to whip, gradually add the remaining sugar, whipping until stiff but not dry.

Add 1 cup of whipped whites to flour mixture and mix until smooth. Gently fold remainder of whites into mixture. Heap onto an oven-proof plate that has the cream on it. Bake at 400 degrees for 10 minutes, turn oven down to 325 degrees and continue baking for 10 to 15 minutes.

Remove from oven and sprinkle with powdered sugar. Serve immediately. Yields 6 to 8 servings.

Touring the Black Forest and Alsace

*T*o design a perfect touring vacation, first choose autumn when most tourists have departed, the air is crisp, and the woods are red and gold. Rent a luxury touring car capable of high speeds. Choose a small area with great variety—Germany's Black Forest and France's province of Alsace, separated only by the narrow Rhine. Both abound in storybook villages and towns, forests, rivers, hills, and mountains. Add friendly locals, welcoming hotels, charming country inns, some of the world's finest cuisine, and the result cannot be topped.

Restaurant preferences are so personal and subjective that we even take recommendations from friends with a grain of salt. But Paul Mann, the noted wine purveyor and bon vivant, insisted we stay at the Schweizer Stuben Relais & Châteaux in Bettingen in order to dine there several times. It was a convenient choice, little more than an hour's drive east from Frankfurt Airport. The hotel's concept was unique to us, a culinary village on the River Main with scattered buildings for rooms and suites, impressive tennis facilities, and three fine restaurants—French, Swiss, and Italian.

After checking into our elegant suite, we inquired at the desk as to a good restaurant for lunch in nearby Wertheim, since we were booked at Schober, the hotel's country-Swiss restaurant, that evening and at its French restaurant the next night. We quickly deduced the reception staff thought us daft to eat anywhere but at the hotel. So Schober it was for both lunch and dinner, and we were well pleased with local fish and game at lunch and a "peasant" platter assortment at dinner. Franconian wines in green canteen-shaped bottles and local beer were excellent. Between meals we toured the pleasant nearby medieval town of Wertheim with half-timbered houses dating from the sixteenth century on winding streets at the juncture of the Main and Tauber rivers. Add a castle, church, and fine shops and the result was charming. Had our nonstop flight not been five hours late, we would have had plenty of time to also see nearby picturesque Rothenberg and Wurtzburg across the Bavarian border.

The included breakfast at Schweizer Stuben may be the most impressive in the world with a selection of twelve elegant miniature preparations such as steak tartare, smoked salmon on a potato pan-cake, *prosciutto* with fresh figs, pâté of foie gras, and quail eggs with dried ham, all accompanied by champagne. One may have as many dishes as one dares.

Our Mercedes 300E took us to the Rheingau wine estate of Schloss Vollrads in Winkel in little over an hour, cruising at 170 kph (106 mph), which I would never attempt in the United States, but which seems natural in Germany. We were given a private wine tasting and a tour of the castle by our host, Count Matuschka-Greiffenclau, who has had private dinners at The Lark. The Greiffenclau family has not only the longest history of wine growing in Germany, but proba-bly in the world, dating back to at least 1211. Their wines are superb. The count's devotion to quality is such that wines are not even bottled in years when the weather is poor.

When we mentioned driving speeds in Europe, he told of a very fast drive he made to Lyon, France, because he was late for an impor-tant business appointment. Arriving at a toll stop, Count Matuschka was met by a reception committee of heavily armed French police who suspected he was a fleeing criminal or terrorist because he was clocked at 264 kph (164 mph). The gendarmes said he was the "fastest man in France in eighteen months," but released him when he explained the reason for such haste.

In addition to his own family's ancient properties, since 1979 Count Matuschka has leased the nearby vineyards of Furst-Lowenstein from their princely owners. Wines from both estates, including *trocken* (dry) dinner-style bottlings, are showcased in a superior restaurant the count has installed in The Grey House, ancestral home of the Greiffenclaus and reputedly the oldest stone home in Germany. Unfortunately, our visit was on a Tuesday when The Grey House is closed, so our hosts drove us up the scenic Riesling Road, paralleling the Rhine, to dine at Hotel Zur Krone in Assmannshausen am Rhein.

Our window-side table in the old paneled dining room over-looked the Rhine where a procession of tourist boats and commercial barges wound its way between vine-covered hills, sprinkled with ancient castles. Lunch included breast of guinea fowl in a light sauce and lamb tenderloin with pâté, wrapped in a cabbage leaf. It was becoming obvious that the food in finer German restaurants has become very, very good—much better than anything we've had in Italy and challenging France. Germans complain that *Michelin* feels France's supremacy threatened and has become very stingy with stars in Germany.

Highlight followed highlight on this trip, and dinner that evening at the French restaurant of Schweizer Stuben was, in fact, the finest meal of our lives to that date. The restaurant has only two stars, but is certainly entitled to three.

The setting was both impressive yet relaxed, with marble floors and oriental carpets, paneled walls and ceilings, cream-colored linens, and solid wood-framed chairs upholstered in needlepoint. Table settings were complete down to knife rests. Maître d' Pedro Sandvoss was only twenty-five but exuded confidence as well as hospitality. He knows that he and the chef are the best!

We chose the seven-course tasting menu to which Chef Dieter Mueller added several more courses. The food was Nouvelle or post-Nouvelle, which is usually pretty to look at and bad to eat. Here every dish was perfect, stunning in both appearance and taste—what many French three-star restaurants attempt but fail to achieve. The Guglhupf goose liver terrine in aspic is famous. One dish was a very small circle of sweetbread with an attached layer of slightly crisp, thinly sliced black truffles on both top and bottom, beautifully garnished and served with a light brown sauce. A circle of oyster pâté (sounds awful—tastes great) had an edge of smoked salmon. Langoustines were perfumed with thyme and served with a dab of black-squid-ink pasta. Sea bass came in a crust of herbs. Mashed potatoes were combined with puréed celery; baby cranberries were a garnish. Gooseberry ice cream had a fresh plum sauce. Chef Mueller has now opened Restaurant Dieter Mueller in an ancient castle near Cologne, which the industrial Siemens firm renovated as a Schloss Hotel.

Needless to say, the wine list is excellent and Pedro Sandvoss is an award-winning sommelier. I rarely permit the chef to choose my food and sommelier my wine, but I recommend that approach here.

We departed Schweizer Stuben with great reluctance the next morning, vowing to return ASAP. A quick zoom on autobahns brought us to the famed university town of Heidelberg on the Neckar River, awash in students and tourists, all in great spirits. Guide books rave of the view of the old town clustered at the foot of the Church of the Holy Spirit and the gaping red walls of the castle against the green of the forest beyond. The view from the castle walls over the town and Neckar Valley is also not to be missed. As suggested by Paul Mann and Pedro Sandvoss, we lunched in the schmaltzy paneled dining room of Hotel Europaeischer—adequate but not memorable.

Our journey to date had been prologue, for we now approached the Black Forest, taking the autobahn farther south, past Baden-Baden to exit at the resort town of Buhl, most famous for restaurant Burg

Windeck. Winding two-lane roads brought us east into mountains and into the Schwarzwald. The first impression is of a beautiful, totally green forest of tall evergreen trees. Next, one notices the order—uniformly spaced trees of one species with no undergrowth or open areas. Cut logs and poles at roadside are arranged with meticulous precision. One wonders if each tree is numbered—perhaps even named!

Our destination was Schlosshotel Buhlerhohe, a palatial edifice 2,600 feet up in the forest with views west of the far-distant Rhine. We were now in the state of Baden, often called Germany's culinary capital. Dinner at the hotel's Imperial Restaurant included a foie gras with truffle presentation. It consisted of a clear cylinder of aspic about three inches across and one inch thick in which was suspended a smaller cylinder of thin, alternating circular layers of white truffles and foie gras. Venison was baked in a salt crust and accompanied by wild mushrooms, warm apple slices, and cranberries from Sweden. Ravioli were layered with caviar and surrounded by *crème fraîche*. A potato pancake incorporated tiny cubes of smoked fish. The maître d', however, was not up to the standards of the hotel or its restaurant.

The genesis of this trip was the desire to look up Mary's great-grandfather Satory's ancestral home in the small town of Otigheim, which is near Rastatt and not too far from Baden-Baden. This was only a short drive from hotel Buhlerhohe after we checked out the next morning. On this stop and another later in our trip, we explored Otigheim, visited and took photos of the circa-1800 Satory house, and met Mary's distant cousins, surnamed Scholl and Kuhn. No Satorys remain, the male line having died out in Germany with only one male left in the United States. The Satory who first came to Otigheim was apparently an Italian serving the Austro-Hungarian army, meaning our children are of German, French, Irish, Polish, and Italian descent.

Plunging back into the Black Forest we soon arrived in the tiny Village of Neuweier, south of Baden-Baden, for a fine and simple lunch at the almost achingly charming Gasthaus Zum Lamm, where we, of course, had lamb!

Relais & Chateaux are extremely reliable. The only one of the many we have stayed in that was not up to standards was the Waldhaus in Switzerland. Our base for the next two days was the Relais & Chateaux Kurhotel Mitteltal of "familie Mast-Bareiss" near Baiersbronn in the heart of the northern Black Forest. This is very much a family-run operation and caters to families. It is wholesome—pool and sauna, planned activities, thirty-kilometer bike rides with return by train, hiking, apple-cheeked maids, hearty food, good cheer—and, of course, squeaky clean.

The principal restaurant at Kurhotel is large and charming. The smaller, more elegant gourmet dining room is magnificent. Place settings are Christofle silver supplemented by a pearl-handled hors d'oeuvre knife and fork and mother of pearl caviar spoon and knife. The flowers rival those of La Grenouille in New York. Dinner highlights included the best venison Mary has ever had—three filets in a pool of sauce topped with a potato and onion pancake. After-dinner delights included chocolate mousse in a cone with chocolate designs, a covered sterling silver dish of chocolate truffles in silver paper, and tiered-silver server of small delights including candied cherries with chocolate leaves. Service was warm and perfect. We were pampered throughout Germany (except at Buhlerhohe) because Pedro Sandvoss had made our hotel and dinner reservations and because we are "in the trade."

A half-hour drive the next morning brought us to Fruedenstadt, tourist heart of the northern Black Forest and a shopping mecca drawing a lively mix of visitors, mostly Germans from Frankfurt and other cities to the north. Cuckoo clocks range in price from $12.50 to $400. We bought and shipped the most grandiose we could find as a twenty-ninth anniversary memento. The challenge later was to find a spot in our home where the cuckoo doesn't drive us crazy during the night. At lunch in the Post Hotel we were lucky to grab two chairs at a table shared with four friendly German ladies.

Becoming spoiled, our stellar dinner that evening was at the Relais & Chateaux Traube-Tonback in Baiersbronn, minutes from our lodging at Kurhotel. The restaurant was elegant, the service perfect. Our host was the shy but friendly Heiner Finkbeiner of the owning family. This may be the best cuisine in Baden. Highlights included rabbit (better than at Alain Chapel); a salmon mousse with head cheese (try it!); sweetbreads in green ravioli with white truffles, *crème fraîche,* caviar and dill; and a pyramid-shaped pastry filled with mocha mousse with three scoops of ice cream on a bed of raspberry sauce. The hotel was jammed and the restaurant fully booked, as it should be.

The River Ill rises in the Vosges Mountains of southern Alsace and flows north, passing through Colmar and Strasbourg before emptying into the Rhine. Our luncheon destination was the gastronomic temple of the Haberlin brothers on the banks of the Ill in the village of Illhaeusern north of Colmar. Alsace has more *Michelin* stars per capita than any other area of France or the world, and its most respected and famous restaurant is L'Auberge de l'Ill. Many consider it the best in the world, and we had long wished to dine there.

Two well-appointed but not overdone dining rooms have large windows overlooking lawn and gardens sloping down to the Ill, about forty feet in width and only some forty to one hundred feet from l'Auberge. A small back room handles overflow. Our reactions were mixed; perhaps we were becoming picky after so much good food. Every fine restaurant in Baden and Alsace features foie gras, often in a variety of guises, and here it was generous and perfect. The famous salmon soufflé with pike-perch (walleye) was ethereal, but a filet in red wine sauce was only fair and the accompanying "Yorkshire pudding *à la moelle*" was bad. As always in this part of Europe, the wine list was excellent. We drank Franken, Baden, and Rhine wines in Germany, and Alsatian wines in Alsace.

A short drive after lunch brought us into the Vosges Mountains west of Colmar to Le Grand Hotel in Trois Epis, where we commandeered its best suite for the next two days. Trois Epis is a health resort known for its mild climate and clean air. At 2,100 feet, there are fine views to the east over foothills to the Plain of Alsace and the distant

Rhine. The hotel has an enclosed pool, saunas, and solarium to supplement the miles of mapped and named walking trails through nearby forests and meadows. No one recommended its restaurant, so for the first time in memory, we simply skipped dinner, giving our sated bodies a rest.

Conveniently, the next day was Sunday, the perfect time to visit Colmar, its medieval old town, the thirteenth-century Dominican church with a Gutenberg Bible and other ancient documents, and the thirteenth-century Unterlinden museum, which is second only to the Louvre in popularity in France and houses the Isenheim altar piece by Grunewald.

We opened up Colmar's two-star Schillinger at noon. It is small, comfortable, and well-appointed—not elegant. The service was excellent and the robust, jolly, teutonic chef-proprietor stopped by our table to chat a bit. My almost daily ration of foie gras was fine, but a main course of veal kidneys was sliced and fanned and, like all such preparations, all appearance and little taste. Mary, as usual, had ordered the winning dishes. My kitchen French told me one starter was sea urchin, but the waiter said no and insisted Mary order it. On arrival it appeared to be a sea urchin, four or five inches across, with a crisscross of spines on top. In actuality, the body of the urchin was a baked and browned seafood mousse that had been filled with boneless frogs' legs and tiny snails in a rich sauce. This almost unbelievable creation was set in a pool of sauce studded with more tiny snails. The flavors were a wonderfully perfect blend in what is certainly one of the best dishes we have ever had. Continuing her winning streak, Mary had the best squab of her life, boneless in a *feuilleton*.

Colmar is filled with fine food shops offering mouth-watering pastries and chocolates. In the fall, all shops offer elaborate candy replicas of chestnuts peeking from half-open husks. Forest roads are littered with chestnuts since, unlike the Black Forest, woods are a mixture of conifers and hardwoods, much more wild and appealing.

We stopped in an exurb of Colmar to watch a funky but enthusiastic harvest parade, complete with a float of a World War I airplane with the two-member crew in old leather helmets. Turning back toward Trois Epis, we visited Munster, atmospheric and old with no great emphasis on its famous cheese. Nearer to Le Grand Hotel was Turkheim, which *European Travel & Life* says is "a quintessential Alsatian fortified village dating from the fourteenth century that recently won a national prize as one of the finest preserved villages in the country." Having toured rather hard, we took the evening off, snacking in our suite with treasures purchased in Colmar.

Alsatian tourist authorities provide an excellent flyer and map, "Alsace Tourist Routes," perhaps copied after the Romantic Road and Riesling Road in Germany. Six routes are mapped and accompanied by brief descriptions of sights and attractions along each one. The Route du Vin (Wine Road) is by far the best, leading one to ridiculously picturesque old villages as well as the major vineyards.

Departing our hotel the next morning, we took the Wine Road south to Eguisheim, which may be the most charming wine-growing village in Alsace. Walking the winding streets one passes home after home of fairy-tale appearance, most with dated stone lintels from the early sixteenth century. The great majority of homes are so perfectly maintained and flower bedecked that we assumed a great deal of gentrification must have occurred and that the few dilapidated dwellings remaining will soon be purchased and restored.

Three minutes down the Route du Vin from Eguisheim is Husseren-les-Châteaux, another ancient village dominated by ruined castles on the highest point of the wine route. Because of The Lark, Mary and I could have arranged private visits to many wineries, but did not wish to impose during the time of the crush or harvest, which by coincidence started that very day. Kuentz-Bas in Husseren-les-Châteaux, however, is very special, so we called on proprietor Jean-Michel Bas, surely one of the nicest men in France, whose many friends even include a group of Texans who visit each year. Son Christian Bas supervised the harvest and missed our festivities, tasting the fine wines of this long-established firm. Père Bas and assistant Coleen had arranged many of our hotel and restaurant arrangements in Alsace as Pedro Sandvoss had done in Germany.

Duty soon called, however, and it was back to work with another lunch at L'Auberge de l'Ill. Somebody has to do it! As repeat customers, we had been promoted to a window-side table in the first and more desirable of the two principal dining rooms, although there is nothing wrong with the second room and our window-side table there had been fine. In contrast to many three-star restaurants, there were few Japanese and Americans. The Haberlin brothers' philosophy is apparently similar to ours, an eclectic approach offering both updated classics and innovative preparations without the excesses of Nouvelle Cuisine. Today's dishes were good examples: a ragout of smoked frogs' legs on a bed of *choucroute* consisting of very fine cabbage, tiny sausage of frogs' legs, and quenelles; an assortment from the smallest of suckling pigs with a miniature stuffed cabbage; and boneless breast of Bresse chicken accompanied by a tiny chicken pie made from the thigh and leg. It is interesting that the menu listed Louisiana crayfish.

Driving back toward the Vosges Mountains, we passed trucks full of the cabbage harvest. Alsatians love cabbage and sauerkraut so much it was no surprise to find it featured in three-star restaurants like L'Auberge de l'Ill as well as humbler establishments.

Our Relais & Châteaux for the next two nights was Hostellerie La Cheneaudier, newly built in the exterior style of an ancient inn. The only accommodation available was the best suite, which one writer accurately described as Hollywood kitsch. The bedroom of the suite directly faced a large archway framing a mammoth gold bathtub. There was nothing kinky, however, about the mountain setting or the two-star restaurant where our dinner included an ambrosial complimentary offering of creamy scrambled eggs and truffles in truffle sauce and excellent wild boar.

The next day was spent touring the nearby Vosges Mountains including Mont St. Odile, a famous convent and place of pilgrimage founded by Saint Odile, the patron saint of Alsace. The well-preserved buildings, which house a convent to this day, are so old that they contain two Roman chapels with magnificent mosaic ceilings. Standing at the old walls, one views the Plain of Alsace far below, distant Strasbourg, the Rhine, and even the Black Forest of Germany.

Andlau was another storybook village that had won the government award granted villages and towns with the highest percentage of flower-bedecked buildings. In the picturesque town of Obernai, we lunched at the large, open, charming and simple La Halle aux Blés, where we had our first *choucroute garnie* of our trip—the groaning-board national dish of Alsace consisting of sauerkraut, steamed potatoes, ham, pork tenderloin, slab bacon, and various sausages. There was, again, no need for dinner that evening.

Called "the prettiest city in the world," few large cities have retained so much of their old buildings and flavor as Strasbourg, the capital of Alsace, where we enjoyed the next day and a half. Our base was the Hôtel Sofitel, conveniently located near the heart of the old city. Père Bas had recommended Maison des Tanneurs, an impossibly romantic, old, traditional restaurant on the banks of the Ill in walking distance of our hotel. It calls itself "The House of Choucroute" and many of the mostly native crowd at lunch were, in fact, tucking into huge platters of the local favorite. Having done that bit the day before in Obernai, we tried other favorites, the thick and rich traditional Alsatian onion tart, and sandre, an excellent fish in Riesling sauce.

Everywhere on our trip sandre was featured, enthusiastically recommended, and priced higher than other fish. But what was it? Beginning a tour of the old city after lunch, we came upon a fish market and asked the proprietor to show us sandre. He did, and it was a walleye, or so close to walleye it would take an ichthyologist to tell the difference. This explains why the Germans and French translate it to English as "pike-perch."

Strasbourg was alive with tourists, even in October. Of the cathedral with its 470-foot spire it is said, "Here for the first time, overtaking even Chartres, the Gothic reaches as far as human art can reach." The Museum and Palace of the Rohan Cardinals and the Musée Alsacien should also not be missed, but the best is the old city itself with its rivers, canals, and ancient-timbered buildings. "The eye can never be weary in Strasbourg."

Père Bas told us that two Strasbourg restaurants deserved three stars, but not wishing to be too free, *Michelin* had elevated only Le Crocodile, leaving equally fine Buerehiesel at two stars. Being somewhat star-struck, we dined at Le Crocodile where a full-sized crocodile hangs outside. Madame Jung was not yet on station at our arrival, so we had to battle a captain who insisted we sit in the front Siberia room before he was overruled by the maître d', who led us to the rear dining room. After my foie gras ration, I had a pig's foot stuffed with its meat, truffles, and other goodies—presumably similar to the dish featured at the hot restaurant on the Riviera, Louis XV in Monaco's Hotel de Paris. Unfortunately, the accompanying overly salty potato pancake was inedible. Perhaps this was because chubby, jolly Chef-Proprietor Emile Jung spent his time talking to us and other tables rather than supervising the kitchen. Madame Jung was friendly and charming, obviously reveling in their three-star status. Mary, as usual, picked the winner—*homard au panache de légumes et fumet de Graves rouge,* an elegant lobster dish with small, fine vegetables in a light, red wine sauce.

Morning was a wonderful walk through the clean brick, cobblestone, and stone sidewalks and streets of Strasbourg, a shopper's paradise. Maison Kammerzell, where we lunched, is one of the few restaurants that is a *Michelin*-starred sight as well as a *Michelin*-recommended restaurant. It is simply the most beautiful old building in the city. I had the sauerkraut *formidable (choucroute garnie)* of "*Strassburger und Montbeliard Wurstchen, Schweineschulter, Pokelfleisch, geraucherter Speck, Blutwurst, Leberknepfle, halbes Eisbein, Landwurst.*" *Magnifique,* as was Mary's *pot-au-feu parisien* of boiled beef short ribs with coarse salt, horseradish, and pickles.

We now sprinted back to southern Alsace, which might lead readers to believe us flaky (back and forth). Our itinerary in Alsace, however, was partly determined by the availability of hotel reservations, difficult even this late in the year. Certainly one of the hardest hostelries to gain access to was the Relais & Châteaux, Château d'Isenbourg, in the Vosges foothills overlooking the old town of Rouffach near Colmar. The château is one of the exclusive inner group of the Relais & Châteaux, known as Grandes Étapes Françaises. Thanks again to Père Bas, we were soon ensconced in an extremely attractive corner room where, taking another break from overindulgence, we picnicked on snacks purloined from the fine shops of Strasbourg.

Earlier mention was made of the tourist routes of Alsace, the southernmost of which is The Fried Carp Roads. Well, folks eccentric enough to host the Michigan Chili Cookoff could not resist The Fried Carp Roads, the path less traveled. The best thing about southern Alsace was getting there, twisting among the higher Vosges Mountains through forests and quaint little towns. We shared the finest scenery of the trip with numerous hang gliders.

The Fried Carp Roads took us through flat and unremarkable countryside. As lunchtime neared, we drove into Altkirch, the largest town of the region, where we could not find a restaurant of even passing acceptability. After forty-five minutes, wishing we had driven to nearby Basel, Switzerland, we were lost in what appeared to be a park. We finally broke out onto a main road. Directly across it was a restaurant of charming aspect, Hotel Restaurant Ottie Baur. Fate obviously intended us to find it for, on entering, we saw the wooden chandeliers were carved in the shape of carp! The front dining room was full of tables of from two to eight, enjoying very good-looking food. Needless to say, we had fried carp and *frites,* preceded by foie gras and excellent snails.

Dinner that evening was in the fifteenth-century cellar of Château d'Isenbourg, which had been transformed into its dramatic and fine restaurant. Highlights included sandre, a fat *tarte Tatin,* and a great 1976 reserve Riesling from Kuentz-Bas. It is interesting that, as far as we can recall, no restaurant of our trip had either live or recorded music. Another notable absence was salad, quite rare and generally curly endive, if offered at all.

Wishing to be reasonably close to the Frankfurt Airport, our last stop was Baden-Baden, a beautiful small city dating to Roman times with many parks, a casino, old spa hotels, and a neat and compact downtown of shops and restaurants. Over the years we had read numerous articles on Baden-Baden and its famous Brenner's Park Hotel in *Gourmet* magazine; as a result, we took a large suite there. This extravagance was the only accommodation we have ever had that was even more expensive than our suite at the Connaught in London.

After a simple and robust lunch in the hotel's less formal Swartzwaldstube restaurant, we joined the throngs strolling and shopping, returning to town again that evening for dinner at a regional restaurant, Badener Stuben, where we especially enjoyed a shared appetizer of white herring in cream with apples and onions.

Our two weeks were everything we had hoped for and confirmed a long-held belief that, fishing or hunting expeditions aside, the most enjoyable and adventuresome trips are driving tours in fairly small areas with a rich history, where food and lodgings are good, there is a diversity of sights, and Americans are appreciated.

(A version of this article appeared in *Gastronome,* the national publication of the *Confrérie de la Chaîne des Rôtisseurs.*)

Paul Bocuse

The world's most famous French chef and principal proponent of now-discredited Nouvelle Cuisine spends his days lamenting the evil he spawned. A few quotes on Nouvelle Cuisine by Chef Bocuse during an interview by Florence Fabricant of *Nation's Restaurant News*:

"It has short-changed us, pulled the rug out from under our strengths…. It may have been easier … that's part of the problem…. The plates were very pretty, but the portions were too small and the vegetables were undercooked … they kept their color better, but when they have no flavor, who cares.... The maître d'hôtel has become a lid lifter.... And everywhere you go it's lentils ... lentils and beet essence. I suppose it's better than kiwi."

When in France

European Travel & Life magazine published a fascinating article by Harriet Welty Rochefort on French manners—*ça se fait* (that is done) and *ça ne se fait pas* (that is just not done). For example, a well-known French restaurant critic cited the things that really bothered him when at a fine restaurant: small children, dogs, smokers, and canned music. Obviously, his list and not mine, since I like dogs.

Ms. Rochefort says that the number of mistakes that can be made at the dinner table staggers the imagination, such as leaving the table after one is seated except in dire emergency. And then, one does not announce where one is going. Bread is broken, not cut, placed on the table rather than a plate, and never used to sop up a sauce.

Almost everything solid except bread is eaten with a knife and fork, even frogs' legs and fruit such as a banana. But cutting salad greenery is unforgivable. If too large, it is folded using knife and fork. Soup is sipped from the end of the spoon, not the side. Roquefort cheese is always eaten with butter.

The worst sin, however, is not to clean your plate at a meal in the host's home. And please note that hands should always be on or above the table to avoid any suspicion of hanky-panky.

Dress Code

The media reported that Don Johnson of Miami Vice and Nash Bridges fame was refused admittance at Doro's, an Italian restaurant in San Francisco, because he was not wearing a tie. The fact that he does not wear shirts with collars was not considered a mitigating circumstance.

In the early days of The Lark, a woman telephoned one morning to inform me that she and her husband had dined with us the night before, but would never return because a man at the next table was not wearing a tie. He was "otherwise well-behaved." When making reservations, new customers often ask about our dress code. We respond that gentlemen should wear jackets and would probably feel more comfortable here with a tie. We have never, however, refused admittance to anyone who was neat and clean, as we do not believe informality in dress is sufficient reason to embarrass someone and spoil a planned evening.

Americans are, of course, much more stuffy in such matters than most Europeans. In France, dress at three-star restaurants varies from ultraformal to ultracasual. At Restaurant Girardet near Lausanne, Switzerland, frequently and inaccurately called the world's best, Chef-Proprietor Fredy Girardet states it is none of his business what his guests wear. We do believe that one should dress for the occasion, and that those who don't are missing part of the fun.

Southeast Asian Cruise

Hong Kong

I was one of 102 people on a small ship for my first visit to Hong Kong. That ship was not one of the new all-suite luxury liners, such as Sea Goddess or Seabourne, but U.S.S. Ford County, LST772, a tank-landing ship. The year was 1956, and I was serving two years before the mast as a petty officer. My most enduring memories are of the old, fabled Peninsula Hotel and of being hunted by the shore patrol, who had learned of my plan to visit then-forbidden Macau. I had been ratted out by a Maryknoll missionary who somehow got wind of my scheme to change into civies in the British NCO Club to be able to board the Hong Kong–to-Macau ferry.

Twenty-two years later Mary and I were in Hong Kong for but a single day on our way to China as one of the first handful of tourists admitted to the Inner Kingdom. Mary was so chagrined by her limited time in Hong Kong that we returned in 1979 for two weeks. On that trip we stayed in the by-then ultraluxurious Peninsula Hotel, before they built a planetarium between it and the harbor.

Skipping to the present, New Year's Day 1996 found us ensconced in the Mandarin Oriental Hotel on Hong Kong Island. This was a precruise stop before boarding the fifty-two-suite Renaissance VI at Singapore for a voyage through the islands of Indonesia. Our package deal with Renaissance included a room on the non-harbor-view side of the Mandarin, but we paid the difference for a harbor-view room and were then upgraded to a harbor suite. We were surprised and pleased that our suite was furnished with binoculars, because the harbor is one of the most spectacular urban sights in the world. The buildings of Kowloon are a glittering background to the harbor's bustling ships, ferries, junks, and sampans. Those who feel that the choice of hotel is not very important, because "I only sleep there," should suspend that approach in Hong Kong, if only to revel in what is perhaps the best service in the world. Also, to quote the very upscale *In World Guide:*

"Hong Kong is probably the only great city in the world where putting on the ritz revolves very much in, and around, its leading hotels. One conducts business breakfasts there, one lunches and takes tea, one meets for cocktails and, as they also happen to offer the city's best restaurants and bars, one goes there to dine. Despite the new hotels ... there are really only four hotels in Hong Kong's hotel crown ... The Regent ... The Mandarin ... The Peninsula ... The Shangri-La."

In World Guide has the same elitist approach to restaurants, declaring:

"Among the many myths of Hong Kong, one, for the sake of exacting palates, must be corrected. For all that the city offers—some thirty thousand licensed eating establishments—those which will truly please a discriminating gourmet are but a small minority. Of course, you can try the floating Jumbo Restaurants at Aberdeen, the junk-dining in Causeway Bay's typhoon shelter ... but don't be surprised if your expectations are disappointed."

Mary and I had enjoyed the floating restaurants on previous trips along with the other almost-obligatory sight-seeing such as Portuguese Macau and the renowned Buddhist Po Lin Monastery and its popular vegetarian restaurant on Lantau Island. Another high-light was the Hong Kong produce market with every imaginable foodstuff, including exotica like live sea snakes and toads, reflecting the Cantonese obsession with freshness. Having "been there, done that," we felt free to concentrate on shopping and dining in three days in the Crown Colony—our last chance to do so before the dreaded Communist takeover on July 1, 1997.

Like many others, we'd become familiar with the diverse Chinese cuisines of such regions as Canton, Shanghai, Beijing, Hunan, and Szechuan. But nowhere in the United States or China had we sampled the food of the other most respected Chinese cuisine, Chui Chow, the coastal region around Swatow in eastern Guangdong Province. Its offerings include seafood, goose, duck, and vegetarian dishes, influenced by Canton to the southwest and Fukien to the north. The Mandarin's Oriental concierge, *In World Guide*, and *Travel & Leisure* magazine all pointed us to one of the City Chui Chow restaurants across the harbor on the Kowloon side, which we reached by the Star Ferry. The ferry's Hong Kong Island terminal is conveniently located in front of the Mandarin Oriental Hotel.

City Chui Chow is in an office building off the beaten tourist track and has one large brightly lit and well-appointed dining room. We were the only non-Chinese, which in upscale Hong Kong restaurants usually portends excellent Chinese cuisine. Once it became clear to the staff that we didn't know what we were doing, we were adopted, amid smiles and tittering, as their pet Americans. Service was cheerful and excellent. Lunch began and ended with unordered strongly flavored Tiet Kwum Yum (Iron Goddess of Mercy) oolong tea, a Chui Chow tradition, plus two other unusual teas, exceptions to the general rule that Chinese do not drink tea at meals other than with dim sum. I greatly amused the staff at one point by sampling what I thought was a bowl of tea, but was in fact a finger bowl of tea. City Chui Chow is obviously not frequented by typical tourists. There was no silverware—period—only chopsticks and spoons, which is all we ever use at Oriental restaurants. Furthermore, there was only one copy of an English-language menu. Our wonderful lunch included shrimp in almost transparent dumpling pastry, vegetarian Chui Chow dumplings with a great sauce, soy goose with large slices of tofu, and crab, which was first presented live, then cooked and served with mushrooms and vegetables. As pet Occidentals, we were presented a complimentary, mysterious (to us) dessert soup. City Chui Chow was a fine beginning to our Asian odyssey.

Hong Kong is a shopping mecca of the world and one need go no farther than the shops in the Mandarin. Some of our (unpurchased) finds were diamonds to twenty carats, huge South Sea black pearls costing up to U.S.$200,000 per strand, and a forty-carat sapphire.

Dinner that evening was Kowloon-side at Plume, the French restaurant of The Regent harbor-front hotel. Plume is superbly elegant with a very high wall of glass giving enchanting views of light-sprinkled ships plying the harbor, with the office and hotel towers of Hong Kong Island beyond. An appealing glass-enclosed wine cellar adds a French accent to this softly lit room. My multicourse, fixed-price dinner included sautéed frogs' legs with Belon oysters, black chicken broth with cèpes sausage and ham, pan-fried venison cutlet with red cabbage and cranberries, plus other courses. It was very elaborate, which explained why no dish was hot enough. Mary had an extremely bland Dover sole starter, followed by a great rack of lamb on zucchini ragout and white eggplant. She also loved her Aribica Surprise dessert—a chocolate saucer with chocolate cup filled with sabayon and accompanied by ice cream.

The next morning and afternoon were spent shopping, mostly at the two Chinese-government arts and crafts shops in Kowloon. Purchases included amethyst and gold earrings, topaz and gold earrings, gold over silver vermeil pins, and silk brocade yard goods. The silk brocade yard-goods selection was much more limited than previously, most of that available being a mixture of silk and polyester. We were told that soon there would be almost no pure silk bolts offered; silk would be blended with polyester to produce more "silk" yard goods and increase profits.

Lunch was at Luk Yu Tea House, an unofficial historic monument, famous as the quintessential dim sum tea house with "unmatched Art Deco *chinoiserie.*" Decor here includes marble-backed chairs, black fans, and brass spittoons. There was one other Occidental couple at this small place behind our hotel, where we have enjoyed dim sum on every visit to Hong Kong. Five different dim sum plus a generous serving of Singapore noodles cost less than twenty dollars. Nostalgia and decor aside, there are better spots for dim sum, including the Summer Palace in the Island Shangri-La hotel, and even the dim sum room of the floating Jumbo Restaurant.

It was permissible for us to bring our own wine and pay corkage at our dinner destination, Fook Lam Moon. Since wine selections at Chinese restaurants are almost always terrible, I brought a 1990 Ch. La Louvière white Bordeaux purchased at the shopping center connected by pedestrian bridge to the Mandarin Oriental. Fook Lam Moon is not to be missed. For convenience we chose the Wan Chai Hong Kong Island locale over its sister restaurant in Kowloon. This is the preferred Cantonese restaurant of Hong Kong's Chinese power elite.

Inside the entry door is a sizable glass cabinet displaying the private, expensive cognac bottles of its regular Chinese patrons. Louis XIII, retailing at about $1,500 per bottle, was much in evidence. Again, except for one other couple who were guests at a table of Chinese, we were the only Occidentals. From their appearance, deportment, and many other clues, we were obviously surrounded by the top echelon of Hong Kong's Chinese society, who all knew each other and table hopped. Some tables had three generations of diners. This is the place to see and be seen, but only for the Chinese. Many tables were delivered their cognac bottle from the entry cabinet. As mentioned earlier, Chinese do not usually drink tea at meals. Beer or soft drinks are in evidence at moderately priced restaurants. At top spots like Fook Lam Moon preferred beverages are fine French wines, scotch, and most popular of all, top-of-the-line cognac.

Our main courses were lobster pieces with bamboo shoots, the house specialty crispy-fried chicken, and a fresh whole crab with

117

black beans. This is an excellent restaurant, which proved a perfect finale to our all-Chinese day.

Lai Ching Heen, the Chinese restaurant of The Regent hotel has been named one of the world's ten best restaurants since 1991 by Patricia Wells, restaurant critic of the *International Herald Tribune*. She rated it second in the world in 1991 and third at last report. Ms. Wells is well-respected and her food books are best-sellers in France. Big, bright and cheerful, Lai Ching Heen is located on the hotel's lower level with harbor views. The menu is inspiring and the place settings are awesome, including a jade base plate, fish-shaped jade chopstick rest, ivory chopsticks, and jade napkin ring. At lunch on our last day in Hong Kong, we liked everything on the menu and had to be guided by the staff, who knew we were "in the trade." We had two dim sum starters—chicken and macadamia nuts in baked puff-pastry dumplings and steamed shrimp and pork dumplings, both with excellent, fragrant sauces, including expensive, very "in" X. O. sauce.

Mary loves eggplant and chose a casserole of lobster and eggplant flavored with X. O. sauce for her main course. I had roast duck breast with kiwi in lemon sauce, the restaurant's most famous dish. All our food was great and the service perfect. Other choices included braised sliced abalone at about U.S.$330 or braised imperial bird's nest with crab roe at U.S.$380. Don't even ask the price of braised whole ouma abalone with oyster sauce. Our complimentary dessert was a shaved ice "mountain" studded with pieces of fresh fruit and berries. The place setting for this course was a jade bowl with a jade spoon.

We had dined at highly rated Man Wah, the Chinese restaurant of our hotel, on a previous trip. In fact, the very first menu of The Lark in June 1981 listed Shrimp Man Wah as a main course. So for variety, we chose our hotel's French restaurant, Pierrot, for our final dinner in Hong Kong. We have very mixed feelings about this place. Main courses of sautéed sea bass on a dill-flavored sweet pepper ragout and a veal chop with pine-nut crust were very good. On the other hand, the staff are either very sloppy in what they serve or there is a deliberate policy of hoodwinking patrons. For example, I ordered

Guigal's Hermitage Côte Rôtie Côtes Blonde et Brune in the 1990 vintage and they attempted to serve a 1991 without pointing out that it was not the vintage requested. Worse, we ordered ossetra caviar, but were served what we believed was sevruga. This should not happen at a fine hotel like the Mandarin Oriental.

Singapore

So, ending a very enjoyable and broadening three days in Hong Kong, we flew to Singapore on its namesake airline and checked into the Oriental Hotel. It is one of this nation-city's finest, outscored only by the Shangri-La.

Singapore has been much in the news because of its caning of an American delinquent convicted of vandalism. That incident made the world more aware of Singapore's unique, present-day culture, developed under postcolonial Prime Minister Lee Kuan Yew and his successor. The democratic but paternalistic government applies draconian solutions to all perceived social problems. Just a few examples, other than caning minor criminals, are punishments that range from the unwavering prompt execution of drug peddlers to huge fines for littering and for failing to flush a public toilet. Traffic jams are avoided by more than a thirty-thousand-dollar charge for a permit to purchase a car and a large additional fee for a license to enter the city center.

On the positive side, every worker has his own individual government retirement account, which he is encouraged to borrow from to purchase his own condominium apartment or house. Thus, almost all citizens have not only an assured retirement income but own their residence. There are no slums and gentrification has renovated virtually every area of the city and suburbs. All of this has contributed to prosperity and stability despite the mixed population of Chinese,

Malay, Tamil, Sikh, and English.

We joined two fellow passengers-to-be at Raffles Hotel, made famous by Rudyard Kipling, Somerset Maugham, and the Singapore Sling. Raffles has been completely renovated at tremendous expense. Hordes of tourists streamed through the lobby and other public areas admiring the restored high-ceilinged, stage-scenery-like decor. All was calm, however, in the famous Grill where Mary had genuine ossetra caviar followed by a navarin of lamb, and I had a starter of warm smoked salmon filet with caviar and a main course of seared scallops with vegetables Provençal. Our wine was our favorite red Bordeaux, the 1989 Ch. Lynch Bages. We were served six different chocolate desserts. The food was good, not excellent, and marred by the service of hot items on cold plates. Those attending a buffet lunch gave a better report.

The next day we toured the city, a melange of Malay, Chinese, Indian, and Peranakan (Malay-Chinese) influences. Highlights included Little India with its stall shops selling jewelry and brassware; the old Malay quarter with its shops featuring precious stones, baskets, silks, sarongs, and much more; beautifully restored homes and the gold-domed Sultan Mosque; and Chinatown where Mary bought tiger balm for her aching back and where we enjoyed a tasting and class given by a Master of Tea at Yixing Xuan tea house.

When asked his opinion of the best restaurant offering local cuisine, the distinguished managing director of the leading tour company recommended Aziza's in Albert Court, a small new development largely occupied by an intimate hotel and the restaurant. What a find! And what a fortunate coincidence, as Aziza's had just reopened for business in this new location that very day. We met Chia Boon Pin, corporate general manager of Far East Organization, owners of Albert Court and, more importantly, Aziza Ali, the proprietor of Aziza's. As apparently few knew they had opened, we were the only patrons at lunch and enjoyed their individual attention. Highlights, accompanied by Tiger beer, were *satay* with a great peanut sauce; prawns with a rich chili sauce; chicken with a sauce that included lemon grass, cumin, and coriander; and a dessert of jackfruit pudding.

The most famous food of Singapore, however, is hawkers' food. In the past, Singapore abounded with street stands at busy intersections, where hawkers shouted their wares to passersby. The perfectionist-minded government decided to remove these traffic obstacles and improve sanitation by establishing planned food courts where hawkers could be gathered in central locations and sanitation supervised by government inspectors. Eating at a hawker center is an essential Singapore experience. We had dinner at the most famous, Newton Circus, browsing among the scores of stalls to see what was available and who had the most appealing food. Then, taking a table, we ordered double-sized bottles of Tiger beer, grilled giant prawns, grilled whole crab, grilled crab in chili sauce, Singapore noodles, and a stir-fried green vegetable with garlic. Other possible choices included oyster omelets, *satays,* barbecued duck, grilled chicken, squid, cuttlefish, clams, mussels, cockles, and much more. The food was fresh and tasty, the price right, and the ambience lively and fun. Would that we had such food courts in the United States.

Our eating festival continued the next day with a dim sum brunch at Tsui Hang Village, a bright and tidy Chinese restaurant in the extensive shopping mall attached to the Oriental Hotel. When in China or any other country where dim sum is conveniently available, we prefer it for breakfast or brunch. Our choices this day were shark's fin dumpling with soup, prawn dumpling *(ha gow),* steamed garlic spare rib pieces, pork spring rolls, barbecue pork puff, and pork dumplings.

Indonesia

Having concluded our precruise sojourn in Hong Kong and Singapore, we now embarked on Renaissance VI for a voyage through the islands of Indonesia. Indonesia, with a population of more than 193.5 million, is the sixth most populated nation in the world. Comprising some 13,677 islands, about half of which are uninhabited, it was ruled by the Dutch for almost three centuries until occupied by the Japanese during World War II. It became independent shortly after the Japanese surrender. Islam is the dominate religion, although there are Hindus, as on Bali, and Buddhists, Christians, and animists. Dozens of ethnic groups and 588 languages add to the complexity of this great nation. Obviously this or any other cruise could only hope to hit a few highlights of so large and diverse a country.

In the fall of 1994 we'd cruised from Athens through the Aegean Islands and up the Turkish coast to Istanbul on a sister ship. Renaissance VI is a small luxury liner with fifty-two, all-outside-facing suites. On both cruises we opted for one of the four top-of-the-line Renaissance Suites with a picture window and sliding-glass door to a private balcony, a king-sized bed, two full-length wardrobes (closets), a vanity-desk, sofa, lounge chair, coffee table TV-VCR, and many cabinets and storage areas.

The captain's welcoming dinner that evening included sevruga caviar on a potato pancake with sour cream, oxtail consommé with lemon grass and local mushrooms, goose liver parfait on lettuce, grilled tiger prawns or baked beef tenderloin, and a cheese cake soufflé with ginger mango sauce. A day without prawns is like a day without sunshine. Our wine was a decent 1989 Gevry-Chambertin from Jadot.

The eruption of the Indonesian island of Krakatoa in 1883 is called the most violent in recorded history. It may have been rivaled or surpassed by that of the Greek island of Santorini, but there is no record of that outburst. The explosion at Krakatoa threw rocks seventeen miles into the sky. Tidal waves 130 feet high destroyed villages on Java and Sumatra, according to Renaissance, and even shook vessels as far away as the English Channel. Dust in the atmosphere caused brilliant sunsets in many parts of the globe, including the United States. Volcanic activity ceased until 1928, when Anak Krakatoa (son of Krakatoa) belched forth. It has been intermittently active and growing ever since, at times shooting forth fire, ashes, and flaming boulders. Krakatoa was the island du jour of our second full day at sea. Anak Krakatoa was reasonably well-behaved but threatening enough to preclude a shore excursion by Renaissance or any other cruise ships. Renaissance VI lay offshore as we listened to a lecture on the island, took photos, and enjoyed an ice cream social on the pool deck. Dinner that night was graced by Newton Merlot—unlisted on the wine list and the last bottle on board.

Jakarta, the capital of Indonesia, is located on the western end of the north coast of Java, a long, narrow island whose central mountain chain includes a number of the nation's approximately 128 smoking volcanoes. Jakarta, known to the Dutch as Batavia, is not only the country's principal port, but is also the center of political, economic, social, and cultural life. Its population has exploded to more than seven million, contributing to Java's overcrowding with more than half of Indonesia's population. After our overnight passage from Krakatoa, we boarded buses to struggle through a continuous traffic jam from Jakarta's port to the central core of this overcrowded, unattractive city. Many of my fellow shipmates, having been trapped on board for two days, were suffering shopping withdrawal symptoms and were in desperate need of a fix. Thus, our first stop was a major department store with good shopping for a wealth of regional offerings. Mary chose four large black mabe pearls at a very good price. We hope they're not white pearls dyed black.

The best thing about Jakarta is the Indonesian National Museum, reputedly the finest museum in Southeast Asia. It has a great collection of bronze items from the Hindu-Javanese era, which preceded the arrival of Islam, stone sculptures from temples throughout the Indonesian archipelago, and a fine collection of ancient Chinese porcelain. The Gold Room is fabulous.

Our typical overnight voyage was east along Java's north coast and brought us the next morning to Semarang in central Java. Under Dutch rule it became an important center of trade with other islands and with China. Its famous Chinese Gedung Batu Temple is unique in that it is used by both Buddhists and Muslims in defiance of orthodox Muslim principles. We drove through the commercial lower town, then up through the old Dutch residential area and south into the countryside where we passed innumerable rice paddies, many terraced, all backed by green hills. The overall impression was that of a lush, green land—quite dramatic.

The principal goal of this excursion was the Buddhist temple of Borobudur, one of many sites alleged to be the "Eighth Wonder of the World." Borobudur is the largest ancient monument in the southern hemisphere, a colossal complex built by the Tantric Buddhists of the Vajrayana sect between 778 A.D. and 856 A.D. using thousands of laborers and slaves. To quote our cruise literature:

"Wrapped around a hill with six square terraces topped by three circular ones, Borobudur represents the Buddhist vision of the cosmos, starting with the everyday world and rising to nirvana, eternal nothingness. The sculptural detail is astonishing with 1,500 relief panels, four hundred images of Buddha in open chambers, plus seventy-two Buddhas partially visible in latticed stuppas on the top three terraces. The huge stuppa on top is empty, symbolizing nirvana."

Borobudur was buried by volcanic eruptions and lay hidden and unknown for almost a thousand years until discovered in 1814 by Sir Stafford Raffles of Singapore fame. A massive excavation and restoration was begun the by United Nations Educational, Scientific and Cultural Organization (UNESCO) in the 1970s and completed in 1993. An essential sight for any visitor to Indonesia, its setting and compelling views from the summit are an added incentive.

We opted the next day for a leisurely private excursion in the town of Semarang and a visit to a locally famous bird market where many hundreds of caged live birds were for sale, including some feisty larks. Other stops were, of course, for shopping, especially for batiks. Batik is a method of dying cloth in which the part of the cloth not intended to be dyed by a color is covered with removable wax. The best are considered notable works of art.

The next day's island was Madura, east of Java. Our approach by sea was marked by hundreds of spidery-looking bamboo fishing platforms erected in the waters between our ship's course and the nearby east coast of Java. These platforms are used after dark when lanterns attract fish to their nets. Each has a hut to shelter its crew. On Madura, we visited the eighteenth-century Sultan Palace Kraton Sumenep and the Grand Mosque Jamik, both a mixture of Chinese and Islamic architecture.

We had been fortunate in our weather until now, having been spared rains in this monsoon season. The skies opened as we drove to Gilling Playground to view the bull races for which Madura is famous. Legend has it that bull racing originated as a playful diversion among teams of workers plowing rice fields. Encouraged by an early king, the practice became entrenched and today bulls are raised for their racing ability. The rains having abated, we watched several races consisting of two competing sets of yoked oxen dragging sleds manned by jockeys across a grassy field. Each race was over quickly at speeds of more than thirty miles an hour. The record time to date is 328 feet in nine seconds, faster than the world record for humans. The bull's (oxen's) diet includes beer, chili peppers, and as many as fifty raw eggs per day.

We think of Lombok, our next port of call, as the Moslem Bali. Although located just east of Bali, only one-seventh as many tourists visit its magnificent beaches or tropical gardens. There is no five-star hotel, the best here being four stars. To quote *The New York Times*, "As Bali suffers from rampant hotel development ... Lombok is being touted the new Indonesian paradise." Moslem Sasak hill tribes make up 80 percent of the population, the rest being mostly Balinese Hindus. Lombok's Balinese culture and temples remain from the days when Bali controlled this island. Our tour included the site of the Royal Balinese Court at Cakra with a floating pavilion in the middle of an artificial lake covered with water lilies. The day's highlight, however, was a buffet lunch at the internationally acclaimed Wayan Café, famous for its Indonesian cuisine. The restaurant is a two-story bamboo structure with a thatched roof, largely open sided on the ground floor and open above table height on the second floor. The very charming attention given patrons reflects its family-run status. Just some of the offerings of the fine buffet were chicken *satay* with corn fritters, Balinese smoked duck, fried chicken with honey sauce, fresh-grilled snapper, vegetable green curry, Balinese vegetables, fried soya beans, fried rice, steamed rice, homemade cake, banana rice pudding, and fresh fruit salad.

Lombok is second only to Bali as the best island to purchase arts and crafts. Space prevents recounting Mary's many purchase coups, but one of Lombok deserves special mention—a 10-by-4 -foot cotton double-ikat weaving purchased at the Sari Kusma shop for U.S.$400 cash. Ikat differs from batik in several ways—most importantly in that batik is dyed after it is woven, while ikat thread is dyed to create the intended design when the many threads are woven together, as in a tapestry. A double ikat means that both the warp and the woof (the threads running lengthwise and side by side) are dyed to create a more precise pattern. The care and work to reach that result boggles the mind. Mary's ikat used all natural dyes for its resplendent figures of birds and deer.

Mary's purchases on this trip totaled more than two thousand dollars. I, therefore, was braced for a hefty tab from U.S. Customs on our return, and was stunned when the customs officer, a victim of Mary's charm, charged her only twelve dollars duty.

Our next island was Komodo, home of the famous Komodo dragon and a premier, almost essential, stop of any Indonesian tour. Reminding everyone of Jurassic Park, these largest monitor lizards are carnivores that can reach a length of ten feet and weight of more than three hundred pounds. Several thousand are found on Komodo, Rinka, and three smaller neighboring islands. Komodo, with the largest population, is a mountainous, sparsely populated national park with a ranger station and Komodo viewing area. Komodos live on deer and wild pigs, which are plentiful. Rather than overpowering their prey, more typically their nip at fleeing animals creates a festering wound that leads to death, with the carcass eventually found by the dragon's acute sense of smell.

The dragons were big and impressive and led one to believe the apocryphal story of the German tourist who fell behind his group and disappeared, leaving only his eye glasses and camera. It is said that dragons have been observed swallowing whole the hindquarters of an adult deer, and that a 110-pound dragon ate an 88-pound wild pig in fifteen minutes. We were glad the viewing area was enclosed, with we tasty morsels on the inside and five Komodos on the outside looking in. We also sighted two dragons on the beach; they are strong swimmers and have been seen far from land.

Our last stop, where we departed the ship and stayed for three days, was Bali. It was a fitting climax to our adventure in Southeast Asia. Known to outsiders and to the Balinese as the "Island of Gods," Bali is unique in many ways. Its location in the Indian Ocean gives it a perfect mix of both adequate rainfall and sunshine. Fertile volcanic soil produces fine rice crops and a verdant background. Because of the mountains, there are many lakes, rivers, and streams providing both natural beauty and water for irrigation. A mountain range contributes to the dramatic landscape with two high peaks and many forested or rice-terraced ravines. White sand beaches stretch for miles.

The natural richness and beauty of Bali has helped foster and preserve a unique, very appealing culture. It is so attractive to Westerners that, from the crew of the first Dutch ship to arrive in 1597 to travelers of the present day, many refuse to leave. Bali is the only Indonesian island to retain its Hindu religion and culture, mixed with animism and Javanese mysticism. Bali's culture has too many aspects to explore here, but essential elements are its peoples' devotion to religion, family, beauty and the arts, and a natural and universal philosophical approach to life. One result is that almost every Balinese practices some art or craft and every taxi driver is liable to deliver a gentle, thoughtful lecture. There is great fear that the ever-increasing tourist invasion will destroy the Balinese culture, which has so far proved resilient.

Our postcruise hotel was the beautiful but large and sprawling Inter-Continental. This beachfront hotel sprawls because of the restriction that no building in Bali may be taller than a coconut tree—four stories. We again upgraded to a suite, which included a marble bath with a large Jacuzzi plus a separate shower room, and a wide balcony facing the gardens and distant beach with its beautiful pools and fountains. We had wanted to stay at one of the justly famous Amanresorts on Bali—Amandari, Amankila, or Amanusa—but Renaissance refused to give us any credit for their included room at the Inter-Continental. I recommend that any reader taking a cruise with before- or after-cruise hotels secure the cruise line's agreement to a credit for any unused room before booking the cruise.

Having had a pleasant lunch at our hotel's pool-side restaurant, we elected to have dinner at the nearby beachfront Four Seasons. Like the Amanresorts, its accommodations are individual, thatched-roof villas, each of which has a marble-floored sleeping and bathing pavilion, a separate open-air living-room pavilion, indoor and out-door showers, and a private plunge pool.

Dinner in the hotel's beautifully appointed, softly lit formal dining room, open sided to gardens, beach and ocean, was supremely roman-tic. Although Chef Vindex Valentin Tengker is from Java, he excels at Balinese preparations. Joined by another couple from our cruise, we enjoyed such dishes as Balinese-style chicken, beef, and seafood *satays,* roasted rack of lamb infused with tamarind palm sugar and chili, and Balinese curry-roasted spring chicken with a charred corn *lawar* filling and wok-fried red rice. Leeuwin Australian Gewurztraminer was slightly spicy and full enough to stand up to those well-seasoned dishes.

Morning found us eager to explore Bali and off early in our hired car and driver. The first stop was a typical Balinese home, which is an open-air compound enclosed by a wall. The Balinese believe the mountain is good and the sea bad, which dictates the layout inside the wall. Nearest the mountains is the family shrine and separate platforms for sleeping, and living. In the less desirable end near the sea is the livestock pen with a pig and a few chickens. The individual villas of the Four Seasons and the Amanresorts are glorified versions of a Balinese compound, their separate pavilions for sleeping and living echoing platforms for the same uses in Balinese home compounds.

Arts and crafts are an essential element of Balinese life; thus the shopper may give free reign without guilt to his or her urges, entering into the Balinese experience. In shopping, avoid the terrible tourist-trap town of Kuta near the airport and port; drive instead to the "art villages": Celuk for gold and silver, Mas for woodcarving, and Ubud for the greatest number of shops. Wayans Gold and Silver Shop in Celuk had great variety, but it would be more rewarding to visit shops of the artisans themselves, like Eddy Santana. Balinese jewelry may be found, without attribution, in upscale American stores under the names of designers such as John Hardy, who purchase their variations or choices of Balinese silver at bargain prices and market them in the United States for great profit.

We stopped at the famous temple at Bangli. Bali is awash in temples, and a common sight is women carrying elaborate fruit or flower arrangements balanced on their heads on their way to deliver these offerings to their local temple. Luncheon was at one of the simple buffet restaurants with views looking out at much revered Mount Batur with Lake Batur in the foreground.

We were so pleased the night before that we returned to the Four Seasons again for dinner, this time with reservations at its seafood restaurant with candle-lit tables overlooking the beach and Indian Ocean. Four of us savored salt and pepper prawns, a mixed seafood grill, local scallops, mahi mahi (worldwide in tropical waters), and calamari. The Four Seasons' superb restaurants, villa compounds with private pools, and beachfront location make it one of the most desirable hotels on Bali.

Our first stop the next day was the famous seaside temple Pura Tanah Lot, which translates as "Temple of the Earth in the Sea." The two small temples with tiered roofs can be reached at low tide. At other times they are offshore, protected by black sea snakes that live among the rocks and caves of the coast. Needless to say, the temples rising from the water with a rocky foreground and the ocean behind are a dramatic sight. A great photo opportunity.

Speaking of drama, we wanted drama at lunch and debated between two small hotel restaurants in the hills: Kupa Kupa Barong and Amandari. Opting for the more famous Amanresort, we nevertheless stopped to check out Kupa Kupa Barong, which means butterfly dance. Its setting overlooking a deep ravine and river is unmatched. Judging only from its menu, the restaurant seemed very promising. Amandari has views over a pool and forested hills. Everything about this resort of twenty-nine suites in private courtyards seemed perfect. Facilities include six private pools, one common pool, a restaurant, bar, library, antique gallery, and tennis courts. Activities include white-water rafting and trekking.

Sitting at a window-side table, Mary sipped a great pineapple daiquiri while I ordered our wine, an Australian Penfolds Chardonnay-Sémillon. Lunch was very good: Indonesian spring rolls with glass noodles, fine rice noodles with shrimp in a mild curry, char-grilled honey and spice-marinated chicken, and prawns with chilis.

Thanks to our excellent guide, we arrived after lunch at the great family-run silver shop of Eddy Santana on Jagaraga Street in Celuk. At the risk of sounding like an advertisement, I must say it not only had the best workmanship but the best prices for fine pins, earrings, bracelets, rings, and much more. One example was a heavy, beautifully elaborate silver bracelet costing twenty-nine dollars, which we preferred to John Hardy bracelets selling in the United States for hundreds of dollars. Later, back on the ship, we compared shopping finds with two other couples. When we showed this bracelet and told them the price, one of the other women surrendered the game of show-and-tell, saying, "You win."

We were all winners on this trip, one of the best of our young lives. I cannot emphasize too much how important were the precruise days in Hong Kong and Singapore and the postcruise time on

Bali. Frankly, those stops were the most interesting and rewarding parts of the package, although we did enjoy our time in the islands. The National Museum of Jakarta, Borobudur, and unspoiled Lombok were the highlights, while Madura and the bull race were a waste of time. Experienced cruisers told us that the Sulawesi stop of prior cruises was a much better choice. We look forward to more cruises in the years to come.

Small World Department

From the *South China Morning Post*, Monday, April 6, 1992: "Jack Nicholson promoted his latest movie, *Hoffa*, while filming in the Detroit area. When the actor dined at The Lark restaurant in West Bloomfield, he visited diners at their tables and 'enlivened up the place like few customers ever have,' owner Jim Lark said. After his meal, Nicholson wrote 'HOFFA' in the snow on every windscreen in the car park."

On the Rim

For years the preferred cuisine of trendy restaurants in this country was "New American Cuisine," mostly California in origin with odds and ends from other regions. Obviously, however, it was not trendy to continue doing the same thing. One can only concoct so many weird recipes using basil, cilantro, and cumin. Salsas, goat cheese, and black beans get a little tiring. And so, the rush is on to the next trendy cuisine, namely Pacific Rim or East-West Fusion.

Writing in *Food & Wine* magazine, Coleman Andrews noted that, while France and Italy still provide the basic vocabulary of the food we eat, the accents are increasingly Far Eastern: Thai, Chinese, Japanese, Vietnamese, Korean, Indonesian, Filipino, and Indian.

Some of the best-known practitioners of Pacific New Wave are Lespinasse in Manhattan, China Moon Café in San Francisco, Roy's and A Pacific Café in Hawaii, and Chinois on Main and Chopstix in Los Angeles.

Paul Bocuse has rightly said, however, that there is nothing ever really new in food. Old cooking bibles like *Larousse Gastronomique* and Raymond Oliver's *La Cuisine* contain many East-West Fusion recipes.

Coleman Andrews pointed out that the founder of East-West blending in this country was not one of the new kids on the block, but that old warhorse Vic Bergeron of Trader Vic's. He not only offered French, Continental, Chinese, Indian, and Indonesian dishes, but also East-West Fusion dishes such as lamb chops with Indonesian spices.

The very first menu of The Lark in June 1981 offered two Pacific Rim main courses, Shrimp Man Wah and Rack of Lamb Genghis Khan. The lamb dish was created by our first chef, Heinz Menguser from Austria. It is probably no coincidence that Chef Heinz was once a chef at Trader Vic's. Rack of Lamb Genghis Khan, which may be the best lamb dish in the world, is the only main course that has been on every menu since The Lark opened. Also of interest, The Lark hosted a Franco-Chinese special dinner in July 1988.

The Lark does its own thing, free of the constraints of trends, and will continue to offer whatever dishes we like in the hope that our patrons will also enjoy them.

*O*ne glance at the Iberian decor of The Lark reveals Mary's and my love for the romance of Portugal and Spain. Trips over twenty years have covered most of the popular central and southern regions of both countries as well as the island of Madeira. Portuguese acquaintances, however, repeatedly told us the north had much more to offer. Travel agent Jeff Slatkin, who likes our advance scouting, also wanted a report on northern Portugal and Spain.

Because of the charm of its towns, the beauty of its countryside, and the warmth of its people, Portugal is one of our favorite countries. Almost every visitor is moved to consider retiring there. Lisbon is also one of our favorite cities—very European but very friendly, and neither too large nor too small. So, as with most of our trips to Iberia, we first unwound with a few pampered days at Lisbon's Hotel Ritz, luxuriating in such old-fashioned amenities as three linen sheets per bed, marble baths, crystal glassware, and a solicitous staff. Since we had seen most of the obligatory sights on earlier trips, we were free to concentrate on dining and shopping.

Three disparate themes are found in today's Portuguese cuisine. Still most popular are traditional rustic dishes such as cabbage soup, salt cod with olive oil and garlic, roast suckling pig and kid, simple fresh seafood, and egg-based convent desserts. Many hotels and older restaurants cling to dated international dishes, while younger ambitious chefs ape Nouvelle Cuisine with some success and some comedy.

All our favorite Lisbon restaurants were still flourishing as were several new finds. Tagide has a clublike dining room with dramatic views over the Tagus River. Although Mary loved her cold stuffed-crab appetizer, a main course cataplana of pork and clams was so overseasoned that it was inedible. When my cold shrimp soup arrived, my nose told me why the maître d' had made a face when I ordered it. I was stunned, however, to discover that my fried crab-leg entrée was *surimi*—chopped seafood analogue from Japan.

Refurbished Tavares is a Lisbon institution—the traditional setting for power lunches. The stuffy atmosphere of mirrors, red silk, and crystal chandeliers is counterbalanced by a charming staff. We feasted too well on a salad of turnip greens, melon and air-dried ham, goose liver and grapes, and *salmis* of partridge. A nearby table had a more sensible lunch of fresh white asparagus, cold stuffed crab, and fresh berries.

One great institution we had inexplicably missed on prior trips was the Calouste-Gulbenkian Museum, housing the art collections bequeathed to the people of Portugal by the Armenian patron of the arts. Mary and I thought it perfect, a diverse but not huge collection reflecting one man's impeccable taste.

Casa da Comida's cuisine is much superior to Tagide or Tavares. Our excellent dinner included baby eels with garlic, frogs' legs with herbs, a tiny rack of kid, duck with cepes, and a praline soufflé with warm chocolate sauce. Dinner at Clara was underwhelming, and a meal at Quim Vua increased our appreciation for our Detroit and Windsor Chinese establishments.

In Portugal, the best shopping in gift shops throughout the country is for pottery from Coimbra, Barcelos, and Caldas de Rainha, and

Vista Alegre porcelain from Ílhavo. Spectacular tile murals, as the one in the lobby of The Lark, are either ready made or made to order. Sixteenth-century and later azulejo tiles are found in antique shops, and hand-woven carpets at Casa Quintao in Lisbon. Copper cookware, including cataplana such as used at The Lark, is widely available. Portuguese Atlantis crystal is overpriced.

On trips to Europe, Mary and I usually reserve a hotel for only the first two or three days, then take off in a rental car, calling ahead for reservations as we wander about. We find it essential to establish a good rapport with the front desk of one's current hotel or inn, who can phone ahead in the appropriate language and produce a desirable room at the next stop. Our general plan was to meander through northern Portugal, pass into the northwest corner of Spain and then turn east, finally arriving at Bilbao in the Basque region to catch our planned flight home. Most stops were at Portuguese-government *pousadas* or Spanish *paradors.*

Heading north from Lisbon in a rental car, which eventually expired in Porto, we bypassed Estoril, Cascais, and Sintra, having explored them on prior trips. None should be missed by the first-time visitor; all are easily reached by day trips from Lisbon. Our first stop was in Óbidos, an ancient, walled fortress, once an important port but now six kilometers inland behind its silted-up bay. The visual appeal of this well-preserved medieval town, replete with castle, towers, and bastions, draws flocks of tourists to explore its streets and gaze over the surrounding green hills and valleys. The perfect way to enjoy the amazing views is to lunch in the castle-top dining room of the Pousada do Castelo as we did, enjoying a shared mushroom omelet, suckling pig, and baby kid. Because Óbidos is such a theatrical tourist magnet, rooms at the small Pousada do Castelo must be reserved many months in advance. The reception desk of Hotel Ritz had, therefore, booked a perfectly adequate tiny suite (two former nuns' cells) at Estalagem do Convento. The owner-manager was hospitable and charming and dinner that evening acceptable, if not memorable.

Following the advice of guide books, we broke our next day's journey at Leiria to view the castle erected in 1135 by the first king of Portugal, the Roman ruins at Conimbriga, said to be among the finest in the Iberian Peninsula, and the monastery and church of Batalha. Even with these stops we arrived at what was to be our lodging for the next three days, Palace Hotel do Bucaco, in time for a late lunch. It began with a quiche and stewed squid and proceeded to an exotic type of chicken pie and Mary's roast suckling pig, a follow-up to her roast kid the preceding day.

It would be difficult to speak too highly of Bucaco. The Bucaco National Forest, protected since the eleventh century, contains seven hundred varieties of mature trees. The entire mood of our journey changed in Bucaco. Life had seemed fairly routine in bustling international Lisbon and impressive but touristy Óbidos. Now, however, we felt ourselves being drawn into an older and very different world. The hotel itself, located in the very center of the forest, is a former royal hunting lodge, government-owned but privately managed. Thanks to another advance call made by Hotel Ritz, we were assigned a fine corner suite with views of the hotel's garden as well as Bucaco forest. The dining room, great hall, gallery, and other public areas were magnificent with huge azulejo tile murals, stone arches, paneled walls, crystal chandeliers, and massive fireplaces. We were so taken with the forest and the hotel that we immediately changed our reservation from two to three nights—an example of one advantage of not booking too far ahead.

Day trips during our stay at Bucaco included several meals in nearby Sta. Luzia at Tem-Tem, a *churrascaria* with unlimited servings of barbecued beef tenderloin, pork loin, lamb, sausages, spareribs, plus salad, rice, and beans at a very inexpensive price—far better than any *churrascaria* we had found in Brazil. Another day we visited the old port of Aveiro, the Vista Alegre fine porcelain factory at Ílhavo, and had a very good simple lunch of wood-grilled chicken at Restaurant Canas in the seaside resort of Praia de Mara. A group at the next table feasted on eel stew, leaving only twenty eel backbones on their plates when done.

At the base of the hill of Bucaco is Luso, a charming spa-resort town complete with tiny gaming casino. In the small central square, spring waters gush from spouts set in a stone wall and many come with plastic jugs for free fill-ups of this mineral water, which is sold in bottled form throughout the country—the Perrier of Portugal. Driving through Luso toward Bucaco, Mary bade me to stop so she might photograph a stunning garden of huge, blue hydrangea. What followed tells much of the Portuguese people. The couple whose home was the setting for this floral display insisted that Mary enter their grounds, inspect the remaining gardens, and accept a huge bouquet of flowers to brighten our lodgings.

Reluctantly leaving Bucaco, we drove east on winding mountain roads into the Serra da Estrela mountain range—the highest in Portugal, although only about forty miles long and twenty miles wide. Boulder-strewn summits overlook wooded slopes and cultivated valleys. The feeling in the higher reaches was identical to our upland desert Southwest. Lunch at the Pousada de Saõ Laurenço above Manteigas was excellent as were the mountain views from a charming dining room with a fireplace in its center. We devoured the baby kid (six tiny ribs), pheasant, and our favorite white wine of the trip, Planalto Reserva '82. The efficient waiter and waitress were both about sixteen years old. After checking in at Hotel de Manteigas, the loser of the trip, we took a narrow unsurfaced mountain road to view the famous Poco do Inferno, or Well of Hell, a waterfall plunging down a rocky and wooded defile.

The next day's journey was the longest of the trip—too long in fact. After driving almost due north for several hours, we crossed the famous Douro River, where all port wine grapes are grown, at Peso da Régua, turned left and followed the north bank of the Duoro west toward the day's destination, Porto. The dramatic drive along the Duoro is one of the most scenic in the world. The road rises and falls, zigzags inland around side valleys and then back toward the river. Views near and far are of the river, vineyards, terraced hills, and red-tiled villages. Since there is no desirable restaurant in the entire valley, a picnic lunch is recommended. At a grocery in a tiny town, we purchased cheese, sausage, tuna in olive oil, a tomato, and wine. The bakery a few doors away had closed for siesta, but opened at the urging of local citizens to sell us bread by weight. It was heavy and good—far better than the pseudo-French bread served in many restaurants. The genuine concern of the staff and customers of the grocery in making certain we obtained bread is typical of the Portuguese. On the other hand, teen-agers seem indistinguishable from teen-agers throughout the Western world, which we assume is an omen of cultural changes to come. Our conclusion, visit Portugal quickly.

As we neared Porto, the rental car stalled with increasing frequency and rain began to fall. Crawling along at rush hour, we fought our way through the city, having to restart the vehicle every minute or two. We also became thoroughly lost, finally hiring a taxi to lead the way to our hotel, the Infante de Sagres, a magnificent converted palace in the heart of the old central city. Tired, rattled, and sweaty, we requested the best accommodations regardless of what had been reserved for us, and were rewarded with the presidential suite. Its elegant rooms and baths quickly restored our sense of well-being at a cost of $225 per night for what would easily bring $1,500 in Paris. Dinner that evening in the hotel's sumptuous dining room included Mary's melon and ham followed by cold lobster and my seafood soup and roast veal from an English-style trolley.

Taking the presidential suite apparently entitled one to almost anything. The next morning the manager assigned a porter to drive me and our crippled rental car to Avis and back to the hotel in its replacement. While I was on this errand, the manager gave Mary a personal tour of the hotel's art collection, which included a painting in the lobby insured for more than four million dollars and Gobelin tapestries worth even more. When we asked the location of the local Vista Alegre porcelain store, a porter led us the three blocks to its location. A large platter of fruit and vases of fresh flowers were delivered to our room; our laundry was returned looking better than new.

Lunch at Portucale on the top floor of a tall building provided unmatched views over Porto, the Doura estuary, and the Atlantic. The meal, our best in Portugal, included a cataplana of clams and sausage with just the right touch of garlic; two perfectly ripe avocado halves stuffed with shrimp, fresh pineapple, and pine nuts in a light sauce; a julienne "Portuguese Hen"; roast partridge; great sautéed onions; rice with sausage; espresso coffee, and rare old Portuguese brandy.

As is our custom in cities new to us, we hired a car with English-speaking driver to see the important sights and obtain an overview of Porto, Portugal's second-largest city. We also visited one of the port wine lodges located south of the Duoro River in Vila Nova de Gaia. Porto has many fine shops featuring local arts and crafts as well as famous products of other European countries. One store had more fine china and crystal than we have seen in New York, London, or Paris.

After our two pampered nights at the Infante de Sagres, we departed Porto in our new rental car, which performed perfectly for the remainder of our journey. It was only a short hop on a quiet Sunday to Guimaraes, the "Cradle of Portugal" and capital of Henri of Burgundy, who was given the "County of Portucale" in 1095 by his father-in-law, Alfonso VI, king of Leon and Castile.

Guimaraes has the distinction of being the only town in Portugal with two *pousadas*. Following the recommendation of *Portuguese Country Inns and Pousadas,* our reservation was at Pousada de Santa Marinha, located in a grandiose thousand-year-old convent overlooking the town. Its architectural grandeur is expressed in its church, cloister, staircases, verandas, doorways, vast public rooms, and impressive examples of azulejo tiles. Most guest rooms, however, are very small, with the few larger ones in great demand. We did snare a good one. The woods, overgrown gardens, untended ponds, and other ruins behind the convent are rather melancholy. At dinner in a vast hall, my rabbit was overseasoned and all vegetables overcooked, but Mary's fresh wild salmon was delicious.

The better lodging choice is the Pousada Den. S. da Oliveira located on the Church Square next to the town hall. Comprising a block of former private Manueline and medieval homes, it is extremely charming and intimate. A fine lunch of melon with ham, Portuguese steak, chicken and rice with vinegar, and chocolate meringue with whipped cream and strawberries revealed the *pousada* in town also has much better cuisine than its sister establishment in the convent.

Lunch in Portugal is generally from 12:30 to 3 P.M. in the countryside and from 1 to 3:30 P.M. in larger cities. Dinner is from 7:30 or 8 P.M. onward and peaks between 8:30 and 10 P.M. Ambitious restaurants always serve a complimentary hors d'oeuvre, and in the larger cities seat patrons in a lounge area for a before-dinner drink and the complimentary hors d'oeuvre. Menus and wine lists are presented, and the dinner and wine order taken before guests are led to their table. After trying this procedure a few times, Mary and I henceforth requested that we be brought directly to our table on arrival, a common preference and not objectionable. Service is always included but a small additional gratuity is appreciated. A meal for two with wine might run from $12.50 in a simple restaurant to $50 in the country's finest, excepting items such as champagne and caviar. Service is always cheerful and generally excellent. In the grander spots it is also polished and professional, courtly but not pompous.

The front desk staff at the Infante de Sagres in Porto had insisted that the next stop, our last in Portugal, be Hotel de Sta. Luzia at Viana do Castelo on the coast, rather than one of the two *pousadas* on the Rio Minho near the border. Viana do Castelo is both a pleasant summer resort and the principal port for the nation's deep-sea fishing fleet. Our hotel, built in 1895, was situated on the highest hill above town to command spectacular views of the Lima River, the port, and sixty miles of Atlantic coast. We were assigned the best suite with the best views, probably a delayed prerogative resulting from taking the presidential suite in Porto. Furnishings of the hotel, remodeled in 1985 by two famous Portuguese architects, are in a fascinating and funky Scandinavian Modern style, which contributed to the otherworldly feel of our stay here. Another component of that feeling, which persisted since Bucaco, was a total lack of Americans. Other than one group in Santiago, Spain, we saw fewer than fifteen countrymen in eighteen days, most of the few tourists being either British or German.

Lunch at the hotel and dinner at a simple restaurant in town were both good. In addition to town, our explorations that afternoon included a walk on a beautiful Atlantic beach, which we reached by fording a small stream. Mary pointed out that women tourists need only bring one pair of high-heeled shoes, since cobblestone streets and sidewalks make high heels impossible except at dinner.

Spain's northwest province of Galicia, which we entered the next morning after fifteen seconds of formalities at the border, was a culture shock after Portugal. While the Portuguese are charming and solicitous, the Galicians are dour—a result of their Celtic origin, poor soil, and general lack of economic resources. Flowers surround most Portuguese homes, but are not favored in Galicia. While many Galicians gave the appearance of having just lost their closest relative, we did find them friendly and helpful. Like most Spaniards they were contemptuous of the Portuguese, whom they consider country bumpkins. The desk clerk of the *pousada* in Guimaraes, who spoke English with a British accent, told us he had pretended he was British when calling into Spain for reservations. He also said we should stay at least two days at our next destination, Santiago de Compestela.

Santiago means St. James (my patron saint and that of Spain), the city so named because the body of this Apostle, who preached in Spain for seven years, was discovered there in the year 813. This caused an amazing centuries-long wave of patriotic and religious fervor, which culminated in the eventual reconquest of the entire Iberian Peninsula from the Moors. In the Middle Ages and until disrupted by the Reformation, Santiago was one of the three principal pilgrim destinations—two million pilgrims a year made the dangerous and difficult trip here when Europe's population scarcely exceeded forty million.

Because Santiago was never destroyed in war, it is an unbelievably well-preserved medieval and Baroque city, and its Plaza de España is one of the most majestic squares in Spain, bordered on one side by the cathedral built over the tomb of St. James and on another by Los

Reyes Católicos, our hotel for two nights. Reyes Católicos, meaning the Catholic Monarchs, was built in 1492 by Ferdinand and Isabella to celebrate the final expulsion that year of the Moors from their last foothold in Andalusia. Built as a hostel, it is today one of the most magnificent hotels in the world. Since "everyone knows where it is," there were no signs leading to Reyes Católicos, although road directions in both Spain and Portugal are much better than in America. Remembering our frazzled arrival in Porto, which led to booking the presidential suite, I asked the desk here for the best-available accommodations and was rewarded with the cardinal's suite, which featured fifteen-foot ceilings, an immense bedroom with fireplace, several sitting areas, assorted antiques and art, and a large compartmented bathroom. Lunch in the hotel's magnificent dining room featured a pompous maître d', wonderful assorted hors d'oeuvres, poached salmon, and salad Niçoise.

No automobiles are allowed in the old city except those of guests at Reyes Católicos and those must be left in the garage until departure. Thus, the sights of the old city may be enjoyed by strolling about, unimpeded by vehicular traffic. The principal attraction is, of course, the cathedral built from the eleventh to thirteenth centuries and its tomb of St. James. But all the streets and squares of the old city are rewarding. There are many restaurants, some with sidewalk cafés where "Tunas" may stop to entertain. Tunas are musical groups of male university students playing guitars and singing, costumed in black medieval hose, bloomers, and cape. Each colorful ribbon hanging from the cape is a favor from a female admirer. Tunas frequent cafés, bars, and restaurants to sing for their drinks and supper, but their obvious goal is fun rather than profit.

If Tunas are the good news, the bad news in the old city is gypsies—beggars and thieves who exist to pester tourists. If totally ignored, they are no problem, except for unescorted women who may be hounded in a not-subtle form of extortion. Gypsies are not, of course, unique to Santiago; they harass visitors in Seville, Rome, and other tourist centers.

In Spain, where the principal meal occurs at midafternoon and dinner after 10 P.M., Mary and I snack at tapa bars from 8 to 10 P.M. and then call it a night. We were dismayed, therefore, to find no tapa bars in northern Spain. A good substitute in Santiago's very cosmopolitan and modern new central city was Ferro at República del Salvador 20, a lively spot whose patrons drank mostly beer, a little wine, and no hard liquor while enjoying air-dried ham, great smoked sausages, olives, and hearty bread. Our real restaurant find in Santiago was Vilas—the original one at Rosalio de Castro 88. Although unpretentious, it had an upscale clientele savoring wonderful seafood such as huge European lobsters, giant crabs, scallops with their roe, fava beans with clams, and many varieties of fish.

Our next destination was Parador National Ribadeo located on a beautiful inlet on the Cantabrian coast. While winding there through lonely forested hills, we were waived off the road by Guardia Civilia (national police). Moments later the first of many bicycle racers swept by. The size of the preceding, accompanying, and trailing police escort indicated this was a very important race.

Other than the wonderful view of the estuary and the opposite bucolic shore, this *parador* is *de nada*—the best rooms merely acceptable and the food and service at lunch both bad. On the other hand, a dinner of clams with garlic, fried squid, and lobster at Voar on the other side of town was excellent. To give some idea of eating hours in Spain, there were still people lingering from lunch when we arrived at 8:30 P.M., and we could not be served until after 9 P.M.

Parador National Molino Viejo is located on a park in the large industrial and resort city of Gijón. We arrived without any reservation and were punished with a room hardly larger than a closet. The food, on the other hand, was so good we had both lunch and dinner at the *parador,* a first for us. The rather young chef was obviously well trained and very talented. White beans and clams, a grilled veal chop, filet of turbot, plum and prune sorbet, and house-made ice creams were all excellent. This *parador* is unusual in that it is used principally by Spaniards in Gijón on business.

After learning that we also were in the hospitality industry, the manager of Molino Viejo atoned for our tiny room by giving us booklets listing *paradors* and by calling ahead to our next stop, Parador National Gil Blas, and arranging that we have their best suite. We were also presented with souvenir menus by Chef Martinez Ortiz. Owning The Lark and bringing along paper menus to indicate its style is one of two secret weapons I use on trips to obtain good treatment. The second is Mary, whose honest charm usually wins over all.

Santilla del Mar with its high, pure Romanesque architecture is often called the most picturesque village in Spain. It is filled with mansions of Spain's old nobility, and one such four-hundred-year-old building houses P. N. Gil Blas where our suite was directly over the front door. Lunch at the *parador* was so forgettable that we had a picnic in our suite for dinner. The sole attraction here is the atmosphere. The Altamira caves with their fourteen-thousand-year-old cave paintings are nearby, but only thirty-five people per day, who have reserved far in advance, are allowed to view them.

Bilbao is the industrial capital of Spain and the largest city in the Basque province of Vizcaya. It was chosen as our last stop because of its international airport, facilitating our return home via Paris and Chicago. The large modern Villa de Bilbao hotel was good if sterile. Basque cuisine is reputed to be the best in Spain, so we were disappointed to learn that Bilbao buttons up on Sunday and the best restaurants were closed. Checking in my *Michelin*, however, the concierge noted that Serantes, a seafood restaurant, was open and recommended it highly. It proved a winner with charming atmosphere and great, very fresh, simply prepared *pesados y marisco*. Ignoring cost for our last meal in Spain, we had goose barnacles, mussels, and two varieties of lobster—a fitting finale to our journey north from Lisbon.

Portuguese Cataplana

The architecture and decor of The Lark, reminiscent of a southern European country inn, was most strongly influenced by nostalgic memories of Portugal. Our vases, carpeting, fireplace design, wall tiles, platters, and tapestry are all Portuguese. On the wall to the left of our larger fireplace are two sets of twin copper bowls. Joined by a hinge on one side, when closed and clamped shut they form a sealed cooking vessel called a cataplana. In it the Portuguese prepare their dramatic national dish of steamed clams and sausage with garlic, wine, and herbs.

Mary and I first had clams cataplana at Alfredo's in Portimao in Portugal's Algarve province in 1971, having noticed the unique dish being served a gentleman at the next table. He was Don Juan, father of the now king of Spain. One cataplana on our wall was purchased in the small village in the hills above the Algarve coast where they are made. Because of our love for things Portuguese, a cataplana preparation is always included on our menu—the only restaurant use of a cataplana outside of Portugal to our knowledge.

Tiles from Portugal

An article in *The New York Times* on Portuguese wall tiles evoked memories of events that led to the tile murals in our lobby and bar.

On a 1970 visit to New Orleans, the standout work in a Royal Street shop was a stunning table and chair set with heavy ornate iron legs and frame, and table top and chair seats of polychrome decorative tile. After revealing the set was Portuguese, the proprietor refused all further information on learning we had a trip planned to Portugal. We did copy a caption in small letters from a corner of one tile, "F. S. Tanna. Lisboa." On arriving in Lisbon (Lisboa), we showed the abbreviation to the concierge of the Ritz Hotel who said it meant Fabrica de Faianças e Azulejos San T'anna, a pottery and tile firm founded in 1741. We visited both showroom and factory, ordering a table and chair set for about one-fifth the New Orleans price, kitchen wall tiles for our new home, plus assorted platters and tiles.

Ten years later, with The Lark under construction, we returned to Portugal as a matter of course to order the antique-patterned tile mural for the lobby, the somewhat funky tile map of West Bloomfield in the bar, plus wall platters, small tile and iron tables, and reserved table signs. San T'anna, in addition to tiles and platters, also offers soup tureens, lamps, bowls, and lavabos. We recommend a visit to the showroom in the ancient Moorish Alfama district of Lisbon.

Latin America and the Caribbean

Pampa, Patagonia, Buenos Aires

I have come to think of us as the Gang of Eight—David E. Davis Jr. and Jeannie Davis, Ham Schirmer and Weezy Schirmer, Joe Frey and Karen Frey, and Mary Lark and me. We've hunted together for pheasant, partridge, duck, and woodcock in Hampshire and Wales; Egyptian geese, shelldrake duck, guinea fowl, pigeon, dove, francolin partridge, sand grouse, and double-banded grouse in South Africa and Botswana; and ruffed grouse, woodcock, quail, pheasant, and duck in the United States. Now, we'd met at Miami's International Airport to continue to Argentina for bird hunting and trout fishing.

With time to kill before our overnight flight to Buenos Aires, Ham insisted we eat at Shorty's, a bare-bones funky barbecue, where one sits at long tables with other barbecue fans. In *sotto voce,* David E. said what most of us were thinking, "On our way to a country where we'll have barbecue three times a day, we pause in Miami to have barbecue at Shorty's." Well, they were very good barbecue ribs, smoky and spicy with no need for red sauce, and since not parboiled, had a good pork flavor.

On arrival in Buenos Aires the next morning, we reclaimed our mountain of clothing and gear, necessitated by three different types of hunting and fishing, and end-of-the-trip wining and dining in Buenos Aires. It's always special fun to bring guns into foreign countries.

A four-and-one-half-hour drive north brought us to El Retiro Estancia, a reasonably charming old ranch house set amid 2,800 acres of rolling grassland and scrub. Mary and I and the Schirmers were fortunate to be assigned the two bedrooms with baths at El Retiro. The Davis and Frey couples were lodged in another country home, some twenty minutes distant, which had great ambience, but only one bathroom. Tent living in Africa was more agreeable.

Having completed an epic journey by various planes and cars with a couple or three hours sleep, we were given a late lunch and led afield to shoot eared doves and large rock pigeons, called "Grande." I was so groggy, my shooting was instinctual rather than considered—a great advantage. Unfortunately, in my daze I mistakenly bagged one of my namesakes, a lark. Back at the ranch, Weezy innocently reported, "Almost all the doves Ham shot were real close."

Jorge Truco and Jorge Richards of Patagonian Outfitters had arranged this expedition for Frontiers, our U.S. booking agent. They were apologetic of the small numbers of doves. David E., who was high gun for our group, later wrote Frontiers:

"I have shot more doves sitting at a picnic table in south Texas with a large red and white cooler beside me."

Food at El Retiro wouldn't hurt you—such fare as rather tough but very tasty steak and always good Argentine wines. Most enjoyable was the Petrossian ossetra caviar I had brought from home.

Other memories of our dove shoot include Ham jamming a shell backwards into his tacky pump shotgun, and the mosquitos, kept at bay by repellent, except on the last morning's shoot, when I neglected to zip up my fly.

After that final dove shoot, we drove north, away from the Pampa to the market town of San Javier in the state of Santa Fé. Our home for the next three nights was the simple Mocavi Hotel, named after a local Indian tribe, now largely extinct. North Americanos tend to think of all Latin countries as a mixture of Spanish and Indian, but that is far from true. The two largest ethnic groups in Argentina are Italian and Spanish. The balance of the population is also mostly of European origin, including many English, Germans, and Jews. The effect, especially in Buenos Aires and in Patagonia, is often European.

Accommodations and housekeeping at the Mocavi were poor, but the staff's attitude was superb. They were very proud of hosting hunters from afar and had built a pleasant dining room in a separate building for our use and also created a new lounge and cocktail area in the main building.

Still rather jet-lagged and weary, a further hour drive from the hotel brought us to flooded ricelands of the Parana River for a late duck shoot. This meant staggering, loaded with gear, through thigh-high water over a slippery uneven bottom. Mary and I were assigned the farthest blind. The good news was that we had the best shooting and bagged the most ducks. The bad news was that we and our excellent guide, Marco, had to gather all the decoys at the end of the hunt. After floundering back in the dark for half a mile, I topped off this ordeal by falling into a channel whose water was over my head. Sometimes it's not easy to be an international sportsman.

The landscape around San Javier, other than in the great marshes with wonderful bird populations, was unremarkable. Here, as in the Victoria area, locals rode magnificent horses, attired variously as Gauchos, Spanish equestrians, or in some other proud costume. In three days we heard only two shots by hunters not of our group.

Our favorite duck hunt was the next morning's. After an hour delay when our escort drove a jeep into a ditch, we boated across open water to sand banks where our guides spread decoys and erected blinds from wood poles and camouflage netting. I again drew the best blind and made a respectable bag while passing on a roseate spoonbill that the guide urged me to shoot, claiming it was a duck and excellent eating. A lasting memory is a passing noble horseman, who forded the marsh followed by two faithful, swimming hounds.

The afternoon hunt on both full days in the area was for snipe, a new experience for everyone in our group, which I enjoyed more than the duck hunting. Attired in Wellies (rubber boots), we marched abreast through fields of alternately wet and dry grass, flushing snipe that flew high at times and low at others. Snipe resemble woodcock with long pointed beaks designed to probe damp soil for earthworms. They were present in fine numbers and provided sporty shooting.

Food at the hotel was very good. One lunch featured duck breasts and snipe. The only other snipe I had ever eaten were in London. An *asado,* or Argentinean barbecue, probably pleased only Jeannie Davis and me as, at our request, it included such oddities as *chinchulin,* an intestine of an unweaned calf, as well as kidneys, sausages, short ribs, and *matambre,* which is skirt steak stuffed with carrots and hard-cooked eggs, rolled, simmered, sliced, and served as a cold appetizer.

Our trip to date had been a prologue. Now we drove to the Santa Fé Airport, flying back to Buenos Aires and a second flight from Buenos Aires to San Martín de los Andes, a small town in Patagonia in the foothills of the Andes Mountains.

Overused adjectives cannot properly describe Patagonia. It resembles parts of Wyoming and Montana—"Big Sky" country with such open space and distant views that the sky is a constant presence. The land undulates, mostly grass with some wooded areas and winding rivers. Mary and I wish we had spent all our time in Patagonia and would happily return the next fishing season.

San Martín de los Andes is an appealing Alpine-style town with a four- or five-block business district of good restaurants and shops, and two good, small hotels, the twenty-three room Hotel le Village and the twelve-room Hostería la Raclette. There are also a large government-built hotel and casino and newly built ski lifts. Some 120 miles to the south is San Carlos de Bariloche, the principal tourist town of the Argentine Andes, which should be avoided.

We stayed about forty-five minutes distant from San Martín de los Andes at remote Hostería San Humberto, a rustic lodge of eight acceptable twin-bedded rooms with private baths. The dining area was attractive, and a huge dramatic lounge had a big open fireplace, high-beamed ceiling, impressive mounts of red stag heads, and a small corner bar. San Humberto, named after the patron saint of hunters, was intended as a hunting lodge, but now draws mostly fisher-people. Since the Malleo River, on which it is located, is strictly catch-and-release, fishing is superb. On the other hand, injudicious shooting of red stag with the largest racks (a crime in Europe) has greatly reduced the quality of stag hunting.

The Malleo River is perhaps one hundred feet wide and, except for pools and holes, rarely thigh deep. Slippery rocks make waders with felt soles a necessity. The river teems with trout, mostly rainbow and brown, but a few brook also. All were introduced around the turn of the century as trout are not native to South America. I caught four rainbows and two browns up to eighteen inches in one hour before dinner on the day we arrived. Mary released the biggest catch, nineteen trout in one afternoon, including a lunker rainbow of at least twenty inches. The guides were very good (although juvenile when together) and took care that none of us took a dunking despite the slipper rocks. Our guide, Marcello, has a fly-fishing shop in San Martín and does free-lance guiding in the Nahuel Huapi National Park for brook trout to twenty-two inches.

The food at San Humberto was excellent, enjoyed at a long table with our four guides. We especially liked the air-dried beef, garlic soup, pastas, vegetable soup, steaks, and a chocolate and mint dessert.

Owners and hosts Carlos and Carmen look German and run a tight ship at their squeaky-clean lodge. We strongly recommend San Humberto, which should be booked well in advance, since it only has eight rooms. The seasons are, of course, reversed with trout fishing ending in mid-April, autumn in Argentina. A double at $325 per angler per day included room, board, ground transportation, guides, and access to fishing on the 175,000 acres of Santa Julia and Tres Picos ranches.

San Martín not having a scheduled flight on the day of our departure, we drove three hours through the magnificent Patagonian countryside, arrayed in fall colors, to the airport at Bariloche, passing only twelve fishermen in all those miles.

Back in Buenos Aires, the Schirmers were to fly home that night, but the Davis, Frey, and Lark couples checked into the perfectly located, refurbished, and grand Plaza Hotel. We strolled the nearby bustling pedestrian-only Calle Florida of shops and restaurants, purchasing tango recordings by Carlos Gardel at Musi Mondo, eventually pausing at Café Richmond. Here we enjoyed drinks and *picada,* hors d'oeuvres that included peanuts, olives, corn crisps, palm hearts, canapes, and English-style tea sandwiches. Eighty-eight dollars bought so much for eight that we skipped dinner. The other famous café on this street for coffee, drinks, light food, and conversation is Florida Garden.

Travel articles say Buenos Aires has a melancholy air. It doesn't, except at tango spots like Casa Blanca. It does have fine old buildings, wide avenues, appealing shops and restaurants, museums, theatres, and other amenities one would expect in a metropolis of eight million *porteños,* as the locals are known.

After an early Easter mass, we taxied to the famous Sunday flea market, Feria de San Telmo, in the colonial barrio's Plaza Dorego. Jeannie Davis was badly cheated by her cab driver, the only villain we encountered in Buenos Aires, whose people were otherwise friendly and accommodating. The flea market is fun, but the good stuff is in the antique shops on bordering Calle Defensa and in other top shopping areas. The quality and variety of antiques is amazing, but there are few bargains. A good lunch in the brick-walled and red-table-cloth ambience of nearby Comité included leek soup, mussels, and mushrooms in a rich sauce, and a filet steak and chicken, both with mushrooms.

Buenos Aires is blessedly free of must-see tourist attractions. All the articles recommend La Boca, (The Mouth), the old Italian working-class area near the docks, but it had no attraction for us. The best area is La Recoleta, Buenos Aires's equivalent of Manhattan's Upper East Side, with elegant mansions, shops, a whole block of fine restaurants, and Palermo Park, modeled on the Bois de Boulogne in Paris. The American ambassador's residence, a beautiful old mansion, is here, as is the ugly modern U.S. Embassy.

Catalinas, near the Plaza Hotel, is often considered Buenos Aires's leading French restaurant. Celebrity-style chef-proprietor Ramero Rodriguez Pardo trained under Chapel, Geurard, and Troisgros. The wood-paneled and steel-beamed room is very attractive and awash in an efficient serving staff. We thought much of the food to be dated Nouvelle. A "big plate of fowls: duck, pheasant and quail, with all the vegetables" was not the hoped-for Italian-style boiled dinner, but ditsy sautéed and sauced little pieces of meat surrounded by not warm, overly arranged, miniature vegetables. In this land of meat eaters, even the most sophisticated restaurants offer grilled steaks and chops. Mary's grilled "veal T-bone" was excellent, although beef, not veal. Designer desserts, a chestnut tulip filled with ice cream and a *feuilleton* with custard and berries, were both very good, desserts being the best of Nouvelle Cuisine.

Mary's favorite Buenos Aires restaurant was Gato Dumas in the block of restaurants in La Recoleta, where she devoured black-ink-squid pasta with bay squid, and scallops of rabbit. I also fared well with bone marrow in a sauce with toast, followed by twenty-five-day-old chicken.

Buenos Aires's principal restaurants fall into two categories, international Nouvelle Cuisine and the famous *parrilla* or *asado* barbecue establishments. La Cabana is the dean of such places. Our limo driver one day called it "The Cathedral of Asado," and it is often described as the best steak house in the world. The interior resembles an old German restaurant with tile floors, dark paneling, wrought-iron chandeliers, red table cloths, and a large-hooded open barbecue in the center of the room where odds and ends such as shrimp, tripe, and kidneys are cooked. Steaks are done on a grill near the entrance. Our starter kidneys and main course of a shared, sliced-thick steak were both served on a miniature grill to keep them warm. The kidneys were chewy but tasty, the steak perfect. We loved the house salad of lettuce, tomatoes, onions, beets, peppers, hard-cooked eggs, and celery.

We lunched one day at Tomo 1, an old house with Art Deco light fixtures owned by two women, Ada and Ebe Concaro. Although only one other table was in use, the food was very good, including an excellent roast leg of lamb and potatoes in the form of uniformly shaped thin discs, arranged in rows, drizzled with butter and lightly crisped in a very hot oven.

Our last meal in Buenos Aires was at Lola's, located in the block of restaurants in La Recoleta. Lola's, which had a brasserie feel with white walls and marble floors, was Buenos Aires's restaurant of the moment and the only one that was fully booked. A mixed hors d'oeuvre assortment was typical Nouvelle, artfully arranged but not tasty. A salad of hearts of palm and thin slices of apple and pineapple over smoked salmon with a vinaigrette dressing was much better. A huge smoked pork tenderloin was accompanied by applesauce, three-inch diameter potato pancakes, and overly arranged tasteless vegetables. Mary's two six-ounce beef filets with Gruyère sauce were very good, although oversalted like most food in Argentina.

The return flight from Buenos Aires was staffed by Argentineans, much less efficient and interested than the American crew on the way down. Overnighting in the Concorde Suite of the efficiently run Miami International Airport Hotel, we took advantage of this pause in our trip home to visit famous Joe's Stone Crab in South Miami Beach. My last visit was so long ago that Ed Sullivan had been at the next table. This very large temple of stone crab, which supplies The Lark and a few other restaurants with these unique crustaceans, was mobbed with hundreds of diners and was lively and fun. Our jumbo stone crab dinner was superb, a perfect finale to a great trip.

Great Wine Lists

The Lark has received *Wine Spectator's* Award of Excellence for many years, one of the first Michigan restaurants so honored. In 1993, that arbiter of wine-list quality promoted us to its Best Award of Excellence, granted to a limited number of restaurants "with very fine wine lists." It noted that The Lark is especially strong in selections from California and France and that our markups are moderate. An impressive array of wines from Germany, Italy, Portugal, and Spain are also listed.

The regular list on the back of our menu plus a separate reserve list now total more than 530 wines ranging in price from fifteen dollars for a 1991 Abbaye de Valmagne from the Languedoc in southwest France to one thousand dollars for the 1989 Château Pétrus red Bordeaux. To those who find it daunting to choose the most appropriate wine from so many available, we suggest telling the sommelier (this writer) the type of wine desired and a price range, requesting the best value in those parameters. There may be sommeliers who do not respond to this challenge to their professional skill, but I have not met one. Especially in France, this is treated as a matter of honor, and one typically receives the wine the sommelier would choose for a friend.

Merlot

"Mare-low," one of the five grape varietals used for red Bordeaux, has become the hottest red wine in America. Always blended with other grapes in Bordeaux, it may be bottled "straight" in the United States or combined with small quantities of Cabernet Sauvignon or other varietals. Merlot generally plays a minor role in Bordeaux blends except in Pomerol, where it is dominant. As a result, Pomerol wines have a reputation for being "plummy and creamy" and for maturing earlier than other Bordeaux. In fact, Pomerol wines are so delicious that they outsell the other districts of Bordeaux and command higher prices. The finest Pomerol, Ch. Pétrus, may by 95 percent Merlot and is one of the two most expensive red Bordeaux.

Hindsight is wonderful, and it now seems obvious that the great popularity and consequently higher prices for Pomerol predicted that Merlot would inevitably become immensely popular in America. Thus, American Merlot bottlings appear on almost every wine list. The rub is, since Merlot's popularity is a sudden phenomenon, demand outstripped the supply of top-quality bottlings, and many of the three hundred or so Merlots now available are mediocre.

Which offerings are best? Richard Nalley, writing in *Departures* magazine, says the ten best American Merlots are: Ch. St. Michelle Indian Wells Vineyard, Washington state; Newton, Napa; Matanzas Creek, Sonoma; Beringer Bancroft Ranch, Howell Mountain; Woodward Canyon, Columbia Valley; Duckhorn Three Palms, Napa; Stag's Leap Wine Cellars, Napa; Silverado Vineyards, Napa; Robert Mondavi, Napa; and Shafer, Napa.

Food Arts magazine praises Clos du Bois, Sonoma; Duckhorn Three Palms, Napa; Matanzas Creek Sonoma; Arrowood, Sonoma; and Beringer Bancroft Ranch, Howell Mountain. *Wine Spectator*'s top scoring California Merlots were Beringer, Justin and Matanzas Creek, but named Washington state's Leonetti Merlot as this country's finest Merlot, giving the 1992 an outstanding 96 rating.

Robert Parker's *The Wine Advocate* also gives high marks to the Leonetti Merlot as well as Beringer Bancroft Ranch, Fisher RFC Vineyard Estate, and Newton. His most lavish praise, however, is bestowed on Matanzas Creek, saying its 1992 "may well be the finest Merlot made in the New World."

Grand Slams at Boca Paila

*B*aseball is not the only sport with an ultimate accomplishment called a "grand slam." To the sporting crowd in Scotland, a grand slam consists of shooting a stag, bagging a grouse, and landing a salmon, all in one day. To the light-tackle, salt-water fisherman in the Caribbean or Gulf of Mexico, a grand slam is the even more difficult task of landing a tarpon, permit, and bonefish in the same day— something Mary and I attempted for years without success. In January 1987, we got serious, giving it our best shot while at Boca Paila Fishing Lodge on the remote coast of Mexico's Yucatán Peninsula.

Getting serious meant first catching sardines with a cast net at 8:30 A.M. On three previous stays at Boca Paila we had thrown everything but our car keys at scores of finicky tarpon without result. Then, the previous August at Boca Grande Pass on Florida's west coast, we learned to catch *mucho* tarpon using menhaden herring on Japanese-style circle hooks (Eagle Claw No. 190, size 6). It's not as sporting as fly or lure, but dramatically effective, even on fish who refuse artificials. Of course, wherever we angle, all fish are released, except for an occasional red snapper or other tasty nongame species.

Boca Paila translates as "mouth of the pan," the pan being a huge skillet-shaped, salt-water lagoon, while the mouth is the pass leading from that lagoon to the Caribbean. After netting the seven-inch sardines just inside the Boca, our Mayan guide, Eduardo Gomez, took our eighteen-foot bonefish boat a half-mile farther into the lagoon where tarpon had been seen rolling on other days. At 9:30 A.M., as we poled along, tarpon were spotted only twenty feet from the boat. Mary and I both cast. A small tarpon hit my bait, did its sky-born acrobatics, and was soon netted and released. We yelled with excitement, knowing the hard part was over with the most difficult-to-catch fish already landed. Or so we thought.

In a cocky mood and determined that Mary should also go for the grand slam, we continued to hunt tarpon, ranging miles north in the lagoon to a deep hole frequented by "silver kings." Three fruitless hours later, we returned to the area just inside the bridge at the Boca and switched to pink wiggle jigs—our favorite lure for both bonefish and permit. While most anglers at Boca Paila Lodge fly fish, I'd left my fly rod hanging on the wall in the bar of The Lark since our vacation mood dictated less challenging spinning gear. Mary and I were both equipped with Berkley graphite rods and Penn salt-water spinning reels filled with eight-pound-test Ande monofilament tournament line, which we had been given to try. We changed our line daily and were well satisfied. The eight-pound test was a compromise since successive casts might be to bonefish, large permit, tarpon, or other assorted species.

At 12:30 P.M., I caught and released two small permit. Very excited to have the second-most difficult fish of the grand slam so easily and untypically out of the way, our mood soared. Mary caught several bonefish, but all ignored my lure. At 1 P.M,. I landed another small permit. Then at 1:15, I cast to and hooked a bonefish. We were already celebrating the grand slam as I fought the fish, waiting out its long runs, when a barracuda flashed after it at incredible speed, slashing the bonefish off the line. At 1:35, I hooked a second bonefish, only to have it slip the hook when a clump of weeds caught on the line, causing slack. Mary, meanwhile, landed two more bonefish and volunteered to let me cast to all the fish from then on, as we were both getting an ominous premonition about my bonefish prospects. At 1:50, I hooked another bonefish, which took off on a tremendous run, breaking line. We then moved to another flat and, at 2:15, amid a lot of shouting, I landed a bonefish. Happy as larks, we quit on this high note and returned to camp to polish our fish story for the cocktail hour.

Those familiar with light-tackle, salt-water angling will find it very difficult to believe this next account of one of our annual New Year's fishing trips to Boca Paila Fishing Lodge. In 1992, Mary and I were accompanied by our "medical sons," Jarratt, an M.D. specializing in emergency medicine, and Kurt, an ophthalmologist. Each two fisherpeople at Boca Paila have their own boat and guide and come and go as they choose. Our guides were Eduardo and Victor, whom we have come to know well since our first discovering Boca Paila in 1984.

The principal species sought are bonefish, permit, tarpon, and snook. Fishing at Boca Paila is almost always excellent. Totals for three trips of our group of four, fishing seven days (from the end of December to the beginning of January), were as follows: (1989–90) 123 bonefish, 13 permit, 0 tarpon, and 0 snook; (1990–91) 121 bonefish, 9 permit, 0 tarpon, and 1 snook; (1991–92) 252 bonefish, 46 permit, 2 tarpon, and 2 snook. For comparison, anglers in Florida, such as former President George Bush, consider landing one bonefish a day or one permit per trip to be a success.

Kurt boated a snook that tipped the scales at twenty-five pounds, the largest in Boca Paila history and an extraordinary size for this best-tasting species of salt-water fish. Because it had swallowed the hook, the creamy white-fleshed critter was kept for dinner. When a snook is kept, we request the kitchen to serve it at the cocktail hour to all our lodge guests, cut into finger-sized pieces, deep fried, and accompanied by tartar sauce and cocktail sauce. We learned this sociable custom in the 1960s at then-remote Cabo San Lucas on

Mexico's Baja Peninsula, where fellow anglers included Jacques Cousteau and actress Amanda Blake.

Other notable fish this year were Kurt's twenty-nine-pound permit, thirty-five-pound jack, and his first Boca Paila tarpon. Jarratt fought and released a twenty-pound barracuda and was first overall with an outstanding eighty-seven bonefish and nineteen permit.

The highlight of the week, however, was Mary's grand slam—landing a tarpon, permit, and bonefish on the same day, an unusual accomplishment for any fisherman and very rare among women anglers. Mary's feat was especially unusual in that she cast to, hooked, and landed the tarpon on the only rod she had rigged at the time, a light bonefish setup with eight-pound-test line and no leader.

If all of this seems barely credible to knowledgeable fisher-people, our final foray will test belief further. Packed and ready for departure on the morning of our return home in 1992, Jarratt and I decided to wade the beach in front of the lodge, hoping to spot bonefish or permit to cast to. There was, indeed, a huge school of bonefish, which we followed down the shore, catching and releasing thirty-one in only one hour.

The lodge at Boca Paila is located on a strip of land about one thousand feet wide that separates the lagoon from the Caribbean. A dirt road parallel to the sea runs up and down the same strip of land, with the camp dock on the western lagoon side of the road and the beachfront lodge on the eastern seaward side. The road comes from Tulum and Cancún to the north and proceeds south to Belize after crossing the rickety bridge at the Boca and turning inland around Ascención Bay.

Boca Paila has eight clean and adequate twin rooms with private baths and showers and pleasant, screened porches in three thatched-roof buildings. They front on a magnificent white beach sprinkled with coconut palms and casarena pines. The clear water is an ideal temperature for a refreshing swim before breakfast, before or after lunch, or at the end of a day's fishing. Also fronting on the beach is the main building, which houses a tiny bar and the dining room of just five tables. A very pleasant outdoor terrace is often used for lunch.

After fishing and lying about fishing, food and drink are next in importance at fishing camps. Breakfasts at Boca Paila are hearty, with a variety of juice and fruit, eggs in almost any Mexican or American preparation, bacon, French toast, and even fish by prearrangement. As at all meals, guests may sit by themselves or with others as they choose. Lunches tend to be preceded by margaritas and are lighter than breakfast. Some of our favorites were black mullet and red snapper grilled over coconut charcoal, sardines attempted the same way at our request, and also at our request, fried sardines in the manner of every seafront bar along the coast.

Guests usually gather for cocktails and nachos or other appetizers at 6:45 in the evening. Boca Paila was full during one stay with fourteen guests—four couples, our two oldest sons, another father and son, and two single men. The two single men were world-class fly fishermen, one being the proprietor of a fishing camp in Montana. Best main courses at dinner were lobster with garlic sauce, Yucatecan-style chicken *pibil*, chicken in dark-chocolate-chili mole sauce, pork chops sautéed with onions and peppers, and a very light preparation of red snapper sautéed in bread crumbs.

Although Boca Paila does not pretend to be other than a fishing camp, different activities might include snorkeling above the offshore reef, scuba diving at Xel-Há or Acumal, visits to the Mayan ruins at Tulum or Coba, and bird watching. Mary and I have spotted eagles, osprey, buzzards, frigate birds, assorted heron, egret, cranes, wood stork, kingfisher, various gulls and terns, roseate spoonbill, flamingos, cormorants, shorebirds, and many others.

The price per person, double occupancy, for a week's lodging and six days' fishing is $2,500, plus gratuities. There are no extras other than modest bar charges. Trips south to what may be even better fishing at Ascención Bay are possible on a calm day by one's own assigned guide and boat at no extra cost, or by plane for $250.

The Birds of Boca Paila
by Mary Lark

I love fishing at Boca Paila. There is so much action—not only hooking fish but viewing the side show of wonderful birds that the lagoon provides. Every turn around a mangrove corner brings a new birding experience. Forget common ones like the periodic great blue heron gliding high with that strange crooked neck, strings of white egret sailing just above the water looking like handkerchiefs on a clothesline, or even the fast dart and trill of a lark as it zips out of the mangrove for thirty seconds. No, I'm talking about some really rare visual treats.

Fifteen minutes by boat from the dock is "bird island"—a small mangrove island we visit often to observe the hundreds of birds that return to roost there each day at dusk. These include egret, pelicans, heron, cormorants (two big fat birds to each itty-bitty nest), roseate spoonbills, and frigate birds. One misty morning in January 1989 we fished nearby and noticed all the birds in residence, probably staying home during the day because of a light rain. Bird sounds from the island have always been a strange discordant symphony, but this day we heard a much louder clacking. Investigation disclosed roseate spoonbills paired off, each bird rapping its wooden-spoon-shaped bill against its mate's. They know what to do on a rainy day. Roseates are almost as large as pelicans but come in a day-glo pink. To see all this was amazing and then awesome when a rainbow appeared over the island. Hard to concentrate on fishing!

On an island in a far corner of the huge lagoon is a small Mayan ruin, and above its doorway nests a pair of great ospreys. They flew at us to warn us off, but we could not take them too seriously as their nest is a multicolored jungle of bright green fish netting, tangled fishing line, and pink styrofoam, while their warning cry is not the shriek one might imagine but a timid, chickenlike *peep, peep, peep.*

Five minutes away in a shallow area of the lagoon live seventy-four day-glo orange flamingos that never let one get close as in a zoo, but fly off waving their black-tipped wings in a block of color.

Although you may have seen ospreys or flamingos, have you ever experienced a flock of frigate birds mating in groups like the spoonbills? When returning by boat from far-off Ascención Bay, we came upon the spectacle of 150 frigate birds alternately soaring above or perched on mangrove branches making loud clacking noises with their beaks. The really rare part of this display was the males expanding their crimson-red throat pouches to the size of balloons and transforming their mangrove perches into full bloom. All this and great fishing too!

Newsletters and Theme Dinners

In October 1981, just four months after The Lark opened, we decided to begin inviting our patrons to a monthly "theme dinner." To inform them of such dinners, we invented the world's first monthly customer-oriented restaurant newsletter. The idea swept the country to such an extent that there are now thousands of restaurant newsletters announcing a never-ending multitude of special dinners, wine, beer or liquor tastings, and any number of other promotional events. Far from resenting the barrage of copy-cat special dinners, we have happily advised other restaurateurs on the planning and mechanics involved, which are tremendously laborious.

All of this was brought to mind by one restaurant newsletter bewailing the tremendous number of no-shows at the restaurant's last special dinner, even though they had been confirmed "TWICE!" Its solution was to adopt the policy followed by most restaurants: reservations can be made only by purchasing tickets for such dinners in advance. Our relationship with patrons who attend our theme dinners is too special to have a no-show problem.

British Virgins

*M*any Americans' impressions of the Virgin Islands are formed when their cruise ship stops at either touristy St. Thomas or St. Croix in the U.S. Virgins. The British Virgin Islands (BVI) are a much better alternative since they are uncrowded, less expensive, have a better selection of appealing resorts, and friendly locals.

Most of the Virgin Islands are in a compact group some thirty to sixty miles east of Puerto Rico with the American islands closest to Puerto Rico and the fifty to sixty British islands, rocks, and cays adjacent but farther to the east. With the exception of the flat limestone BVI of Anegada, isolated fifteen miles north of the other Virgins, the islands are volcanic in origin and larger ones have rounded hills rising to a maximum of 1,780 feet covered with secondary forest and dry scrub, including cactus. If this sounds unattractive, the reality of gentle hills rising from multicolored seas is in fact beautiful and, for some reason, especially tranquil and soothing. While the American islands have a population well over 100,000 and a density of almost 900 people per square mile, BVI is home to but 12,500, of whom over 9,000 are on the main island of Tortola, leaving the other islands sparsely populated or uninhabited. The temperature during our mid-February stay ranged from seventy-two degrees at night to a daytime high of eighty-six with the sunny weather interrupted only by one or two very brief showers per day, often occurring while we slept.

On prior trips, Mary and I and children had stayed at Caneel Bay on St. John in the U.S. Virgins and Little Dix Bay on Virgin Gorda, BVI, when both were owned by the Rockefellers, and Peter Island Yacht Club, BVI, when it was owned by Peter Smedwig, a Norwegian shipping tycoon. All three have since been sold, and Peter Island Y. C., in particular, is reported to have slipped badly. Because we would be accompanied on this trip by three sons on winter break from the University of Michigan and daughter Adrian on vacation, we chose Bitter End Yacht Club on Virgin Gorda for its relatively moderate prices and all-inclusive water sports policy.

Bitter End is located on the isolated North Sound of Virgin Gorda, one of the larger BVI, and can be reached only by boat. In twenty years it has grown from a beach bar and restaurant with five cold-water rooms to a sophisticated resort of eighty-two rooms strung on hillsides stretching along more than a half mile of shoreline. Accommodations vary greatly, ranging from our childrens' simple motel-type rooms to Mary's and my hillside chalet with porch, which we preferred to our accommodations at either Little Dix, Caneel Bay, or Peter Island. Rates included full American plan and the use of all boats including sailboards, Sunfish, Lasers, Rhodes nineteen-footers, J-24s, as well as outboard-powered Boston Whalers. Nonsailors may do what daughter Adrian did—take two sailing lessons and then sail away, preferably in the company of more experienced hands.

Bitter End is water oriented; it does not have golf or tennis. In addition to sailboarding and sailing, we took snorkeling and beach-combing trips to George Dog by a large crew-manned catamaran; to Anegada, Necker Island, and nearby reefs by crewed power boats; and to nearby islets and reefs on our own by Boston Whaler. One may also go by catamaran to the famous boulder-enclosed "Baths" on

Virgin Gorda and by power boat to the BVI capital of Roadtown, all at no extra cost. In addition to the excellent snorkeling, a variety of scuba diving is readily available. Many consider the BVI the best of sailing grounds, and Mary counted eighty-two sailboats and eight power boats anchored off Bitter End one typical day. Included was the Sea Goddess superluxury cruise ship and the huge yacht of a French prince.

Although it could not be seen from Bitter End, the other North Sound resort of Biras Creek was but a ten-minute walk from our chalet. It features stunning views, tennis, and a good wine list, but a limited menu and few water sports. The setting makes its bar a perfect destination for late afternoon cocktails. Another nearby restaurant and bar is Drake's Anchorage on Mosquito Island, a ten-minute boat ride up the North Sound. Extremely atmospheric and with good, not great, food, it is the restaurant where Bitter End staff members dine on their evenings off. It is also open for lunch.

Despite the dry BVI climate, Bitter End has lush, colorful plants thanks to head gardener John Albert, his trusty staff, and their trickle irrigation system. In contrast to the flower-bedecked grounds, the view from our chalet of multicolored sound and sea and distant rounded islands was austerely grand.

A continental breakfast at Bitter End may be taken in the room or around the magnificent fresh-water pool, while a full breakfast is available at the 150-seat waterfront Steak and Seafood Grill. For lunch, a club sandwich or main course salad may be enjoyed on the pool deck, while hot selections plus an attractive buffet are available daily at the Grill. In the evening a second large restaurant, the 100-seat English Carvery, is also open, offering a buffet selection of three roast meats and poultry, such as rack of lamb, beef tenderloin, and Cornish hens.

Minor complaints aside, we highly recommend Bitter End to those interested in either a very relaxed vacation or one based on water sports. A high percentage of guests are repeat customers. Those who wish may live aboard and sail Cal 27s (taking their meals in the dining room or in their galley as they choose) for the same low rate as the least-expensive room on shore. We strongly recommend the chalets. Their rate per day drops in early April and even lower in early May when they must become one of the best vacation values in the world.

That's About the Size of It

Many factors contribute to the success or failure of a fine restaurant. First and foremost is the need for a restaurateur, not a restaurant owner. It is easier for a rich man to enter heaven than for a fine restaurant to prosper under absentee ownership.

A competent restaurateur will see that the ambience is agreeable and the staff competent. But location is location and, if one is too far from one's patrons, it's an awful handicap. As Casey Stengel said, "If the fans don't want to come out, you can't stop 'em."

One factor that is given too little attention is size. If a fine restaurant seats many more than forty guests, the head chef becomes a supervisor rather than the chef. It's a given that those who then do the cooking will not do it as well as he or she would.

Size also affects the dining room. Obviously, it is easier to find three good waiters than ten. Furthermore, it's a lot harder to fill an expensive large restaurant, especially during the week. One can't attract the best waiters, since tips don't come from empty tables. So, to attract good waiters, it is necessary to cut down their number to give each of them more tables on slow evenings. But that means there are not enough staff on busy nights, especially Saturday. Catch-22. Putting it all together, a successful fine restaurant will most likely seat less than fifty guests, be well located, and have a competent on-site proprietor.

Viva Mexico!

I still wear my "old fishing shirt," which debuted in 1966 at Cabo San Lucas, the then-remote fishing village at the southern tip of Mexico's Baja Peninsula. Life was exciting there in the old days, beginning with arrival by small plane at the dirt airstrip. Our craft had a dog for a copilot and a fuel gauge that read empty. One morning, we witnessed six men on an eighty-five-foot boat out of San Diego fighting six marlin at the same time, standing up with belt-rod holders.

Deep-sea excursions in succeeding years included marlin fishing off Punta Canero, Ecuador, where Lee Wulff caught the first marlin with a fly and hordes of pre-TV locals followed me down the street, gawking at my white hunter outfit.

Mary and I, of course, have enjoyed light-tackle, salt-water fishing each January for years at Boca Paila Fishing Lodge. On only three occasions in the first seven years of annual trips, however, were seas calm enough to allow the two-hour run farther south along the Yucatán Peninsula to fish the virgin waters of Ascención Bay. Fishing for bonefish there was the best in the Tres Marías Islands—big schools of five-to-six-pound fish with occasional loners over ten pounds.

In 1989, Texas brothers Bobbie and David Settles leased the private Ascención Bay estate of Mexican tycoon Roberto Hernandez and converted it to a new fishing lodge, regrettably called Casa Blanca. Mary and I jumped at the chance to fish there in early March 1990 with sons Jarratt and James. The last leg of our trip was by a small charter plane from Cancún Airport and finally by boat. Located on the beautiful rock and sand point of Punta Pájaros, the camp accommodates fourteen fisher-people in seven rather luxurious double rooms. Casarena pines and coconut palms contribute to the tropical mood. Other than the typical young chef's overuse of musty cilantro, Allen Phillips turned out very good meals.

Although handicapped by high winds, which made the best flats unfishable, our sons landed and released ninety-six bonefish and one permit in six days while losing three tarpon. Mary and I released sixty "bones." Our guide introduced us to a potentially unbeatable fishing experience—casting from the beach to huge permit feeding in the surf. In the few minutes of this trip when the surf was calm enough, three large permit followed my wiggle jig. One was hooked, but broke off. The chance to attempt that again and to fish the even more remote southern Bahía del Espíritu Santo are reason enough to return to Casa Blanca. Mary was especially intrigued by small Mayan ruins, including some remains right outside our bedroom window.

Fisher-people's near-exclusive enjoyment of the southern Yucatán coast, away from the mob at Cancún, is about to end. Coincidental with our visit in January 1994, both *Condé Nast Traveler* and *Travel & Leisure* magazines ran feature articles on the "about-to-be-discovered remote Yucatán coast" and described the early resorts that have sprung up. Brits, Germans, and Italians, all harbingers of soon-to-be popular destinations, are on the scene. Readers of The Lark's newsletter, *Food for Thought*,™ heard it from us first—more than ten years ago.

Another recent Mexican adventure was at El Tejón hunting lodge in the state of Taumalipas, about seventy miles south of Brownsville,

Texas. Our party of six "guns" consisted of Trevor Jones, Clint Lauer, Ed Mabley, Dick Place, Jerry Rivard, and this writer. This is a bachelor group with which I've fished in the Queen Charlotte Islands.

Our agent for the El Tejón hunt was Sporting Charters of Austin, Texas. One of its owners, Tosh Brown, accompanied us in our drive by van from Brownsville to the lodge and was part of our shooting party, which insured a quality hunt. His brochure says of El Tejón lodge, "Unpressured geese out of dry pit blinds and wild quail hunting that is beyond comprehension. If you are looking for a different twist in old Mexico, try our quail and goose combo."

This sounded especially appealing to me, as I had never bagged a goose and had only quail hunted in Michigan, which is a lot like never having quail hunted at all. Owner Barry Batsell's lodge has simple but adequate twin-bedded rooms with private baths, and the food is good. Each of our three days began before dawn with a hearty breakfast and a predawn drive to open fields. There, the staff had dug seven pits during the night, one for each of the six hunters plus one for our Mexican guide, who called the geese to the decoys.

The hunting was fabulous and exciting. We crouched out of sight in the blinds as rafts of geese cautiously circled closer and closer until the guide yelled "shoot!" The three species present were snow, blue, and white-fronted or speckled—all magnificent birds. The bag for three mornings totaled eighty-eight, just two short of the limit of five per man, per day. There was, of course, lots of banter back and forth and teasing over missed shots. I especially enjoyed dropping one goose that landed on Trevor and which he blamed on another innocent hunter.

If the goose hunting was spectacular, the quail hunting was, indeed, "beyond comprehension." Our total for three hours of shooting on each of three afternoons was 530 bobwhite and blue quail. Hunting fields and hedgerows behind Mexican beaters meant that, unlike shooting behind pointing dogs, there was no warning of flushes and birds were farther out. Also, unlike hunting in the southern United States, where quail are essentially farm raised, these birds were totally wild. One afternoon we flushed an estimated one thousand quail. It doesn't get any better.

Sopaipillas

Most fine restaurants serve French bread with their meals. The Lark is unique in serving sopaipillas, a deep-fried bread common to southwest United States and to nearby areas of Mexico. In Mexico the "little pillows" are slit open to receive honey and dusted with powdered sugar to become dessert. In New Mexico they are used as a dinner accompaniment, as at the Lark. Mary and I first experienced them at Rancho de Chimayo, an authentic country restaurant between Santa Fe and Taos. Our recipe is derived from Jane Butel's Tex-Mex Cookbook, Harmony Books. The original recipe called for cooking the bread in lard. We use canola oil and, if fried at the proper temperature, the sopaipillas contain less fat than French bread and butter.

4 cups sifted all purpose flour
1 ½ teaspoons salt or more to taste
1 teaspoon baking powder
1 tablespoon shortening or butter
1 package active dry yeast (optional)
1 cup warm water (105 to 115 degrees)
1 ¼ cups (approximately) scalded milk
1 quart canola oil

Combine dry ingredients and cut in 1 tablespoon shortening or butter. Dissolve yeast in the water. Add yeast to scalded milk, cooled to room temperature. If not using yeast, use 1½ cups milk; omit the ¼ cup warm water.

Make a well in center of dry ingredients. Add about 1¼ cups liquid to dry ingredients and work into dough. Add more liquid until dough is firm and springy and holds its shape, similar to yeast dough. Knead dough 15 to 20 times, then invert the bowl over the dough and set aside for approximately 10 minutes.

Heat 1 quart oil to 400 degrees in deep-fryer.

Roll one fourth of the dough to ¼ inch thickness or slightly thinner, then cut into squares or triangles; (do not reroll any of the dough).

Cover the cut dough with a towel as you fry the sopaipillas, a few at a time, in the hot oil. They should puff up and become hollow very soon after being dropped into the oil. To assure puffing, slightly stretch each piece of dough before lowering it into the fat, then place the rolled or top side of dough into the fat first, so it will be the bottom side. Hold each piece of dough in the fat until it puffs. Drain sopaipillas on absorbent toweling. Serve as a bread with any southwestern meal. They are specially good served with honey.

Shopping at the World's Markets

All travelers have priorities. For some it's museums and art galleries; for others, fine shops. Mary and I head for the local market.

Mexico is a market freak's paradise. Guadalajara boasts the largest in the Western Hemisphere—two stories tall and covering several square blocks. The best marketing area south of the border, however, is Oaxaca in south-central Mexico. Foreign markets are frustrating to any cook since, aside from fruit, there is little that is practical to buy. Mary and I bought some flowers for our hotel room at Oaxaca's market, which seemed to amuse the locals who saw us carrying them about. We learned our selection was considered an aphrodisiac.

Oaxaca is surrounded by villages populated by different Indian groups who have maintained their separate cultural identities. Each village has a market one day a week featuring its particular handicraft such as black pottery or colorful weavings as well as local produce. Our regimen was to visit a different ancient ruin and a different market each day. The photographic possibilities were endless, but there were risks. One lady, who did not appreciate her picture being taken, bounced an overly ripe banana off Mary.

The marketing equivalent of the hat trick is to tour a separate fish, meat, and produce market in the same morning. We achieved this in London, completing the rounds of Billingsgate, Smithfield, and Covent Garden, and ending up with the market workers in the Nag's Head Pub at 7 A.M. They weren't too happy at first with Mary's presence and banished us to a corner table, but things got jolly after a while. Dirtiest market honors go to Santo Domingo in the Dominican Republic, of which the less said the better. The cleanest markets and our favorites are in northern Italy. Although their scale is human, the variety is great, as meat, seafood, and produce are all featured. Oddly, all of the signs telling one not to touch the precise displays are in English. The market past the Rialto Bridge in Venice, interlaced with canals and surrounded by small cafés, is a special favorite. The prize for exotica goes to the Hong Kong central market where toads, sea snakes, land snakes, sea pens, countless fish, poultry, pigs, you name it, were all alive and wiggling.

Countless other markets in Europe, the Americas, and Asia crowd our memories, and, except for Santo Domingo, we enjoyed them all.

*R*ising inland from the Sea of Cortez on Mexico's west coast are the Sierra Madre Occidental. Deep in the center of this fabled mountain range are the Sierra Tarahumara, named after the local native American tribe. The Tarahumara are unique in many ways: some live to this day in cliff-front caves, run in nonstop, three-day, 170-mile races, and hunt deer and other game by chasing them on foot to exhaustion and capture.

Intrepid travelers are drawn to North America's most rugged wilderness, not only to learn more of the Tarahumara, but to view the continent's most awesome scenery—tens of thousands of square miles of mountains, streams and rivers, ponderosa pine and oak forests, and most especially, the almost unbelievable *barrancas* (canyons), deeper and far greater in area than the Grand Canyon of the Colorado. Most famous of the five major *barrancas* is Barranca del Cobre, or Copper Canyon, named when first seen by Spaniards for the resemblance of its walls in the light to the green color of oxidized copper.

Prior to the completion in 1961 of the Chihuahua al Pacífico railroad, linking Chihuahua to the Sea of Cortez at Los Mochis, the region was accessible only on foot or by burro. Since then, an increasing number of tourists have viewed the area from the train, which takes fourteen hours for the trip between Los Mochis and Chihuahua while traversing seventy-two tunnels and four miles of bridges spanning thirty-eight chasms. Most visitors make the very arduous round trip, breaking their voyage each way with an overnight stay at one of the rustic lodges that have sprung up since completion of the railroad. These stops provide an opportunity for exploratory side trips that could occupy a lifetime.

None of the available travel brochures or articles provides advice on how best to plan a trip to this area, and none of the packaged tours is intelligently planned. As a result, almost no one enjoys their visit as much as they might. One purpose of this chapter is to suggest an ideal trip.

Our odyssey in offbeat Mexico began with a pleasant flight from Tucson to Guaymas, a port on the eastern mainland shore of the Sea of Cortez. Other than several good restaurants, Guaymas has little to interest most visitors, so we drove our beat-up, rented VW Vanagon twenty minutes north from Guaymas Airport to the resort town of San Carlos. We had reserved a large sedan, but in many trips to Mexico, we have rarely received the type of car promised, nor one that had either air conditioning or automatic transmission.

San Carlos is within easy driving range of southern Arizona and California; thus many Americans have purchased homes or condominiums here. Oddly enough, there is no decent hotel on a beach other than a large Club Med ten miles north of town. Not being given to adult camping, we rented a well-designed but well-worn condo at Solimar Hotel, adjacent to the equally well-worn San Carlos Country Club. The lack of a suitable hotel has by now been remedied on completion of an attractive Howard Johnson's high-rise on a good beach near Club Med.

The hot restaurant in San Carlos is Papas Tapas, which doesn't offer tapas but is casual and tidy with tiled floor, stucco walls, good decorations, and white tablecloths. The only loser after two visits was inedible chicken wings. A complimentary cheese and bean dip was excellent, as were large garlic shrimp, very fresh sea bass, and meaty spareribs with a mellow pork taste rather than the typical American par-boiled approach where the only flavor is that of barbecue sauce.

The northern Mexican states of Sonora, Sinaloa, and Chihuahua, those we visited, are famous for tasty beef. Almost every restaurant offers all the standard cuts in a multitude of preparations ranging from steak Tampequeña with chilis, onions, tomatoes, and refried beans to steak with mushrooms, priced from eight to eleven dollars for a generous cut. Seafood, however, was the stellar attraction in coastal towns. Guaymas is famous for its shrimp, some as large as small lobsters. Sea bass is also omnipresent and is listed on menus as simply *pescado,* or fish, since everyone knows the fish will be sea bass.

The Terraza and Paradise restaurants in San Carlos were acceptable, although not as good as Papas Tapas. The star of the area, however, was the Del Mar, a short drive away in downtown Guaymas at Avenida Serdan and Calle 17. This locally famous seafood restaurant of three adjoining rooms and a bar has a well-maintained, simple but attractive interior. As in every restaurant on our trip, waiters were extremely eager to please. The best dishes of two visits were small hard-shell clams steamed with onions and celery, coconut-fried shrimp, almond-fried shrimp, and a serving of two small broiled lobsters, which cost twelve dollars. Another enjoyable restaurant in Guaymas was El Oeste, a steak house in the Armida Hotel. A filet steak was too thin and unremarkable, but a strip sirloin was thick, tasty, and cooked as ordered, as were grilled, lean, meaty, and tender beef short ribs.

Mexico is the top choice of Americans who retire abroad, attracted by proximity to the United States, low-cost living, and romantic ambience. Because of one of the world's most perfect climates, requiring neither central heating nor air conditioning, most settle in the Bajio in or near former colonial towns such as Guadalajara and San Miguel de Allende. Toward the west coast, however, all of the colonial towns have been trashed save one—the somnolent former silver town of Álamos, our next destination.

Looking like aged hippies in our van, we sped ninety miles south from San Carlos, passing through prosperous Ciudad Obregón, thence to Navojoa, where we lunched at Motel del Rio, subtitled La Casa del

Cazador (House of Hunters). Ciudad Obregón, Navojoa, Los Mochis, and other towns in the area are all famous as bases for excellent white-wing dove and duck hunting from November through March. This costs only about one hundred dollars per hunter per day, plus the modest expense of lodging in good accommodations such as Motel del Rio, where all of the other guests were men. The food here, as at most spots catering to hunters, was fine, especially steak Tampequeña and very large garlic shrimp.

A thirty-five-mile drive after lunch completed our move to Álamos, once capital of the state of Chihuahua, with a population of forty thousand. By the early part of this century, exhaustion of mineral resources, attacks by Mio Indians, and the 1910 revolution had turned Álamos into a near ghost town with 1,700 residents. After World War II, American retirees and artists, drawn by pleasant weather from October through April, colonial charm, and relative proximity to the sea and the United States, began restoring old mansions and haciendas.

Álamos, at an elevation of 1,050 feet, has been declared a national monument and construction or renovation not in the colonial style is forbidden. Some two hundred American singles, couples, or families have either restored old homes or built new ones in the approved style in "Gringo Gorge." A Mars candy billionaire and Mary Astor were once homeowners. Actors Carroll O'Connor and Rip Torne are recent purchasers, helping to bring today's population to over ten thousand. Most Americans choose to restore an old mansion or build a new home of their own design. Because this is Mexico, either course can take several years, but restored mansions and haciendas can be readily purchased, with most running from $115,000 to $170,000.

Our lodgings in Álamos were at Casa de los Tesoros (House of Treasures), an ex-convent covering a half-square block. Simple, but very charming, it boasts two enclosed courtyards on which most rooms face. We recommend rooms number 11 and 12, which we and our accompanying couple snared at the far end of the most inner and private courtyard, where bougainvillea blossomed and water splashed into a swimming pool surrounded by a stone-paved patio. The large courtyard near the entrance was the site of lunch and dinner, dinner being accompanied by a four-piece mariachi group. This was the "in" spot where locals gathered nightly for drinks and dinner.

The food is mediocre, but Los Tesoros is the only hotel of the three in Álamos at which most readers would be happy. Rates are one hundred dollars per couple, including all meals, or forty-five dollars without meals. An American, Mel Larson, is converting an old hospital on the edge of town to a hotel with the Mexican owner of Los Tesoros as his mentor. Six rooms had been completed by the time of our visit, with five or six to go before the grand opening.

We explored Álamos (cottonwood) the next morning under the tutelage of "Candy Joe," the guide of preference with a bulging belly resembling Big Stuff in *Smilin' Jack* or Wimpy in *Popeye*. Highlights included the old church, a lively plaza, a bustling market, an old silver mine, the town jail, magnificent restored mansions with bougainvillea draped over courtyard walls, impressive homes in Gringo Gorge, and an old hacienda where American hunters rent studio apartments for $150 a month during the dove season.

The Americans of Álamos, who wish to do so, live a life of cocktails, dinner parties, and revolving card games in flower-bedecked inner patios. Newcomers are welcomed with open arms. Other than one touring group that stopped at Los Tesoros for one night, only eight or nine American couples were present during our two-night stay, and the local community prompted two couples to make offers on homes. Of course, many Americans come to Álamos with that in mind.

For those to whom a seaside setting is not essential and who are content to limit Mexican visits to October through April, Álamos may well be the best place to purchase a Mexican home. Although it does not yet have good shopping and restaurants or a variety of activities, those are sure to come as the American community grows. Of course, when everything is in place, prices will be much higher. But, as always in Mexico or any foreign country, anyone considering a home purchase should rent for six months before taking the big step.

We skipped the included last lunch at Los Tesoros, preferring to purchase another good meal at Motel del Rio in Navojoa before proceeding down the coast 110 miles to Los Mochis *(loss moe-cheeze)*, the Pacific terminus of the Chihuahua al Pacífico railroad. Los Mochis was also the terminus of our rental van as our foursome now joined three other couples in a package tour, which included our time in Los Mochis, the Copper Canyon, and Chihuahua, and our transfer by air from Chihuahua to El Paso at the end of our trip.

In Los Mochis, Hotel Santa Anita had just been completely remodeled with marble lobby, halls and baths, as well as new carpeting, furniture, and bath fixtures. Visitors should request an inside junior suite such as number 200 or 300 on the second (third) or third (fourth) floors, since outside rooms are assaulted by traffic noises and those on the first (second) floor rock to the wee hours from the loud band below them in the bar off the lobby.

Hotel Santa Anita also serves as an upscale base for dove and duck hunting, which is about the only reason an American tourist would come here other than to catch the train to the Copper Canyon. The hotel restaurant is quite good, serving a variety of shrimp preparations, steaks, and lobsters, plus Mexican specialties. More appealing, because it was lively, real, and full of Mexicans, was nearby El Farralon, a seafood restaurant. Oysters are never eaten on the half shell in most of Mexico, but rather in oyster cocktails. Here, the cocktail contained two dozen small local oysters.

Led by Pablo, we left the hotel at 5:30 A.M. for the train station and our 6:15 rail departure with comfortable reserved seats in a poorly maintained and not very clean third-world train. Otherwise, it was pleasant enough, and there was even a dining car where we had eggs and toast for breakfast and steaks and chicken for lunch. Beverages were limited to soft drinks, beer, and coffee.

After two hours climbing from coastal flatlands into the Sierra Madre, much of the time was spent not in our seats, but on the platform between cars where there was nothing to impede photography or enjoyment of the passing scenery. This was a never-boring fascination of mountains, tunnels, bridges, gorges, forests, streams, and rivers—a vast, almost unpopulated wilderness.

Shortly after noon, the train approached the famous Copper Canyon itself and stopped on its rim at the settlement of Divisadero. Here, we disembarked to view a *barranca* deeper than the Grand Canyon. Immediately to the left of our viewpoint was the rustic Divisadero Barrancas, a lodge perched on the very edge of the canyon. The other best hotel possibility here is Hotel Posada Barrancas, which has the same owners as the Santa Anita in Los Mochis. It boasts modern rooms, fireplaces or individual heaters, and a handsome dining room and lounge. It is not, however, on the rim of the canyon like Divisadero Barrancas, although it has attempted to remedy that with a *mirador* viewing building, a fifteen-minute walk from the hotel.

Whistled back on board the train, we continued through more mesmerizing scenery before arriving about 3 P.M. at Creel, with several thousand residents, the largest town along the way. A fifteen-minute ride through a Western movie set of pines, rocks, and streams brought us to Copper Canyon Lodge, whose rustic log and adobe construction reminded us of a dude ranch. There is no electricity; on chilly nights some of the twenty rooms are heated by fireplaces, others by iron stoves. Ours had a large corner fireplace and three kerosene lamps, one in the bath, one on the dresser, and one on the bedside table. Charming! A long, long porch in front of our rooms was the setting for chairs and benches, a perfect spot to relax and enjoy views of a stream and the forest beyond.

The extremely atmospheric and tiny bar, lounge, and restaurant were crowded for cocktails and dinner that evening as the lodge was fully booked. Our latest "it's a small world" feeling came on learning the lodge's owner is Skip McWilliams of Oxford and Troy, Michigan, and that Liliana Carroso, the very competent lodge manager, once resided in Bloomfield Hills. Following cocktail entertainment by a Mexican guitarist with a terrible voice but *mucho* enthusiasm, we enjoyed an adequate baked chicken dinner. Next morning's breakfast of scrambled eggs, bacon, ham, beans, cheese, and tortillas was better, as was lunch based on chunky chili.

We hiked downstream along the river the next morning through jumbled worn rocks and pine and oak forest, finally arriving at a forty-foot waterfall where the river plunged over an escarpment. Tarahumara Indian girls along the way sold inexpensive but wonderfully wrought woven pine-needle baskets. Similar baskets made by Indians in northern Michigan sell for thirty dollars or more.

After lunch, we visited a Tarahumara cliff dwelling consisting of a cave, one end of which was enclosed as a bedroom by a pile of flat rocks without mortar. Chickens were cooped nightly at the other end of the cave. Tarahumara arts and crafts and three-day foot races are the bright side of the coin, unfortunately offset by 50 percent infant mortality and the average one hundred days a year spent drunk.

After buying more pine-needle baskets, we bade adieu to the Tarahumara and boarded the 3:15 P.M. train at Creel for Chihuahua, passing Mennonite farm settlements along the way. After upgrading our rooms at the Hotel San Francisco, at a cost of U.S.$3.40, we caught a late supper across the street at Trastevere. This lemon was Pablo's only goof.

Our tour of Chihuahua the next day revealed an attractive, compact city of almost a million souls without sprawling suburbs, surrounded by low, dusty-looking mountains. Chihuahua means dry and dusty. As with all of the larger towns in northern Mexico, there is a growing prosperity founded on booming agriculture and expatriate U.S. factories, of which Chihuahua has some 100 and Juarez 280.

The historical star of the region is Pancho Villa, the Mexican revolutionary who raided New Mexico, was chased by General Pershing, and was murdered by political enemies after his retirement. His widow, one of fifteen wives, lived in his Chihuahua home until her death in 1981. It is now a spellbinding, not-to-be-missed museum, which reveals Villa not as a rough, tough rustic, but a consummate, sophisticated role player.

Lunch at Los Canastos was the most enjoyable of our trip. This

185

new restaurant has a Euromodern interior, a dynamic proprietor, and very bright attentive waiters. A variety of fine dishes included crisp-fried tripe with mushrooms, bacon, and miniature tortillas as a wrapper; artichokes with *béchemal* sauce, bacon, and cheese; grilled beef short ribs; jumbo shrimp; and crêpes with caramel and nuts.

Dinner our last evening in Mexico was at the old-line "best restaurant in town," La Calesa (The Coach), which had a spacious, established, clubby ambience. The menu was dated, the staff unbright, the specialty steak. Mary's was medium rare as ordered, mine overdone. Here, as everywhere, not one man wore a jacket, let alone a tie.

The Copper Canyon region was the high point of our trip. We would have enjoyed it more if the authors of the articles on the area had sense enough to recommend what a trip should be, rather than merely reporting what they had done. We suggest flying to Los Mochis, overnighting at Hotel Santa Anita with dinner at El Farralon, and taking the train the next day for a three- or four-night stay at Hotel Divisadero Barrancas while touring that area. We suggest staying at Copper Canyon Lodge for three or four nights while exploring there, proceeding by prearranged van from Creel to Chihuahua, stopping for lunch at a Mennonite home, and staying in Chihuahua at Castel Sicomoro with dinner at Los Canastos. This would shorten the train trip and divide it into two shorter periods, give time for exploration, and get one much more quickly from Creel to Chihuahua, with an interesting visit with Mennonites.

Reserve Wine Lists

We have always had a strong conviction that a restaurant's wine list should be included on the menu, either on the back of a one-sheet menu, as at The Lark, or as a page or so of a multipage menu. Such a list should be extensive enough to meet the needs of most diners, yet brief enough to be neither intimidating nor a chore to peruse. As in all things, the goal is to make patrons' visits easy and pleasant.

A fine restaurant, however, will almost certainly have more wines than are suitable for inclusion on its menu. These compose the reserve wine list, in our case 430 wines supplementing the 100 wines on our menu. A note on the bottom of our regular wine list states that a reserve wine list is available on request, but relatively few guests so request. I suspect this is because of an assumption that these wines will be very expensive. Not true. Rare and expensive wines are usually placed on the reserve rather than regular list, but most wines on the reserve list are there simply because there is not enough room for them on the regular list. In fact, many are moderately priced. At The Lark, we are flattered to suggest the best value.

Opinions on Food

Mary and I have strong opinions on food and restaurants or we would not put up with the hassle and long hours. We chose a country-inn format because we believe the physical setting and the related approach to food are best suited for a perfect dining experience.

Put another way, we do not like food that has been fussed with too much. Everyone enjoys a beautiful presentation, but when food begins to resemble a work of art, beware! The senses of taste and smell are interrelated and inseparable in the enjoyment of food. We smell food because evaporation transmits odors to our nose. When we chop, purée, mash, form, and so forth, to make works of art, we speed up the evaporation process and the food cannot possibly taste as good. The culinary arts approach to food may be called the last refuge of nontasters. Chefs, deficient in their own taste buds, become more and more decorative, searching for the approval that eludes them.

Nouvelle Cuisine is receding because it was excessive and, when the novelty had worn off, ridiculous and precocious. In France, its replacement is called Cuisine Bourgeoise and in this country, regional cooking. It's alive and well in San Francisco and New Orleans, and The Lark does its best to foster this exciting and sensible movement in Michigan.

United States and Canada

Autumn in New York

*M*ary and I were married in October 1960, and spent part of our honeymoon in my ancestral homeland, Quebec, and the rest of the happy time in Manhattan. Foodies even then, we dined at the top restaurants, such as 21 Club and the newly opened Four Seasons.

So began a custom of an autumnal visit to New York. On our twenty-fifth anniversary, I arranged with the maître d' of the newly rejuvenated 21 Club for Mary and me to be given the same table in the horseshoe facing the bar where we sat on our honeymoon. The lure of far-off places as well as northern Michigan in the fall eroded this annual pilgrimage, and we'd not been to Manhattan for some years. Fittingly, our hiatus ended on our thirty-fifty anniversary when Mary and I, together with Chef Marcus and his kitchen brigade, accepted the long-standing invitation of The James Beard Foundation to present a special dinner at the late cookbook author's home in Greenwich Village.

Our staff stayed at the New York Vista Hotel in the World Trade Center, fairly convenient to the James Beard House. Mary and I lodged at the St. Regis more centrally located at Fifth Avenue and Fifty-Fifth. We chose the St. Regis, not only because of its location, but to enjoy the advantages of its participation in the Amex Platinum Card Fine Hotel program, such as free room upgrade, free breakfasts, and 5 P.M. check-out. Also, the St. Regis was the beneficiary of a complete renovation, which not only restored the hotel to its original grandeur, but added improvements such as marble baths and video-screen telephones. The bath had a separate tub and shower, two sinks, plush robes, and Bijan toiletries. Both *The New York Times* and *The Wall Street Journal* were delivered early each morning. Room service was excellent. Breakfast, always promised in twenty minutes, actually arrived in less than ten minutes. Every floor had its own butler; ours saw to our faxes, laundry, and other needs. Management and service were nearly perfect, reminiscent of London's Connaught in the old days.

Needing a simple, not-too-distant Saturday lunch after hotel check-in, we accepted the concierge's suggestion of Coco Pazzo on East Seventy-Fourth off Madison. Our lusty repast began with starters of sautéed chicken livers and giblets flavored with *vin santo* for Mary and three fresh sardine filets on a bed of mixed greens for me. Mary had the winning main course—sautéed shrimp flavored with chestnut honey, accompanied with deep-fried julienne asparagus. Coco Pazzo's cuisine is from Italy's Emilia-Romagna region, a refreshing change from Tuscan fare. Our wine, however, was an obscure but fine "Super Tuscan" blend of Sangiovese and Cabernet.

In times past, Mary and I have made the mistake of rushing to restaurants all over town, later to find out we missed one of the best in our own hotel. Not this trip. We joined Chef Marcus that evening at Lespinasse. Like Le Cirque in the Mayfair Hotel, Lespinasse in the St. Regis is separately owned and managed, the hotel merely its landlord. Chef Grey Kunz, not yet forty, was born in Singapore but raised in Switzerland, where he trained under famed Chef Fredy Girardet. He next returned to the Far East, cooking at The Regent Hotel in Hong Kong before opening Lespinasse in 1991. *Wine Spectator* says his cuisine "may be the most confident and convincing example yet of one of the culinary world's most exciting experiments, the integration of French and Asian foods." The dining room is totally French with the opulence and space unique to fine hotels, which alone can afford to subsidize the cost of such spaciousness. Soothed by the elegant ambience, our sense of anticipation and contentment grew when the maître d' suggested that, if agreeable to us, we need not order because Chef Kunz would prefer to prepare a special menu he had designed for us. Assuming first courses might display Oriental influences, our first wine was a Gewurztraminer—the single-vineyard Hengst Grand Cru of Zind-Humbrecht, the pre-eminent Alsatian vintner.

This was the season for fresh white truffles from Alba, and they were delicately shaved over the miniature risotto first course. Next came sea bass and currently fashionable fava beans in a Thai fish-sauce broth seasoned with fresh ginger, garlic, and Oriental sesame oil. This was followed by delicate lobster chunks with snap peas over crisp rice crust with saffron sauce. Like the sea bass course, this was a melding of French and Oriental ingredients and techniques.

Our main course was purely French: twin medallions of venison tenderloin, crisp on the outside and rosy and tender within, garnished with huckleberries and a red wine sauce. Accompaniments were two cabbages, mashed potatoes, and candied chestnuts. A La Jota Tenth Anniversary Cabernet was a fine match. Our first dessert was a cold papaya soup, with sorbet cradled above on a decorative lattice. The real dessert followed—a warm chocolate tart with a delicate sesame *tuile* and rhubarb sauce, accompanied by a *tuile* cup of vanilla ice cream. All courses were appealingly arranged on a variety of china shapes and patterns, different for each dish. Service was perfect. Lespinasse is rated in the top four for cuisine in the *Zagat Survey* and is certainly one of New York's finest restaurants.

On Sunday morning, it was only a four-block stroll down Fifth Avenue from the hotel to St. Patrick's Cathedral, adorned with draping in the gold and silver papal colors for Pope John Paul's visit.

Another short walk after mass, this time up Fifth Avenue, brought us to Harry Cipriani, the Manhattan outpost of Harry's Bar of Venice. As usual here, patrons engaged in entreaties and conniving for favored tables. Two dowagers demanded a window table for four and later admitted no one else was joining them. Then they only ordered a salad. The intended foursome, who had reserved that table, stormed out when they arrived to find it occupied. My card garnered the customary professional courtesy and a corner table near the window. Whoopee!

Mary had the *de rigeur* Bellini cocktail invented at Harry's Bar, while I sipped a red. Our waiter, the maître d', and Giuseppe Cipriani (owner Arrigo Cipriani's son) all urged us to have the risotto with spinach, and we relished the order we split as a first course. Harry's risotto is made special by the use of rare and costly Carnaroli rice. Our favorite risotto with black squid ink, which we have enjoyed here and at Harry's in Venice, is only available on Fridays. Complimentary zucchini chips were followed by main courses of grilled halibut with fresh artichokes and the quintessential Venetian dish, thinly sliced calf's liver with onions. Our feeble attempt to limit calories by skipping dessert was sabotaged by Giuseppe, who insisted we at least share an order of crêpes *à la crème* flamed with liqueur. Great!

Danny Meyer's Union Square Café in lower Manhattan is the number-three favorite of New Yorkers, according to the *Zagat Survey* (1996) and the logical choice to host our kitchen staff that evening. So, joined by Chef Marcus, Sous Chef Rick Ormsby and Cook Tony Cotton, we tucked into a variety of American vittles. Wines were the allocated 1993 Kistler Durrell Chardonnay and the 1990 Ch. Montelena Cabernet, both excellent. Service was attentive and efficient. Danny Meyer is also a partner in one of New York's new hot restaurants, Gramercy Tavern.

Madison Avenue is even more fun to stroll than Fifth Avenue, and Monday morning found us at James Robinson Antiques, whose wares are so special that one is viewed through a locked door before admission is granted. Having passed that test and after browsing among such stuff as heavy George I sterling tankards, Mary inquired as to whether they had any Francis I pieces. New daughter-in-law Cinda's silver pattern is Reed & Barton's Francis I, and she covets odd bowls, platters, and serving pieces, especially older ones. The saleswoman said she had a Francis I platter and led us to it. Mary and I had to control ourselves to keep from laughing. The very large, heavy platter was indeed Francis I, not Reed & Barton, but a 250-year-old beauty from the time of Francis I, Holy Roman Emperor from 1745 to 1760, probably worth a year's salary. Other shops we enjoyed included Nelson & Nelson on Park Avenue for silver, crystal, and "small" antiques, and Scully & Scully, also on Park Avenue, for home furnishings and gifts.

But now it was midday and time to return to work—luncheon at Aureole on East Sixty-First. Because of the constraints of its long townhouse shape, some tables are in what resembles a corridor. Other than that, the ambience is very agreeable, with the larger rear space, where we were seated, underlooking (yes, underlooking) a garden.

Service is outstanding, and the food (despite Chef-Proprietor Charles Palmer's absence in Brazil) superb. The only caveat we have heard is the objection by some to Palmer's architectural, sometimes towering, approach to presentation, especially of desserts.

Mary and I both chose the bargain-priced, thirty-two-dollar *prix fixe* luncheon, which offered two choices for each of its four courses. We both had the white bean and new potato salad appetizer with wild mushroom vinaigrette (immensely better than it sounds), as neither one of us coveted the other choice, tuna and salmon tartares. For the fish, main, and dessert courses, we had one of each: pepper-seared salmon filet with grain mustard, and pepper-seared cod with green onion risotto and green endive; veal medallions with wild mushroom cannelloni, and grilled venison with crisped gnocchi, red wine sage sauce, and *ratatouille;* and warm blueberry compote for Mary's final course and Hawaiian chocolate *timbale* with white chocolate cheesecake *pour moi.* The wine list revealed two excellent half-bottle selections: 1993 Talbott Chardonnay and the 1990 Gaja Barbaresco. Aureole is now one of our favorite New York restaurants. We just hope Chef Palmer didn't pick up any crazy ideas in Brazil.

Monday evening was our turn for center stage at the James Beard House in Greenwich Village, which has been preserved and is owned and managed by The James Beard Foundation. To quote its brochure:

"The idea of saving James Beard's home in Greenwich Village was conceived by Julia Child as an important step in her personal quest to establish gastronomy as a recognized art and bona fide discipline. Today the Beard House is North America's first and only culinary center. Each week, chefs from America's finest restaurants and hotels cook in Jim's famous kitchen, presenting their work to members, friends and the press. Great American chefs, whose names are readily recognized across the country, and Rising Stars, whose names soon will be, come to the House, as do Best Hotel Chefs, Great Regional Chefs and visiting chefs from abroad, honored by the invitation and committed to showing their best. A dinner at James Beard House has all the excitement of opening night—for chefs and members alike."

Chef Marcus's dinner was eagerly anticipated and, of course, sold out. The menu:

Discovery Series Marcus Haight
<u>*The Lark, West Bloomfield, Michigan*</u>

Chinese salt-baked shrimp

Tartlet of curried duck salad

Roasted venison tenderloin and candied onions
  on toasted brioche

Champagne Veuve Clicquot Yellow Label Brut

Shrimp and crab cake with spicy palmier

Trimbach Gewurztraminer 1992

Roasted squab and foie gras in phyllo with a
  Michigan sun-dried cherry sauce

Domaine de la Roquette, Châteauneuf du Pape 1992

Lemon and rosemary granité

Rack of Lamb Ghengis Khan with wild mushrooms
  gratin and duchess potatoes

*Château Clos des Jacobins, St. Émilion Grand
  Cru 1986*

Chocolate mint emerald

*Domaine de Coyeux Muscat de Beaumes de
  Venise 1991*

Mignardises

Veuve Clicquot had kindly donated their champagne as well as the Muscat de Beaumes de Venise dessert wine. The other wines were chosen by officials of James Beard House. As one might assume with the cuisine of Chef Marcus assisted by Sous Chef Rick Ormsby, Pastry Chef Paul Burnash, and Cook Tony Cotton, the evening was a great success. Several foundation members, who are frequent Beard House diners, said it was the finest dinner they had ever had there. Mary and I were privileged to dine at this event and were charmed by the hospitality of Penny Trenk, a proprietor of Rubicon in San Francisco, Robert Farber of the New Jersey *Chaîne des Rôtisseurs*, and many other foundation members. Penny Trenk even returned us to our hotel and secured reservations for us at Restaurant Daniel. Dinners at the James Beard House are certainly one of the best dining values in the world.

We've many long-standing invitations to lunch or dinner any time we land in New York, but were only able to squeeze in one lunch with a long-time friend and patron, Al Levine. He chose Tuesday lunch at his favorite Chinese restaurant, Chiam on East Forty-Eighth Street, which earned top-four Chinese status in the *Zagat Survey*. Chiam has the rare distinction for a Chinese restaurant of a *Wine Spectator* Best Award of Excellence wine list—the same as The Lark. The proprietor, like the proprietor of The Lark, is convinced he deserves the ultimate accolade—the Grand Award—but will not receive it because "it's who you know." Wine prices are modest; in fact, the almost-impossible-to-obtain 1990 Ch. Margaux was listed far below current wholesale cost. We ordered the great unfiltered Newton Chardonnay.

Our most enjoyable course at Chiam was the especially good dim sum appetizers: scallops St. Mue, steamed shrimp dumplings, and steamed chicken dumplings. Chiam has a dim sum lunch every Saturday and Sunday and that's when we would return.

No visit to New York is complete for us without browsing a wine shop, so our after-lunch stroll found us in Morrell's on Madison Avenue. When a red Bordeaux becomes "in," I notice the price escalating until finally there are no offerings. Such was the case with the

1989 Lynch Bages. Now it is happening to the more modest 1989 Ch. Gloria, but Morrell's still has it.

In its special "Best of New York" issue, *Wine Spectator* called Les Célébrités in the Nikko Essex House on Central Park South, "The Jewel Box of Manhattan," and its choice for the best restaurant in New York. Giving it a perfect 100 for ambience, *WS* says:

"Extravagant is putting it mildly. The five-million-dollar dining room is so opulent it barely escapes vulgarity, yet the whole effect is so lush and harmonious, it's perfection. Paintings by celebrities such as James Dean and Phyllis Diller give the place its name; they're framed and lighted like Rembrandts, but gilt and marble are used so lavishly that the art fades into colorful accents. Enormous black columns and crimson drapes add drama. The table settings drip with Bernardaud china and Christofle silver. If it seems ostentatious at first, after a glass of wine the ambience draws you into a world of luxurious comfort."

I couldn't have said it better. In this room of only fourteen tables, we were honored at dinner with a large comfortably upholstered booth scattered with matching pillows. Service was solicitous and friendly, yet professional. Wine markups were a bit of a problem, but that five million dollars must be recouped somewhere. We settled on the 1989 Ch. Beychevelle, St. Julien at $105 as not too far out of line, and it was delicious.

Chef Christian Deloubrier's restaurant is very French, as evidenced by Mary's first course of filets of red mullet *(rouget)* and my fresh lasagna with mussels, oysters, and clams, especially adorned with white truffles. In this fall season, New York restaurants lean to fur and feather: venison, rabbit, and pheasant. Mary spoke up first and stole my intended main course of roasted wild pheasant with Alsatian *choucroute* and turnips, so I made do with saddle and leg of rabbit roasted on the spit and stuffed with wild mushrooms and spinach. Mary's Jamaican Dream dessert consisted of coconut *tuille* (yum) with banana compote and vanilla ice cream with dark rum sauce. I chose a chocolate soufflé with praline ice cream. The typical professional courtesy we encounter was exemplified by a third complimentary dessert—a rather large white chocolate painter's palate, adorned with a variety of sherbets with a garnish of fresh fruit. Another wonderful experience.

Our museum of choice on this trip was a new one for us, the National Museum of the American Indian, a unit of the Smithsonian Institution at One Bowling Green in Lower Manhattan. A variety of programs and even interactive formats are available to visitors, but we were entranced by the show of some six hundred works until recently buried from sight in a warehouse in Queens. Sources ranged from Alaska south to Bolivia. If they are still on display, don't miss this on your next trip to New York.

Over the years, a restaurant most recommended to us by our patrons has been Il Mulino on West Third Street in the Village. It is routinely voted the best and most popular Italian restaurant in New York. So off we went for lunch, using the name of a patron of ours from *The New Yorker* magazine to secure a reservation. Be warned that Il Mulino is so small and popular that they sometimes do not even answer the phone.

We loved Il Mulino, neat and trim with white tablecloths, but relaxed and comfortable. Owner Fernando was a working guy in shirt-sleeves. Our waiter, Claudio, had Detroit connections. Complimentary cold antipasti were sliced cacciatorini sausage, marinated zucchini, and *parmigiano reggiano* cheese. Cheese and herb *crostini* were hot. Mary had the new crop of shaved white truffles from Alba, which she had at most meals except breakfast. I was far from suffering with a starter of porcini mushroom ravioli in a cream sauce flecked with black truffles. Mary's main course of skinny-clawed European lobsters sautéed with garlic were the largest we've seen since Bilbao, Spain. They were perfect, as was my veal chop with shallots, garlic, and sage. Tiramisu and complimentary cherry and grape grappa were the finale to our first meal at the best Italian restaurant we've found in America. Our wine was the rare and lush 1989 Solaia of Antinori.

One of the two or three hottest restaurants in town is Bouley in the TriBeCa area of lower Manhattan. For three years in a row it has topped the *Zagat Survey* in both popularity and food rating, creating a big problem obtaining reservations. Given that, I was baffled by the ease of booking my table, even allowing for professional courtesy. All became clear when Mary and I arrived at the appointed hour. A young staff member introduced himself as the reservation manager and said he received copies of our newsletter from a good patron of Bouley and The Lark.

The crowded but comfortable dining room resembles a French country manor with fabric-covered chairs, high wooden cabinets, mirrors, and candles. Service was, as usual, friendly but professional. Our 1990 Ch. Lynch Bages at ninety dollars was one of the better buys of this trip. Dinner began with a complimentary *amuse-gueule* of Spanish mackerel in a light sauce, followed by appetizers of Maine day-boat lobster with marinated cucumbers and unexpected ossetra caviar for Mary and a panache of three "salads" for me: roasted hot foie gras, grilled shrimp, and wild mushrooms. This was followed by a complimentary course from Chef-Proprietor David Bouley of fresh Japanese yellowtail "white" tuna braised with rosemary and scallions in an aromatic sauce with ginger. Mary's main course was organically fed rabbit roasted with Italian chestnuts, artichokes, and seckel pears. My choice was roasted lobster scented with Tahitian vanilla. Dinner concluded with an array of complimentary desserts too numerous to list or note, but including an especially crisp-topped and tasty *crème brulée* and a trio of tropical fruit sorbets. We were led to the kitchen before departure, where we met the dynamic Chef Bouley and thanked him for his gracious hospitality and wonderful evening. Long may he reign. We now understand why we hear such raves for Bouley—not surprising given that David Bouley trained under Joel Robuchon in Paris.

Two more of the hottest restaurants in New York occupied much of our last day. Mary and I had met Nobu Matsuhisha, chef-proprietor of Matsuhisha in Los Angeles, when we were inducted into the food industry's Fine Dining Hall of Fame together. His L.A. restaurant is widely considered to have the finest cuisine in that city. Matsuhisha scored a perfect 100 for food on the first *Condé Nast Traveler* "Readers' Poll" but received "a disastrous 13.6 for decor." When he paired with restaurant guru Drew Nieporent (Montrachet, Tribeca Grill, Rubicon) and actor Robert DeNiro to open a Manhattan outpost of Japanese cuisine named Nobu, designer David Rockwell was retained to raise the decor rating, and he has created a space both vibrant and soothing. Despite my Navy days in Japan, I relied on the maître d' and savored rock shrimp in a light tempura with ponzu sauce; a pasta with squid, shiitake mushrooms and asparagus, and a soft-shell crab sushi roll. Drew Nieporent appeared at our table at this point with greetings and recommendations for more food, including tiradito "Nobu" style, raw fish with hot seasonings found by Nobu on a recent trip to Brazil. Our co-proprietor (Nobu was in Los Angeles at this time) then sent out complimentary desserts: Asian pear granité, vanilla and chocolate mousses, champagne grapes, raspberries, and Asian pears. We were being killed with kindness. Thank God it was almost time to return home.

A postprandial stroll took us to the new Barney's store at Madison and Sixty-First, which Mary pronounced "great" for the best and most unusual designer clothes, shoes, jewelry, and accessories. They also have a popular casual restaurant named Mad 61 (location of store) and an adjacent wine bar, originally the Wine Spectator Wine Bar with *Wine Spectator*'s ratings listed for the wines offered. Unfortunately, that concept has been shelved. Unfortunate, because the wines now offered rate very poorly.

Restaurant Daniel, the site of our last supper, is the other establishment with the most sought-after tables in town, although opinions do differ. We receive a constant stream of dining reports from patrons at The Lark, and while Bouley receives almost universal raves, Restaurant Daniel is frequently criticized for the attitude of its dining room staff. We, however, received excellent, friendly, and solicitous service from the sommelier, our captain, and waiter. The maître d' did exude an officious aura.

There were no problems whatsoever with the sublime food and wine. Our wine choice was another familiar bottling, the 1985 Ch.

Pichon Lalande. A complimentary first course went beyond the usual gesture with shellfish bisque with purple basil and shrimp for Mary and chilled lobster consommé with caviar in a coral sauce for me. Our ordered first course came next—Mary's daily truffle extravaganza at sixty-five dollars consisted of shaved white truffles over a baked potato and it was worth every penny. My *rillettes* of wild hare, pheasant, partridge, and foie gras with spiced raisins and pine nuts was the best pâté I have ever had, encasing a large core of slightly pink foie gras.

Another gift from Chef Daniel now appeared: sautéed foie gras with wild blueberries, *frisée,* sweet and sour orange zest, and hazelnuts. Mellow and great. Mary's main course was a perfect rendition of roasted black sea bass in a crispy potato shell on a bed of leeks and red wine sauce. Mine displayed the chef's versatility and lack of pomposity—a duo of braised beef short ribs and roasted hanger steak with fall root vegetables and mashed potatoes with black truffles. The meltingly tender short rib was one of the tastiest beef dishes I have ever had, and my potatoes with black truffles rivaled Mary's first course.

Weakening at last, we split a dramatic milk chocolate *bombe* with espresso sponge and bitter chocolate sorbet, but the chef added desserts of pears poached in red wine with currant sauce and a lemon sorbet. Here also the staff brought us to the kitchen to meet Chef Daniel Boulud, a handsome and charming man, whom we thanked for his kindness and our superb dinner.

So ended our gastronomical odyssey, which began, continued, and ended on a very high plain. I doubt that anyone else has ever dined at so many of the finest Manhattan restaurants in so brief a time.

New, Hot, and In

New restaurants are not "hot" and "in" because of cuisine or service. When everyone rushes to the latest restaurant, it is because of an exciting concept and ambience. Yet, almost all such restaurants fade and die. Why?

Poll after poll has shown that ambience is more important to most diners than good service, and that cuisine is least important of all—thus the crowds that respond to an appealing decor and theme. But, it is also proven that the impact of any setting lessens over time and is eventually taken for granted. The inhabitants of the most beautiful locales in the world rarely appreciate their surroundings.

The rare new restaurant that has fine cuisine and service, in addition to ambience, becomes an established institution. Perhaps the best example is New York's Four Seasons. But when food and service are poor, the restaurant is doomed in the end, although it may prosper for several years if the setting generates enough excitement.

But why do proprietors of more new, hot, and in restaurants not ensure their survival by providing good service and cuisine? The simple answer: it's beyond their ability. It is a hundred times easier to find a good decorator than a good chef, and it is a thousand times easier to develop an exciting restaurant concept than it is to manage a dining room to provide superior service day after day, week after week, month after month, year after year. As Joe Baum, the founder of The Four Seasons and other famous restaurants, emphasizes, "Execution, execution, execution."

The Best Restaurant, the Best Steak

Bob Talbert of the *Detroit Free Press*, Michigan's leading columnist, visits as many restaurants as any critic and affirms that The Lark is "the best restaurant Michigan has … they've established the criteria by which all other fine restaurants around here are judged."

Bob quoted his wife, Lynn, as saying that her sirloin steak at The Lark "was the best I've ever had in my life." Former Detroit Tigers announcer Ernie Harwell, a sophisticated world traveler who has resided on Spain's island of Majorca, called his steak "world class."

Many guests are hesitant to have our sirloin steak with crisp onions and red wine sauce because they feel obligated to order a more "sophisticated" dish at a fine restaurant. But, steak is on the menu because it has almost universal appeal. When Marchesi Leonardo de Frescobaldi, proprietor of Italy's oldest family wine estate, dines at The Lark, he orders steak. So also does Count Matuschka-Greiffenclau of famed Schloss Vollrads, whose family has the oldest history of wine making in Germany and the world. As long as one can remember, the most popular dish and meal in France has been "steak *frites,*" which is steak with French-fried potatoes. When we visited the *Michelin*-starred restaurants of France and Germany, we found steak featured on virtually every menu.

Our steak is properly aged Black Angus prime beef. Many restaurants begin with quality beef, but then dry it out by broiling it. Ours is prepared in the French manner in a heavy cast-iron skillet, accented with a magnificent but not distracting sauce, and topped with a heap of crisp, thin onions. And, unlike any other restaurant we know of, you may not only tell your waiter how you like it done, but how thick a steak you prefer.

Touring the Pacific Northwest

*W*hile Mary and I love to travel, we only wish to go where we'll have a great time. One gap we've long wished to fill is the Pacific Northwest, and we accomplished that in a one-week whirlwind visit.

Arriving in Seattle via a nonstop flight, we drove by rental car three hours to Vancouver, British Columbia. The city of Vancouver (not to be confused with the nearby island of the same name) is Canada's "Gem of the Pacific" and the Northwest coast's most appealing metropolis with 1.5 million residents in the city and environs. Shielded by mountains from Arctic air and warmed by the Japanese Current, the climate is pleasant year-round. The prosperity of a city may often be judged by the number of huge cranes constructing skyscrapers: they dot Vancouver's downtown. Here, the racial minority is Oriental with the second-largest Chinatown in North America. Hordes of Japanese tourists also help create a cosmopolitan feeling. Vancouverites are extremely polite and try to be "with it," favoring casual Euro-style attire when not at the office. Men rarely wear jackets to restaurants.

The city has many striking postmodern office buildings as well as unfortunate, ugly glass boxes from an earlier era. It is a fine and safe city for walking with Rio-type mosaic sidewalks, Parisian-style trees, mini parks, shops, cafés, and restaurants. But Vancouver's greatest asset is its setting among mountains falling into the sea. Stanley Park is minutes from the city's center, one thousand acres of forests and flowers where one may walk or bike the nature trails and seawall, view killer and beluga whales at the zoo, see bald eagles perched in trees, and dine at a variety of restaurants.

Another "must see" convenient to downtown is Granville Island, which boasts a fascinating public market, a hotel, live theatres, restaurants, and shops packed into thirty-eight acres. Great for strolling, browsing, shopping. Other local attractions include the Botanical Gardens, Grouse Mountain by cable car, and the Capilano Salmon Hatchery.

Canada Place is a harbor-front development that includes the Canadian Pacific Railway's Pan Pacific Hotel, which has an Oriental flavor and is dramatically located atop the World Trade Center. We, however, chose to stay at the Four Seasons Hotel, which may have the best service in Canada.

Visitors to Vancouver should drive the forty-five-mile Sea to Sky Highway north to road's end at Squamish, not to see Squamish, which is unremarkable, but to experience the coastal mountains, forests, and shore. This is the northernmost coastal road in North America since rugged mountains and many fjords make any farther northern extension hopelessly impractical. Mary and I turned inland at Squamish, continuing forty-five more minutes to the ski resort of Whistler Mountain where we lunched at Umberto's Trattoria and took a gondola to high ice fields where skiing continued even in midsummer. One 6,500-foot run is reputed to be the longest in North America.

Everyone's favorite Chinese restaurant in Vancouver is the Beijing, where many of the patrons are Oriental and where we feasted on the finest meal of our trip——especially enjoying half of a Peking duck as a shared appetizer and a two-and-one-half pound Dungeness crab in spicy black bean sauce, displayed whole and live before preparation. We also had a good steamed crab at the simple Kettle of Fish, but were unable to obtain last-minute reservations at the popular Salmon House on the Hill—more famous for its views than cuisine. We were underwhelmed by the Thai food at Salathai, although the locals seem to love it.

Victoria on Vancouver Island was almost two hours distant by car and car ferry, so for a day-trip we opted for the half-hour jump by helicopter over the island-dotted Strait of Georgia. Victoria is a tourist city—clean, charming, a little tacky, and dull compared with vibrant Vancouver. However, the wooded mountainous beauty of Vancouver Island and the mild climate have made Victoria and the surrounding woods and islands a retirement and tourist center, attracting some two hundred thousand residents from all over Canada and the United States.

After touring the small city and its suburbs, our chauffeured limousine brought us to Butchart Gardens, thirteen miles from Victoria and one of the area's two not-to-be-missed sights. The fifty acres of gardens, begun in 1904, feature a world-famous deep sunken garden that magically transforms a former gravel pit and is so overwhelming as to be called "the outstanding showplace of the Pacific Northwest." The grounds also include a rose garden, Japanese garden, and formal Italian garden as well as restaurant, greenhouse, and gift shop, together drawing some ten thousand visitors per day including almost every passenger on the cruise ships that stop at Victoria on their way to or from Alaska.

The cliché about Victoria is that it is "more English than England," and the English tea with appropriate snacks served at the Empress Hotel is always cited as proof. The restored landmark hotel should be seen by all visitors, but be forewarned, as we were, and skip the mob scene at tea. *Fodor's Guide* calls the formal dining room of the Empress, which has entertainment and is only open for dinner, "the gem of elegant dining in the West," which I suspect is an oxymoron. The crowded Bengal Room, serving a curry lunch, oozes North Indian atmosphere and is almost as jammed as the lobby where the tea is served.

Fleeing the crowds, we headed to Don Mee, a large Cantonese restaurant where excellent dim sum (snack-sized offerings) were presented and served from rolling trolleys to a mixed clientele of Orientals and non-Orientals.

The next morning found us wafting 180 miles north in a well-worn, single-engine, four-seat Cessna floatplane to North Pacific Springs (NPS), a floating sport-fishing lodge tied to an island in the Inland Passage to Alaska. This thirteen-room fish camp is moved two or three times each season by tug, following the best fishing. The views from our chartered plane of mountains, forests, fjords, and sea along this popular cruise-ship route were themselves worth the cost of our two-day excursion. An anomaly we flew over were the many fish-farm pens of Atlantic salmon *(Salmo salar)*. In addition to twin-bedded rooms with private baths and showers, NPS boasted a rustic communal-style dining room, large lounge with twenty-four-hour self-serve bar (no extra charge for liquor or wine), and a smaller lounge with VCR. Meals were good for a camp, the highlight being all the just-caught Dungeness crab wanted at lunch each day.

At NPS the idea seemed to be to stuff as much fun (fishing) as possible into each day. Guests were roused from bed at 4 A.M. for a hearty breakfast, on the water by 4:40, and trolling herring with downriggers by 5. Lunch back at the lodge ran from about 11:40 A.M. to 1 P.M., before returning to the water until 5. Cocktails were at 5:30, dinner at 6. Mary and I fell into bed at 8:15, while other guests went fishing for giant haddock after dinner and then, encouraged by "free" booze, partied to 1 A.M. What stamina!

All the other guests were at NPS for a week, compared to our two days. Generally, there were two fisher-people to each boat. Some had paid a supplement to have a guide; some had not. Our twenty-three-year-old guide had eleven years' experience. We refused to let him touch our rods and were soon setting the downriggers and other gear ourselves. This contrasted to the other guided boats where the paying guests were all but superfluous as guides set all lines, hooked the fish, and then handed the rod to the "fisherman."

The tranquil, magnificent setting of the lodge and of areas we fished consisted of water, rock islands covered with evergreens, and distant mountains. Twice, cruise ships passed on their way up the Inland Passage to Alaska. The most common birds were bald eagles, which perched in nearby trees as we fished, begging handouts. Pods of killer whales frolicked nearby, and a sea lion amused himself by tossing and retrieving a fish he had caught. Weather was generally good, but cool on the water in the early morning.

Reels were direct drive, like large fly reels. Bait was trolled from twenty-five to eighty-five feet deep. We lost eight or nine fish by refusing our guide's assistance, but after getting the knack, landed chinook to twenty-five pounds as well as sockeye, coho, and pink salmon, scoring the highest average daily catch.

Finding the fishing slow our second afternoon, we took a break and wound our way through scattered islands to an abandoned Indian village, gloomy with its ancient totem pole and weathered cedar buildings. Other possible diversions from salmon fishing included fly-in trout fishing at wilderness lakes and flight-seeing the Coastal Mountain Range to view and photograph ice fields and glaciers, waterfalls, and deep fjords.

A large twin Otter float plane returned us to Vancouver where we retrieved our rental car and drove to Seattle, checking into that city's Four Seasons Hotel. Although agreeable enough, it had less sumptuous accommodations and poorer service than Vancouver's Four Seasons.

Metropolitan Grill is located in a former bank in Seattle's financial district and is reputed to have the town's best steak, which is what Mary wanted after our recent surfeit of seafood. Her bone-in Delmonico was tasty, huge, and properly done, as were my twin double-thick lamb chops.

Being food market aficionados, the next morning found us at Seattle's Pike Place Market featuring attractive displays of seafood such as Manila clams, scallops, squid, mussels, oysters, geoduck clams, salmon, haddock, ling cod, Dungeness crab, and prawns. Fruit and vegetable stalls completed the array along with unfortunate tacky gift and craft stalls. On the brighter side were appealing delicatessens, restaurants, and snack stands, one of which even served Chinese dumplings.

After Vancouver, Seattle was a disappointment since flight to the suburbs has left a ravaged but rebuilding downtown. Although its metropolitan area as a whole may be prosperous, the central city was not very appealing.

Ray's Boat House, perhaps the city's best-known seafood restaurant, served us a fine lunch of steamed Manila clams, salmon, and haddock. Neither Ray's nor any other seafood restaurant of our trip did anything, however, to shake our conviction that Detroit is blessed with the best seafood restaurant in North America—Joe Muer's. Professional courtesy precludes a description of our last dinner of the trip, at Seattle's Café Sport.

No-Shows

Fine restaurants consider a reservation as a contract—the restaurant promises to have a table available and the patron promises to occupy that table. An empty table at The Lark generally indicates a "no-show"—a coarse person who failed to honor a reservation.

No-shows, if not controlled by an effective avoidance program, can run as high as 30 percent of reservations. Larger restaurants know from their individual experience what to expect and, like airlines, overbook accordingly. Their continuous turnover of tables and numerous walk-ins without reservations minimize the problem. Fine small restaurants, however, can only book the number of tables they have, and one no-show can mean operating at a loss that evening.

The Lark's no-show program is unique in the industry and has been reported in several trade publications, including the magazine of the National Restaurant Association. Reservations are not given without obtaining both a home and office phone number, and all reservations are reconfirmed. As an additional safeguard, a credit card number is required of parties of more than four and from out-of-town visitors. By these precautions, no-shows have been reduced to about 1 percent, which still creates a loss of more than ten thousand dollars per year.

André Soltner, the former chef-proprietor of New York's famous Lutèce, called no-shows at 3 A.M. to ask if they were still coming. We prefer to send a card that reminds the no-show, "You failed to honor your confirmed dinner reservation" and that this behavior: "(1) caused a loss to our restaurant; (2) deprived customers on our waiting list of the opportunity to dine here; (3) in effect, took money from —————, your assigned waitperson, who is dependent on gratuities to support his/her family. Obviously, you will not be given any reservations in the future."

The Caymus Caper

Some of our practices are a reaction to irritations endured at other restaurants before opening The Lark. For example, our carte blanche dessert policy resulted from Mary being charged double after asking for a small slice of two pastries at a Southfield, Michigan, eatery. Requests for a single glass of wine at French restaurants in Manhattan brought European jug wine at unconscionable ten-time markups. This inspired our introduction of the Cruvinet wine system to Michigan, making feasible the sale of fine wines by the glass. That in turn led to the invention of a "wine bouquet," a package of fine wines designed to accompany the various dinner courses.

Plagued or blessed with an inbred drive to improve, we have inexorably upgraded our wines by the glass culminating in such anomalies as Bollinger Special Cuvée Champagne, Ch. La Louvière

Bordeaux Blanc, and Vieux Télégraph Châteauneuf du Pape—rare, exceptional wines offered by the glass.

What we think of as "the Caymus Caper" began as an insider joke—adopting one of California's most famous Cabernets as a house "pour" wine. When guests asked for "a glass of Cabernet," know it or not, they received a glass of the finest. None of this makes economic sense. While house wines are typically low in cost and high in markup, this is impossible when our cost is two-and-one-half to three times the industry average. *À votre santé!*

Chicago

*O*ur willingness to sacrifice ourselves searching out good food is becoming famous. Noted novelist, screenwriter, essayist, and poet Jim Harrison wrote us after our mission to New York:

"I was a bit startled by your newsletter. Way off in the future, perhaps fifty years from now, when you decide to cash in your chips, you might very well will your bodies to the University of Michigan Medical School so they can figure out how you were able to stomach that New York trip. You have my admiration."

Indeed, Mary and I had such a grand time in New York in October that we drove to Chicago in November. Yet more willing sacrifice—for science.

My *Condé Nast Traveler* "Readers' Poll" booklet listed the Four Seasons Hotel Chicago as the best in the Midwest and the Ritz Carlton Chicago in second place, so I fought victoriously to reserve a suite at the Four Seasons. Subsequently, I got around to reading a new issue of *Condé Nast Traveler* and learned that the latest poll reversed its rankings, with The Ritz Carlton first in Chicago and third in the

United States and the Four Seasons second in Chicago and fourth in the United States. Ownership of the Four Seasons and Ritz Carlton has now merged and together they comprise fifteen of the twenty-five top-rated U.S. hotels. In any event, the Four Seasons was very good and also well located on Michigan Avenue in the center of the fine restaurant and shopping area. Our rooms had dramatic views of many landmark buildings, and Lake Michigan and the lakefront.

Chicago, of course, is much loved by Detroiters as a convenient destination with enough good sights, shops, restaurants, and hotels for an enjoyable short vacation. It is most important, however, as the temporary home of number-three son Kurt Karl Lark, a resident in ophthalmology at the hospital of the University of Illinois Chicago, and his delightful friend, Becky Long, a resident in internal medicine at the hospital of the University of Chicago. They proved willing accomplices in some of our dining forays, allowing us to sample a wider variety of vittles than would otherwise have been possible—even for us.

We've learned that if you intend to dine in your hotel, the best time to do so is the evening of arrival, thus avoiding more travel on an already travel-filled day. So Sunday evening found us seated in considerable luxury at the hotel's eponymously named Seasons dining room. It is one of Chicago's top-rated restaurants, with high marks for cuisine, decor, and service. It also has a superb selection of American wines, like the unfiltered Newton Chardonnay, Matanzas Creek Merlot and Journey Chardonnay, and the Leonetti Reserve Cabernet. Dinner was preceded by a unique experience—a complimentary tasting of apéritif wine vinegars made from traditional grapes such as Gewurztraminer and Sylvaner from Doctorenhof, a small wine estate in Germany's Palatinate. These very carefully crafted vinegars are intended to "stimulate the appetite, sensitize the taste buds and neutralize the palate for the upcoming meal." I'm not sure about that, but they were very tasty and dramatically served in long and elegant hand-blown, artistically painted bottles. The hope is to promote vinegar as a trendy drink.

Mary began with a perfect crab cake, crisp on the outside with a tender interior of blue crab and shiitake mushrooms accompanied by charred pumpkin chutney and roasted bell pepper oil. My dramatic starter was sliced medium-rare-to-rare Sonoma Valley squab breast with figs, served over mixed greens with orange blossom vinegar and a circle of foie gras on the side. A large seared sea scallop on a lobster pancake was an equally good complementary second appetizer. Roasted Colorado lamb rack with potato peppercorn gnocchi followed for Mary, missing the promised eggplant olive fritters accompaniment. If any menu lists a dish I've never had, I usually order it, as was the case here. Thus came my braised Iowa ham hock with sweetbread stuffing, turnip-potato risotto and roasted marrow bone. This proved to be a circle of the outer shell of the ham hock wrapped around the sweetbread with a little ham. Although a trifle salty, I loved it, as did Mary. We shared tastes, as usual. Plates here were not heated, and warm dishes were not warm enough. Desserts are not a strong point, the best dessert being a warm chocolate soufflé cake with hazelnut, caramel, and coffee ice creams.

217

Chicago's top *Zagat*-rated seafood restaurant is Nick's Fishmarket, followed closely by Shaw's Crab House and then the Cape Cod Room of the Drake Hotel. We found Nick's Fishmarket to have a comfortable clubby ambience and were ensconced for lunch in a large maroon-leather corner booth. The small traditional menu held no surprises, but we were very pleased to find the first stone crabs of the season, which we both chose as our first course. One claw of Mary's serving was "off," and it was cheerfully replaced. The rest were sweet and delicious. Mary's cold lobster salad, which overflowed the Maine lobster shells, was garnished with artichoke hearts and accompanied by a fine potato salad. My large whole Dover sole, boned tableside, was barely lukewarm and should have been served on a hot plate. Our wine was the now impossible to obtain 1993 Beringer Private Reserve Chardonnay, which has mellowed into a great wine in the last few months. We enjoyed lunch, but the larger dinner menu would be even more appealing.

The Four Seasons Hotel is conveniently (or dangerously) located atop the Chicago branch of Bloomingdale's. Mary foraged there between meals and other outside excursions. Since the first two evenings of our trip fell on Sunday and Monday, days many top restaurants are closed, dining for those two evenings was restricted to hotel dining rooms. Not that we suffered, for if Seasons had been very good, The Dining Room of The Ritz Carlton was superb. The setting was opulent: rich wood paneling, a forest of crystal chandeliers, and a large, soft-upholstered, raised booth. Thirty-one-year-old Chef Sarah Stegner, who has been at The Ritz for twelve years, was named the James Beard Foundation "Rising Star Chef of the Year for 1994" and Pastry Chef Sabastien Canonne the "1995 Champagne Taittinger Pastry Chef of the Year."

Sarah kindly came to the table, introduced herself, and asked if we would like to have the special menu she had planned for us. Well, Mother Lark didn't raise any fools, so we gave Sarah free reign. Our perfect caviar "parfait" starter had fresh ossetra caviar and *crème fraîche* over creamy eggs and tender onions, all atop a small bowl of shaved ice. This was accompanied by silver-dollar-sized blini. The evening continued magically with sautéed duck liver served on a duck *confit* "cake" with toasted brioche drizzled with truffle oil. Our wine was the extraordinary Château Montelena Napa Cabernet in the 1991 vintage, the only year equal to its great 1987.

One of Sarah's staff is Mike Burns, an alumnus of The Lark with an obvious knack for finding top kitchens. Mike came in on his day off to see us and to prepare our next course of squash and leek ravioli with black trumpet mushrooms, while Sarah sautéed salmon with potato-hazelnut purée, carrot, and parsley sauce with a petite herb salad. Mary and I shared these two exciting dishes. Mary's main course was a tender pink veal chop in a mustard herb crust with braised leeks, apples, and acorn squash. I savored a venison steak with potato-celery root terrine and thyme-honey marinated pearl onions. We had a little cheese from the very proper cheese trolley, saving ourselves (a little late for that) for desserts to follow. First a crisp coconut *tuile* filled with vanilla ice cream, fruits, and berries garnished with quenelles of ginger ice cream. Next chocolate obsession for two served on a big marble slab—opera cake, and a honey-wheat *tuile.* The grand finale (pun) was a hot Grand Marnier Soufflé. Chef Sarah is a charming and immensely talented professional and deserves any and every honor she may receive.

Few Chicago restaurants have received more national exposure than Rick Bayless's two Mexican knockoffs—ultraplain Frontera Grill and the adjoining slightly more upscale Topolabampo. Frankly, we were as puzzled here as at Jean-Louis at Watergate in Washington, D.C. Visions of the emperor's clothes danced in our head. Maybe we've been spoiled by thirty-some trips south of the border, but the highlight of our lunch was the complimentary guacamole—well seasoned and chunky the way we like it—not a bowl of mush. I had been looking forward with anticipation to finally trying *huitlacoche,* the fungus that grows on corn. And, although crêpes *de huitlacoche* were the first item on the menu, our waitress said they had nada. As a consolation to myself I ordered Pato en Mole de Calabaza: "Muscovy duck (grilled breast, braised leg) with rich mole of chili ancho, Mexican pumpkin and sweet spices." I've long-treasured memories of a wonderfully hot but deeply flavorful mole experienced at a roadside restaurant named Cabo Kennedy, south of Oaxaca on the way to Tehuantepec. Topolabampo's version was so bland I asked for hot sauce to add. I was brought an ounce or so of what I was warned was an extremely hot sauce made from habanero chiles. Habaneros are the fiercest chile, many times hotter than jalapeños. After a very cautious taste, I dumped the whole container into my mole, and it was still bland. *Que pasa?*

One of the glories of Chicago is the John G. Shedd Aquarium, the world's largest aquarium, unless recently supplanted. Budget close to two hours and include the dolphin show at the oceanarium. One of our favorite critters was a beluga whale, which stayed where we leaned over the wall of its tank and seemed to give us special attention, demonstrating how he or she could spout like a drinking fountain. Perhaps it appreciated our applause.

Our favorite Chicago restaurants from previous trips were, of course, Le Français, where our Chef Marcus had worked with Chef-Proprietor Jean Bancet, and Ambria. We would not have dined at either on this too-brief visit, needing instead to try new venues, but Kurt requested a dinner at Ambria, the most popular restaurant in the Chicago area according to the *Zagat Survey.*

My notes and memories of this visit to Ambria are that it has either slipped a lot or was having a very off day. Service was extremely slow and the food only average. Vegetables were very poor in contrast to The Dining Room of The Ritz Carlton, where even the vegetables were exceptional. Our best dishes were a starter of roasted sweetbreads with langoustines and port-shallot jus and a main course of veal tenderloin with a fricassee of wild mushrooms and stuffed onions.

We worked up an appetite for lunch on Wednesday, our last day in Chicago, with another excursion to by-now-familiar Bloomingdale's. I was able to order another Italian tuxedo (my third) at a 30 percent discount. Continuing this Italian motif, we lunched at Spiaggia, which vies with Gabriel's as Chicago's top Italian eatery. We loved Spiaggia. The cheerful room is lavish with Italian marble and our window-side table overlooked Oak Street Beach. Service, supervised by assistant maître d' Gianni Toffanello, was perfect, attentive, yet professional. Our wine was the great 1990 Castello dei Rampolla Sammarco, a "Super Tuscan." Like most of the best wines mentioned in our travels, it is listed on the reserve list at The Lark.

Chef Paul Bartolatto created our special menu, which began with Mediterranean red mullet *(rouget)*, pan-fried in a polenta crust and served with a light mayonnaise and mixed greens. Next came a seared sea scallop with porcini mushrooms and white truffle oil, topped with one large shaving of the best *parmigiano reggiano*. Our meal of perfect ambience, food, wine, and service continued with three pasta samplings: tortellini of turkey, pork, and *mortadella* in chicken broth; ricotta-cheese-filled ravioli with a light cream sauce and beef glaze; and a seafood rissoto with a light tomato sauce. Our seafood course was plump and tender mussels in a white bean soup with tiny cubes of ham. I now guessed our main course would be fowl or game and was right on both counts, as we were served tender breast of guinea hen in a flavorful Chianti sauce with porcini mushrooms and braised Brussels sprouts (Mary's favorite vegetable). I am almost embarrassed to list our desserts, of which there were five. First a chocolate *semi-freddo* with coffee ice cream and chocolate sauce; followed by *babas au rhum* with orange segments and orange sauce; mascarpone cheese-cake with chocolate ice cream; an apple tart with vanilla ice cream; and a finale of three sorbets.

We could not fault any of the food at Spiaggia, and it is very difficult to prepare so many and varied dishes so perfectly as to please critics such as Mary and me. Readers should know that there is a more informal restaurant under the same ownership nearby named Café Spiaggia, which I have no doubt is very good, but I'd recommend going for the gusto as we did and reserve at Spiaggia.

Trio, located north of Chicago in Evanston, is a small and intimate restaurant, where we were served a variety of courses in or on a bewildering assortment of offbeat vessels or slabs. These included duck *confit* over green dumplings with squash purée; crayfish and mascarpone wontons with chanterelles and leeks; grilled shrimp with *pancetta* and four different *aiolis* served on a marble slab; an oyster with Bloody Mary sauce served in a raised soap holder; warm lobster with garlic mashed potatoes in a glass; hazelnut-crusted rack of lamb; applewood smoked tenderloin of beef; a triple banana *marquise* on a mirror; brownie sundae in a cup; and a passion fruit chocolate truffle. Obviously the cuisine of Trio as well as its presentation is inventive— meant to startle and amuse. Since many diners have indifferent taste buds at best, this can work very well, even when the food itself is not exceptional apart from presentation.

This was the last supper of this adventure, which hit many gastronomical highlights in a mere three and a half days. Because number-three son Kurt and friend Becky are residents in Chicago, we hope to return often, revisiting old favorites such as Le Français and new favorites like The Dining Room of The Ritz Carlton, Spiaggia, and Seasons. We'll also dine at Everest, of which we've heard such praise, and their Chef Jean Joho's new Brasserie Jo. Others on our list are Arun's, Gabriel's, Yoshi's Café, and Charlie Trotter's.

A Garden of Dreams

A restaurant's success or failure is determined by its ambience, service, and cuisine, and the order of importance is as given—ambience, service, and then cuisine. Most new restaurants concentrate on concept and decor (ambience) and eventually fail because of poor execution (service and cuisine). While The Lark is noted for its service and cuisine, Mary has also created a magical ambience. She is up and about and at the farmers' market by 6:30 A.M. many mornings, buying the best and freshest flowers at reasonable prices. Even more impressive are the flowers for cutting, which she grows on the grounds of The Lark. Boggling the mind further, Mary not only has blooms flown to us from Belgium, but is the only restaurateur importing exotic florals from Maui. In addition, of course, she grows orchids in her greenhouse and transports them to our dining room when in bloom. As a result, The Lark has been chosen as Michigan's most romantic restaurant over and over again by the readers of various publications. An important part of this romance is our walled garden, which seems almost a part of the dining room as viewed through an entire wall of windows.

Features include an imported stone fountain with spouting lion's head and Pewabic tile frogs; beds of herbs and vegetables divided by flat stone paths; ivy-covered brick walls; dramatic tall, thin, skyrocket juniper; white-plastered columns supporting a timbered arbor heavy with grapes; flowers and herbs in stone, clay, and Chinese pots; and masses of colorful flowers ranging from simple marigolds to lady slippers. Goldfinch, purple finch, and mourning doves are resident. Outdoor tables are available for cocktails and hors d'oeuvres, coffee and dessert, or even dinner.

Pomposity

Pomposity is the disease of a fine restaurateur. If he is competent and successful, compliments are showered upon him. If very successful, more patrons wish reservations than there are tables available, and he is wooed like a beautiful woman. He will easily meet and talk to more famous people in a week than the average person would in a lifetime. When he dines out or travels, professional courtesy results in the finest service and the best accommodations. After months and years of such treatment, he may come to accept all this as justified and fitting. If accused of being pompous, he might well respond as in the old joke, "Pompous! *Moi?*"

Pomposity by the proprietor effects the whole restaurant. Waiters and especially maître d's ape the attitude. A general feeling spreads through the staff that the restaurant is doing their guests a favor rather than the reverse. Celebrities are treated differently than non-celebrities. New customers are not treated nearly as well as regulars. A Siberia is created in which the young, old, less affluent, or less well-known are assigned tables. Unlisted preparations are offered to the privileged few. A pompous style of service may be affected—rife with tableside cooking and dishes served on napkins. The menu may be in French or Franglais. The Lark has been successful enough that we have been subjected to some of the blandishments noted above, which we lap up. But the good-old-boys with whom we hunt, fish, play poker, and cook chili keep our ego pretty well punctured with their caustic comments. If we succumb and become pompous, however, please tell *moi*!

*L*ying in bed, I looked out the window through an open grove of mature oaks to Lake Michigan with Beaver Island on the horizon and the white lighthouse on Ile aux Galets in the middle distance. Goldfinch and grosbeak sampled the three bird feeders on the oaks, while grey squirrels policed the ground below. Since it was morning, the gulls over the lake flew from right to left, or north to south, toward Harbor Springs and Petoskey. They would return at sunset, drifting north to the Beaver Island archipelago. We would see that passage also, since almost everyone on M119, between Harbor Springs and Cross Village, makes a point to pause and enjoy the daily wonder of sunset over Lake Michigan. M119, or Shore Drive, is a two-lane asphalt road through the woods on the bluff overlooking Lake Michigan. It's been dubbed "the tunnel of trees" and voted Michigan's most scenic highway by the readers of both *Michigan Living, Traverse Magazine,* and the *Detroit News.*

Michiganders have always known they had something very special in their hundreds of miles of Great Lakes shoreline, thousands of inland lakes, hundreds of rivers and streams, and thousands of square miles of unspoiled forests and fields. The concept of "Up North" is magical to residents of various New England and northern Midwest states, but none equal Michigan. Locales "Back East" with much less to offer receive redundant praise. But that's for the best, keeping our Up North relatively unspoiled and uncrowded.

Periodically, we're made nervous, however, when a media spotlight focuses on northern Michigan. Fortunately, it has always swept back to the usual overexposed tourist destinations. A few years ago, *Town & Country* carried a glowing report on what it called Michigan's Gold Coast, the northwest part of the Lower Peninsula. No permanent damage was done, as much of its sophisticated readership already knew the glories of Charlevoix and Harbor Springs. But then, *W* (of fashion fame) featured a glowing special section on the Lower Peninsula's Lake Michigan coast. Naturally, the piece was written from a Chicago point of view. It was reasonably informative and accurate on attractions on Michigan's southern coast close to Chicago, but fell apart as it went north, thank God! Also, thank God there is no expressway up this coast from Chicago.

My own involvement Up North has roots in French-Canadian ancestors and childhood summers spent on a remote island in Lake Huron's Georgian Bay. Our log cabin was built by Ojibway Indians for seven hundred dollars. There was no electricity or plumbing, just kerosene stove and lanterns, water pumped by hand from the bay, and an outhouse. The environment was stark and beautiful: water, rock islands, evergreens, blueberry bushes, ground cover, and the sky— nothing else. Each day passed like any other, exploring the woods or catching fish and gathering the blueberries that were a great part of our diet.

After the island was sold, northern vacations were spent at Manitoulin Island, Burt Lake, Mullet Lake, Lake Charlevoix, the Leelanau Peninsula, and near Harbor Springs and Petoskey. We would enjoy mushroom hunting, woodcock, partridge, and turkey hunting, fishing, and foraging.

Mary and I were at our lodge in the northwest part of Michigan's Lower Peninsula, which we were "forced" to purchase when we ran out of rental digs that would permit our black Lab. We had always rented, fearing ownership of a place Up North might limit our world travels. But one rental spot after another banned dogs, and real estate prices zoomed to as much as six thousand dollars per front foot for Lake Michigan shoreline. Faced with now or never, we took the plunge and purchased a home on North Lakeshore Drive. This wide single-story home with a fieldstone and elm-bark exterior is actually fourteen miles up the coast from Harbor Springs near Good Hart. The view of Lake Michigan and Beaver Island on the horizon is awesome. Please note that all of Emmett County has only six traffic lights! Purchase of this property, however, did not signal imminent retirement, nor does it provide more than temporary hiatuses in our travels.

Our supposed goal on some stays is to pick wild morels and leeks for The Lark, but we'll grab any excuse to drive Up North. The morels in recent springs have been spotty. Some foragers do very well. We do fair. Mary feels we've "lost it" after twenty-some annual excursions. I suspect we never "had it," and our best scores were actually made by our children. In any event, moreling for us is only the excuse that leads into Michigan's magical spring woods, when the ground is carpeted by wildflowers. We were also charmed by sightings of deer, fox, skunks, rabbits, raccoons, red fox, and grey squirrels, ruffed grouse, wild turkeys, ravens, and many song birds. Lately, we even see black bear and coyote.

Up North seems to provide more dining pleasure than "Down Below," but that may be attributed to our temporary life of leisure and holiday mood. We, of course, eat at our old favorite restaurants. The Crow's Nest in Cross Village for superb pan-fried walleye and rack of baby lamb with chutney; Dam Site Inn in Pellston for a world-class chicken dinner; funky Cunningham's and Darrow's in Mackinaw City for roadfood such as chicken and biscuits and local walleye, whitefish, and perch; The New York in Harbor Springs, the most charming of Michigan's resort towns, where standouts include veal and shiitake mushrooms over pasta and boneless pork loin stuffed with cranberries; and Stafford's Bay View Inn just north of Petoskey for a bountiful Sunday brunch with Stafford Smith himself manning the griddle.

A recent addition to both the golfing and dining scene is Little Traverse Bay Golf Club Restaurant and Bar, located on high hills above Harbor Springs. Its dining room has the best views of the coast with mesmerizing panoramas of the golf course itself, forested hills, Little Traverse Bay, and distant Lake Michigan. Its food, which was good on opening, has improved a lot, and that food, together with fine service and unmatched ambience, combine to create a unique dining experience that should not be missed. Golden brown perch, a bountiful seafood pasta, bouillabaisse, and a special of two honey-glazed seven-ounce boneless grilled pork chops were all fresh, good, and properly prepared.

Another new golf course with a fine restaurant is Charlevoix Golf & Country Club, north of Charlevoix on the west side of U.S. 31. Huge ceiling beams and trusses in the dramatic clubhouse inspired the name Mahogany for the well-appointed main dining room with a massive stone fireplace and unimpeded view of the golf course. Chef de Cuisine Kevin Dunn produced a memorable dinner that included large ravioli with eight varieties of wild mushrooms; veal *mialander schnitzel* in a Parmesan cheese crust with a lemon and caper sauce with *spatzel,* the finest *schnitzel* I have ever tasted, and my first chef at The Lark was Viennese; and a toothsome osso buco of tender braised veal shank with a garlic, mushroom, and tomato sauce served over pasta. My *crème brûlée* made a fitting finale, but was outshone by Mary's special dessert, which included fresh strawberries, ice cream, and liqueurs. Service at Mahogany is attentive. Ninety-one wine selections on the regular and reserve lists include a good choice of Cabernet Sauvignons, Chardonnays, and champagnes.

We'd had good reports on Andante, which opened a couple of years ago as Petoskey's only upscale restaurant. We finally got there accompanied by Mike and Linda McElroy, host and chef, respectively, and owners of the very popular Crow's Nest. Despite Andante's location in a charming old building in downtown Petoskey, this small, relaxed, nonsmoking spot has views of the town harbor and lighthouse. We especially enjoyed Acadian peppered shrimp on crisp polenta with a white wine butter sauce; three char-grilled semiboneless breasts of quail with a cherry-gooseberry glaze; grilled pork tenderloin with a hard cider sauce; and grilled rack of lamb with a warm garlic and mint balsamic vinegar vinaigrette.

As if all of the above described self-indulgence were not enough, we had one of our best Up North meals ever at The Rowe in Ellsworth, on a lake south of Charlevoix. Warm, woodsy-tasting pecan-stuffed morels were arranged upright in a cluster, evoking their typical appearance in the woods. A wild rice and morel soup was a perfect balance of complementary flavors. My rack of lamb with an apricot-ginger sauce worked very well, the tang of the sauce offsetting the tender richness of the tiny chops. Mary, who "doesn't even like trout," loved her almost-impossible-to-obtain brown trout, stuffed with shrimp and leeks, and served with a fresh sorrel sauce. The Rowe has always been very close to our hearts and was one of the favorite restaurants that inspired The Lark. We are happy to see that its cuisine has endured under Chef Kathy Ruis. Its wine list is of the two finest in the state. Proprietor Wes Westhoven doesn't just serve dinners, he creates memories.

Having dined at The Rowe in Ellsworth and Andante in Petoskey, we completed the big three with a fine dinner at Tapawingo, down the road from The Rowe. A few of the fine dishes served to our table were shiitake mushrooms, snap peas, and jicama and peppers in a crisp spring roll with seared sea scallops and plum sauce; boned quail marinated with herbs, brandy, and mustard, char-grilled and served with brown and wild rice pilaf, roasted corn and pepper sauce, and thin chili-dusted onion rings; and an individual pastry shell filled with silky chocolate, toasted pecans, and a broiled caramelized coconut-top crust, accompanied by house-made caramel-pecan ice cream.

Accompanied by wives Anne and Mary, brother Larry and I

made a voyage into the past by lunching at Hack-Ma-Tack Inn at Mullet Lake on the Inland Waterway that begins at Lake Huron and winds through rivers and lakes. We had simple but very good barbecued beef sandwiches and hope to return soon to sample the appealing dinner menu.

Larry and I had stayed here in our early teens when an illegal slot machine was hidden behind a cedar-log wall. This beautiful log structure on the water reeks with northwoods ambience, greatly enhanced by hunting and fishing art constructions by Mort Fadum III, two of whose works also grace The Lark—one at the head of the circular stairs to the wine cellar and one in the wine cellar itself.

Another voyage into the past was dinner at the Argonne, north of Charlevoix. Once a true roadhouse with great atmosphere, it has regrettably been yuppified in an ultrabland manner and retains no feeling of Up North. We did enjoy the food, most especially the long-featured steamed and fried shrimp combination, available at varied prices for either six, eight, ten, or sixteen large shrimp, or all you can eat.

Labor Day found Mary and me, together with Mike and Linda McElroy, gathered in the predawn darkness at the Upper Peninsula end of the mighty Mackinac Bridge. At 7 A.M., we followed Governor John Engler across the bridge on the Annual Mackinac Bridge Walk. The five-mile walk was not much of a workout, since the crowd prevented a brisk pace. It was a jolly group that enjoyed the sunrise and crisp air, many of whom later had a truck-stop style breakfast at Cunningham's in Mackinaw City, as we did.

We look forward to our trips Up North and, as usual, break the drive with lunch at either the Sugar Bowl in Gaylord (ask for a table in the bar), Iva's old-fashioned chicken restaurant in Sterling, or a new favorite, Austrian-chef-owned Hermann's at Cadillac. During the many years of renting condos Up North, the best were Windward, one and one-half miles north of Harbor Springs, and Sunset Shores on Little Traverse Bay in Petoskey. Rentals may be arranged with a simple phone call to Garber Realty.

Morel Mania

May is morel month in Michigan's fields and forests. Each year Mary and I and whatever offspring are available mount an expedition to the Harbor Springs area to replenish our supply of morels. Years ago we had the woods to ourselves. Since morels have become very "in," moreling has mushroomed. Hunting for morels has the appeal of all foraging—the thrill of finding and gathering one's own food, which makes its preparation and enjoyment very special. But, as with hunting and fishing, the greatest reward is the natural setting, in this case, Michigan's woods aglow with spring wildflowers.

Going First Class

While attending Georgetown Law School in the 1950s, I and six other future lawyers leased the elegant and historic District of Columbia home of the then-appointive governor of Alaska as our pad. Eighty-five dollars per person per month had to cover rent, utilities, household supplies, and food. We rotated the Saturday morning chore of food shopping for the coming week. Bill Wahl from Kansas invariably purchased steak and other costly fodder, citing his motto, "It only costs a little more to go first class." As a result, food ran out on Wednesday and canned corn and one-slice bologna sandwiches were our fare for the balance of the week.

We know at The Lark that it costs more than a little more to go first class. But like Bill Wahl, we are committed to the best. This dedication manifests itself in myriad ways, most of which are unknown and would never occur to guests. A few of scores of possible examples are the use of Guernsey (not Holstein) dairy products, fresh strained (not canned, cooked, and salted) tomatoes, Caribbean white (not brown) shrimp, live Maine (not frozen) lobsters, prime (not choice) meat, and extra-virgin (not virgin or "pure") olive oil. Our bar Scotch is Dewar's White Label; the bourbon pour brand is Maker's Mark. A periodic irritant is the on-and-off availability of Boissiere French Dry Vermouth, which is incredibly superior to any other brand. All this is your fault, Bill Wahl.

By Mary Lark

*T*he Upper Mississippi Valley has always been special to me because my mother and father were from there, and I spent several childhood vacations on the river's banks. Having decided on a nostalgic visit in May, I left Jim and daughter Adrian in charge of The Lark and headed west in a comfortable Chevy Suburban, accompanied by my sister Joan and her husband, Ron Steinmayer. Joan and I decided where to stop; Ron was our "chauffeur."

We left early to avoid the worst of Chicago traffic and arrived at the Wisconsin Dells shortly after noon. Familiar with limited lodging choices from a previous trip, we checked into the Holiday Inn, reliable and unremarkable. We soon discovered there were several attractive new hotels and motels, which surprised us until we learned the reason. About twenty minutes from the Dells, south of I-75 on Highway 12 before Baraboo, is the huge new Ho Chunk Indian Gambling Casino. Many new businesses were being rushed to com-

233

pletion before the summer season, giving the area the resemblance of a miniature Myrtle Beach with new hotels and motels, every fast food restaurant possible, golf courses, putt-putts, superslides, go-carts, and so on, stretching from the Dells to the casino. Will anyone ever want to hike or take a boat ride to see the beautiful rock formations of the Dells now?

Our only activity at this stop was a visit to an old favorite, Parsons Indian Trading Post on Highway 12 in Lake Denton. Beyond the left entrance door is a vast room of Indian art and artifacts. A museum of authentic old Indian art is displayed in showcases along the walls—everything from clothing to war implements and housewares. Tons of newer Indian-made goods for sale are piled on counters in the center of the room. But, if you are really a collector, ask to see the treasures locked away in trunks behind the counters—museum-quality works, expensive but beautifully made old pieces. Of course, we didn't leave empty-handed. I purchased a charming Navajo Yei rug decorated with eleven strolling maidens.

On the way to Baraboo, Wisconsin, the next morning, we passed the impressive Ho Chunk Casino. At 9 A.M. on a Monday in May its vast parking lot was packed! We were drawn to Baraboo because it is the home of the Circus World Museum. This museum was of particular interest to us because Joan's and my father, a commercial photographer with the Jam Handy organization for thirty-five years, had donated to it some of his work, which we had never seen. Scenically located on the Wisconsin River, this indoor and outdoor museum was the original winter quarters of the Ringling Brothers Circus from 1884 to 1918 and is a National Historic Monument. The Circus World Library and Research Center, a few blocks distant in Baraboo, is the largest circus archive in existence and did have many of my father's photos, slides, and a 16mm movie, *Behind the Big Top,* labeled "top priority." We were thrilled when told that they would try to make copies of this movie for Joan and me.

At La Crosse, Wisconsin, our next stop, we love to stay at the downtown Radisson Hotel with rooms facing the park on the Mississippi.

Old Granddad's Bluff, the river, and the rolling landscape make La Crosse a beautiful city. My aunt and uncle like to dine at the Freight House Restaurant, and so we did, enjoying very good roast beef.

My great-uncle George Satory (my maiden name) decorated scores of churches with painted frescos and was known as "The Michelangelo of the Midwest." A cousin was excited about a church he had discovered in Dyersville, Iowa, decorated by Uncle George and previously unknown to my family. Our cousin's video revealed frescos splendid enough to justify a day-long detour to Dyersville, whose claims to fame are its role as the setting for *The Field of Dreams* and as the home of Ertl Toys. The church did prove magnificent, but surprise, it was not the work of Uncle George. An easily accessible pamphlet attested to that fact. We assuaged our disappointment by purchasing fine toys at the Ertl factory.

Driving through the flat farmland of Iowa would have been boring without our audio book—Elmore Leonard's *Killshot,* which made it seem no time at all until we were back in lovely Minnesota at Lake City. We stay there because it is central to many wonderful small towns, and the Americana Hotel in Lake City has fine views of the great wide part of the Upper Mississippi known as Lake Pepin. The "Great River Road" along the Upper Mississippi around Lake Pepin, crossing at either Wabasha or Red Wing from Minnesota to Wisconsin, is one of America's great drives. The barges on the river, trains along its banks, great waterfowl populations and soaring eagles, all in a valley between bluffs, create a unique environment in which my parents grew up, and for which I envy them.

In La Crosse, Ron, a certified collector of old paving bricks, found a stash where the old town had bordered the river. In Red Wing, a short distance north of Lake City, he again struck pay brick while Joan and I antiqued. Red Wing is an interesting old river town. I especially enjoyed seeing the huge kilns of the now closed Red Wing Pottery. In Red Wing one should only dine at the St. James Hotel. Most of our relatives were raised in Wabasha, the setting for the movie *Grumpy Old Men.* Perhaps that is why most left. We return for memories, to visit Joe Suilmann and his private museum, and to watch the river from the same banks our dad did.

We also drove to Kellogg, my mother's hometown, to chat with a cousin and visit the cemetery, but spent most of our time there at the shop of L.A.R.K. Toys. The name is a coincidence, but our grandchildren now enjoy toys incised with the family name. For two years we have watched the progress of the resident carver as he creates what will be the most magnificent hand-carved carousel imaginable. There is only one horse, the rest of the pieces ranging from a pelican to an eight-foot-high moose, each more charming than the next. My favorite is a bear running with a honey jar in his mouth, pursued by bustling little bees. Although costly, one can order similarly artful animals carved into rocking critters. All are charming, and each piece is registered and numbered. These unique treasures cost Grandma Lark a lot of money!

Most dining in the area is simple and good, but two establishments deserve special mention. Anderson House in Wabasha, Minnesota, is famous for its "room with a cat," referring to the option available to guests of having a cat stay in the room for the night. It also serves tasty meals in an appealing atmosphere. Breakfast is properly caloric and excellent. Crossing the river at Wabasha Bridge and heading north to Pepin, Wisconsin, we found another winner—Harbor View Café. Main course offerings from the creative chef included pheasant and veal sweetbreads. Unfortunately, it accepts no reservations and, even in the off-season, we waited forty-five minutes for a table. Pepin is the birthplace of Laura Ingalls Wilder, but there are really no other sites to fill one's waiting time.

The River Road on the Wisconsin side of the Mississippi is equally as beautiful as Minnesota's on the far bank, with many inviting small towns along the way. It evoked memories of the Lot River in southwest France. On another trip we'll explore the Amish country and plan to be around for the famous Eighty-Five-Mile Garage Sale. We couldn't understand why hotels were so full in the first week of May. The day we left we were told that visitors came from outstate to indulge themselves during the two designated days of eighty-five miles of garage sales around Lake Pepin. Leaving to dine at Mader's in Milwaukee that evening, we passed thousands of garage sale signs. We did stop once or twice.

Mader's is special—the best German restaurant I've ever dined at outside Germany. Ron and I had big tender pork shanks (not hocks) with sauerkraut, while Joan enjoyed her Kasseler Rippenspeer (smoked pork loin) with excellent red cabbage. The warm strudel for dessert was also the best I've had, even though the first chef of The Lark was from Vienna. The old German decor of Mader's is very authentic and contributes much to the great dining experience. Save a moment to peek at the gift shop upstairs.

The Upper Mississippi Valley is a pleasant change of pace from Up North in Michigan. The scenery is magnificent, the locals pleasant, the shopping appealing and different, and the food and lodging quite good.

Harrison in Esquire

Our country has plenty of good food journalists at both the local and national level. For some time, however, there have been no food writers of the stature of Waverly Root, Lucius Beebe, A. J. Liebling, or M. F. K. Fisher. But, to this bleak scene appeared Michigan's own Jim Harrison, an outstanding poet, novelist, essayist, and screenwriter. Following his food, travel, and hunting essays collected in *Just Before Dark*, Harrison briefly was the monthly food writer of *Esquire* magazine. Even though those pieces were only a part-time calling for this prolific author, they may be the best food writing done in America of late. Thus, our hearts were gladdened to have him write so highly of The Lark:

"In The Lark there is a curious amplitude and grace, warm colors and light spirits, which you identify with Europe at its best, rather than fine restaurants in New York and California, where self-consciousness can sodden the air and the help is straight out of *The Mikado*.... Since I entered The Lark in a fuchsia slump, I was caught off guard when a trolley of pâtés and oysters arrived. How gorgeous and direct with nothing, including my appetizer of pasta and fresh chanterelles, looking like it had been wrapped at Bloomingdale's.

"There is a moral stance here that reminds one of Robuchon's revolutionary notion that food should taste like itself, that it need not wear a wig and earrings. A roast Maine lobster with elephant-garlic hollandaise tastes real good, as does a copper cataplana of large, white gulf shrimp, clams, mussels, and chorizo, as does a veal chop with porcini mushrooms, as does the utterly prime beef and lamb and the Salzburger Nockerl Austrian soufflé. I drank a Dunn Howell Mountain Cabernet that was as good as those old, wonderful '68 Heitz Martha's Vineyards.... On either of the dream coasts ... [The Lark] would be an enchanting relief, like a warm rain after a good movie."

Zinfandel

The resurgence of red Zinfandel, several years ongoing in California and other hot wine markets, has only begun to surface in other locales. So popular in the 1950s, 1960s, and 1970s that twenty-six thousand acres of vines were planted in California, Zinfandel sales faded as interest shifted first to Cabernet Sauvignon and later to Merlot. The Lark's first wine list of June 1981 offered the outstanding 1978 vintage of Ridge Paso Robles Zinfandel. Popular demand prompted the addition of newly created "white" Zinfandel in May 1985. By 1987 there were no sales at The Lark of red Zinfandel, and it was removed from the list.

Zinfandel's origins were once shrouded in mystery, but Jancis

Robinson's *The Oxford Companion to Wine* declares that the application of DNA fingerprinting to vines in the early 1990s "irrefutably demonstrated that Zinfandel is one and the same as Primitivo of southern Italy." It is also beyond doubt that berry-tasting Zinfandel, in addition to its ubiquitous white Zinfandel blush version, can make outstanding lush red wines.

Wine guru Robert M. Parker Jr. said in the June 1995 issue of *The Wine Advocate*, "I am thrilled to see the renewed interest in high-quality Zinfandel, California's 'own' wine. Nothing like it is produced anywhere else in the world. Moreover, it is fairly priced and, most importantly, a wine of fun, pleasure, and exuberance."

Responding more to reports of red Zinfandel's resurgence than to actual demand by our patrons, we have judiciously acquired some of the finest bottlings, all but one of which are hidden on our reserve list. Knowing that demand in Michigan was still slack, we concentrated our purchases on what many consider to be the best Zinfandel—Ravenswood Winery of Sonoma. Parker says of Ravenswood and its proprietor, "If California is ever to realize its maximum potential for producing compelling wines, there will have to be more people with Joel Peterson's vision.... There is no fast-food processing wine approach at Ravenswood. All of the Zinfandels go into the bottle unfiltered.... The results are among the most individualistic, splendidly rich, and delicious wines made on earth."

Ravenswood produces a large quantity of Sonoma Zinfandel without vineyard designation, which is a fine, highly rated wine and readily available. Its glory, however, is the small quantities of single-vineyard-designated wines, and those are what we have cellared. Demand for these is so great that the Michigan distributor receives calls from other states attempting to purchase part of its small allotment.

In the Land of Ancho Chili–Kumquat Butter

On the Sunday when we held the annual Michigan Chili Cookoff at The Lark, Mary and I, together with Chef Marcus and his wife, Susan, rushed to the airport immediately after the awards ceremony to begin our vacations. Marcus and Susan were off to tour the restaurants of France; Mary and I flew to San Francisco and proceeded by rental car the next morning to the Sonoma and Napa wine country.

The wine areas of Sonoma County begin about a forty-five-minute drive north of San Francisco and stretch some fifty miles farther north. The Sonoma Valley itself, including the prestigious Carneros area, is in southern Sonoma County. The northern viticulture areas of Sonoma County are the Alexander, Dry Creek, Knights, and Russian River valleys. The fact that the Sonoma Valley is only one of five principal wine valleys in Sonoma County causes much confusion. Our base for the first two days was in the town of Sonoma

241

at Sonoma Mission Inn and Spa. Our rooms were plain but adequate, overpriced if one did not use the spa, and we did not. A better choice for active visitors would have been Vintners Inn, up the valley near Santa Rosa.

Sonoma is the site of Mission San Francisco Solano de Sonoma, consecrated in 1823, the last and northernmost mission of California's Spanish and Mexican past. Sonoma was the birthplace of California's wine industry, as it was here in 1857 that Hungarian Count Haraszthy established the first major plantings of *Vitis vinifera,* the classic European wine grape. His example was quickly followed by General Mariano Vallejo, the former and last Mexican governor of Sonoma.

Our first vineyard visited was, appropriately, Buena Vista, California's oldest premium winery. Its property includes the historic Haraszthy press house as well as the count's cellars, dug in 1857 by Chinese workers. A series of disasters, including the count being eaten by a crocodile in Honduras and America's experiment with prohibition, led to the abandonment of the vineyards. Buena Vista's recent renaissance has accelerated since its purchase in 1979 by the wealthy German Racke family, whose extensive European holdings include the Champagne House of Bricout. The Rackes' Buena Vista vineyards total some 1,700 acres in Carneros, straddling the Sonoma-Napa county line. Our tasting with the gracious staff began at a table under the trees in front of the rugged-stone press house.

All of our tastings were private, prearranged by the Michigan distributor of each winery. The wineries' reception of visitors not in the hospitality industry varies greatly. Some have prominent signs and tasting rooms open at specified hours where one may sample wines for a nominal charge and purchase wines at favorable prices. Others may be visited only by appointment and may even have unmarked entrances to discourage unannounced visitors. Jordan, Domaine Michel, and Lyeth all had electronically controlled gates.

Our bane and blessing was that our arrival in California coincided with the crush of harvest. While there was much to see, many vintners had scant time for visitors. Such was the case that afternoon at Carmenet, a sixty-acre Sonoma mountaintop vineyard of Chalone Corporation, producing a Bordeaux-style blend of Cabernet Sauvignon, Cabernet Franc, and Merlot, which wine guru Parker had called one of the twenty hottest wines of California. Winemaker and General Manager Jeff Baker took time from supervising the crush to show us the huge open-topped metal vats used for initial fermentation. These were not enclosed, but merely covered by a dramatic beamed roof, suspended from which was a powerful mechanical device that could be moved into position over each vat to punch down the solids that had risen to the top.

We felt almost obligated to have dinner at Sonoma Mission Inn that evening, since we heard that our hotel had scored a coup, luring their new chef, Charles Saunders, from much publicized Maxaluna in Boca Raton, Florida.

The cuisine of Chef Saunders and of most upscale California restaurants may be described as California Cuisine or New American Cuisine. Sauces of the French repertoire with a base of long-simmered stock are shunned. Used instead are flavored butters, olive oil, salsas and other condiments that require little labor or skill and are defended as being "lighter" than traditional sauces. Most offerings are either some form of salad or simple sautés or grills, except chicken, which is often roasted. Other roasts and braises are rare, as are any preparations that require more than combining flavored ingredients at the last minute. This is lauded as cuisine that is light and fresh and in which the true flavors come through, although almost all dishes are drenched in strong herbs. Emphasis is not on skill or perfection of preparation, but rather on "creativity." This has led to a veritable contest between chefs, and such inventions as Chef Saunders' ludicrous ancho chili–kumquat butter. We were reminded of Oliver Conant's comment on this cuisine in *The New York Times:* "improbable ingredients, implausibly combined, an excess of gimmicky contrivances, above all, too little substance."

Other strange offerings that evening included filet of beef with rosemary and garlic oil and corn pancakes, as well as something described as pink peppercorn linguini, baby clams, olive oil, leeks, garlic, bacon, and radicchio. Modern Cuisine, of course, dictates that meat, fish, and vegetables be undercooked, but even my pasta on this occasion was rarer than al dente, tasting like little strips of cardboard. A dessert of three varieties of fig, meringue, and caramel sauce was superb as was a Trefethen Chardonnay.

There is something to be said for the light effect of simple ingredients, simply combined—an admirable approach for salad, a summer luncheon, or to feed an invalid or the obese. But an entire cuisine and menu is too much. As a long-time resident of France and a good French-style cook said to us of her recent meals in California, "The food is so awful. After a while I just longed for a good stew." Mary and I also soon longed for food with some substance or depth of flavor—real food!

Years ago Mary and I were introduced to Sonoma-Cutrer's Les Pierres Chardonnay at the then-new French seafood restaurant in Manhattan, Le Bernardin. We were so impressed by this wine, then unknown in Michigan, that it was immediately added to our list. Our second morning in Sonoma found us driving north to the Sonoma-Cutrer winery in the Russian River Valley. Oddly, each mile took us farther from Les Pierres Vineyard, since that particular Sonoma-Cutrer vineyard was in the Los Carneros region of the Sonoma Valley, far from the winery and its other holdings in north Sonoma County.

Sonoma-Cutrer is an impressive facility with such amenities as beautiful croquet lawns, the site of the world championship croquet matches. The winery is also consciously state of the art in winemaking techniques—so much so that subtly worded resentment exists toward Sonoma-Cutrer at other wineries. Examples of Sonoma-Cutrer's dedication are the transporting of grapes from the field in small forty-pound lug boxes, rather than larger boxes or truck bins, to reduce premature crushing; chilling the grapes on arrival to forty-five degrees to retard oxidation; removing imperfect clusters, twigs and leaves by hand on specially designed oscillating sorting tables;

utilizing expensive membrane presses rather than a stemmer-crusher; and aging the wine in barrels on a floor of river rock over a bed of sand to mimic conditions in Burgundy.

We lunched at what may be the most famous Sonoma County restaurant, John Ash & Co., in the Vintners Inn just off Interstate 101 near Santa Rosa. Our very pleasant table on the outdoor patio was within a few feet of the vines of the adjacent winery. A duck *rillettes* was crumbly and bland because, unlike French pork *rillettes,* which are rich and moist with fat, John Ash's version was lean and dry—that old healthy California approach.

Flank steak marinated in garlic, red chilis, and herbs grilled with a green chili and goat cheese topping and served with a black-bean-serrano-chili salsa, in addition to being a mish-mash of ingredients, was gray and greasy and overwhelmed by cilantro, musty and dead tasting. On the other hand, grilled Pacific haddock was excellent. A clue to Mr. Ash's approach is that he raises and serves seventy-five varieties of edible flowers.

Returning to Sonoma County we visited Sandra MacIver at her Matanzas Creek Winery, originally famous for its Chardonnays but now equally known for Sauvignon Blanc and strictly rationed Merlots.

The next morning, after checking out of Sonoma Mission Inn, we proceeded seven miles north on Highway 12 for breakfast at the Garden Court Café, highly recommended by the staff of Buena Vista. We loved this diner-like spot—an antidote to California Cuisine. A wonderful Hungarian omelet and eggs benedict and biscuits were as good as any we had ever experienced. Intriguing touches included the presentation of chocolates with the check at so modest an establishment, plus the sight of one man who entered, proceeded directly behind the counter, filled his coffee cup, and departed.

A short drive east into northern Napa County brought us to the old mining town of Calistoga, now a vacation and weekend retreat for San Franciscans with a good assortment of quaint inns and bed and breakfasts. Next, we backtracked to the Petrified Forest, a California Historic Landmark where giant redwoods, then 3,500 years old, became petrified 3.4 million years ago following the eruption of California's Mount St. Helena, not to be confused with the similarly named volcanic Mount St. Helens that blew recently in Washington state.

The same Calistoga-Petrified Forest Road brought us to the turnoff to Fisher Vineyards, whose winery and Sonoma vineyard is carved from a hilly, deeply forested setting. A second vineyard is owned in Napa. Proprietors Fred Fisher, of the Fisher Body family, and Juelle Fisher served us a fine alfresco luncheon in the gazebo overlooking their home, pool, gardens, and vineyard. Lunch was accompanied by Fisher Coach Insignia Chardonnay and Fisher Coach Insignia Cabernet, both of which have received rave reviews and are featured at The Lark.

If the principal reward of hosting The Lark is the people we meet, the best of our wine journey was meeting vineyard owners and their staffs. Almost of necessity, they were not only intelligent and competent, but had good taste and were genuinely nice. The owners themselves form a natural aristocracy, and like most practitioners of unique professions, such as doctors or journalists, tend to choose their friends from co-professionals. Thus Fred and Juelle Fisher were good friends of the Jordans to whose winery we drove directly on bidding farewell to the Fishers.

Jordan Winery is an extremely elegant Bordeaux-style château overlooking 1,300 Alexander Valley acres whose grapes produce seventy thousand cases of Cabernet Sauvignon and Chardonnay. Oilman Tom Jordan was not in residence, so our host was a charming and efficient ex-Detroiter, Shelly Eichner. In our tasting, the Cabernet Sauvignon and Chardonnay scored high with Mary and me, and both were added to our wine list.

The residential west wing of the château, overlooking the vineyards and valley, has a first floor comprising an elegant reception and dining salon with a cathedral-like oak cask ceiling, the site of dinner parties for marketers of Jordan wines. Stone, brick, and tile exterior stairways lead to a second floor of three guest suites, reserved virtually every day of the year for the exclusive use of wine merchants and restaurateurs. The central suite was ours for the night. The accommodations at Jordan eclipse those of famed hotels such as the Bel Air, The Connaught, Reid's, Crillon, Peninsula, Mayfair Regent, and others. Sally Jordan did it right!

The tremendous differences between wineries makes the wine country especially interesting. Our hosts at a large winery might include the proprietor, national marketing vice president, hospitality director, and winemaker. Facilities would be large and impressive. In sharp contrast was Spottswood on the west of St. Helena, to which we drove the next morning for our first venture into the Napa Valley.

Television goofed choosing Falcon Crest (actually Spring Mountain Winery) as a setting for the TV series. It should have been Spottswood with its charming Victorian house, giant palm trees, exotic gardens, swimming pool, tennis courts, and world-class wine. The barrels are in the basement; proprietor Mary Novak lives upstairs; and the forty acres of vines are out the back door. Thanks to the dedication of Mary Novak and her daughter Beth, the skill of winemaker Tony Soter, and the qualities of the grapes, Spottswood's Sauvignon Blanc and more especially its Cabernet Sauvignon are a great success with demand far exceeding their two-thousand-case production. We tasted the 1985 Cabernet, which exudes class and received a 95 rating. Wine writer James Laube speculated that the 1986 and 1987 may be even better than the 1984 and 1985.

Napa County now has well over two hundred wineries, compared with the thirty that existed at the time of our first visit in 1963, and is much more congested than Sonoma—so much so that there is a moratorium on new wineries. Main towns, running from south to north along Highway 29, are Napa, Yountville, Oakville, St. Helena, and Calistoga. Examples of the tourist atmosphere were high gasoline prices, a wine train to haul visitors up and down the valley, and a tasting center with wines from numerous vineyards to end the need (and joy) of visiting individual wineries. Given those few negatives, Napa is still wonderful with many wineries to visit, fascinating stores like Vanderbilt's in St. Helena, and a variety of fine restaurants such as that of Domaine Chandon, where we had lunch after departing Spottswoode.

Domaine Chandon in Yountville is the sparkling wine estate of Moët et Chandon, the French champagne house. Its visitors' complex includes a tasting bar, gift shop, and large restaurant with both indoor and outdoor tables. Although the commercial air and the crowds were off-putting, the restaurant itself provided by far the best food of our trip to that point, including fresh tomato soup with a puff pastry dome, sweetbreads with Cabernet sauce, and a fish and shellfish *pot-au-feu*. A William Hill Reserve Chardonnay was excellent as was service from the senior waitress.

Not having planned a logical itinerary, we returned to Sonoma County by way of the wonderful road winding through the hills from Calistoga to Healdsburg, whence we continued on a few more miles to Domaine Michel in the Dry Creek Valley. The Swiss owner, Jean-Jacques Michel and family, good friends of the Jordans, have built a mission-style winery surrounding a central court with a fountain, gardens, and comfortable chairs for lounging. Their guest quarters were our lodgings for the night, so after taking a brief tour and settling in, we enjoyed a picnic dinner in the now-deserted courtyard accompanied by their Chardonnay and a Cabernet that was very drinkable and which we especially enjoyed.

Thank God I drive fast, because as addicted to farmers' markets as we are, it was back to St. Helena the next day for the Friday morning market. Best finds were locally grown pistachios, Hawaiian pears, and Sweet 100 tomatoes, as small as blueberries.

Back past St. Helena off the Silverado Trail, we checked into Meadowood Resort, where we rejected a dank cottage in favor of a bright and airy suite overlooking croquet courts, obviously the coming sport in California and elsewhere. Meadowood also has a golf course and tennis.

We dined that evening in Yountville at The French Laundry, a beautiful, old, brick building, once a laundry, but now a fifty-seat, fixed-price, country-inn-style restaurant, open just five evenings a week. This was the restaurant most recommended by locals—extremely popular and booked well in advance. It is also an obvious gold mine with very low food costs and overhead for its fixed-price dinners. Highlights of this enjoyable evening were polenta with chanterelle mushrooms and a salad accompanied by wonderful local cheeses. A Far Niente Chardonnay left us without care.

Since private tours and tastings are not commonly available on weekends, Saturday and Sunday provided an almost welcome break from winery visits. Two ex-classmates of Mary's drove up from San Francisco to join us for lunch near St. Helena at Mustard's Grill, Napa Valley's most famous restaurant. This bright, pleasant, and casual roadside eatery had a charming staff, who were very indulgent despite the fact that our guests were an hour and a quarter late. By then, we knew everyone at nearby tables, and on my signal, all applauded the entrance of our late arrivals.

Although we enjoyed our visit to Mustard's because of the ambience and service and the presence of our guests, Mary's onion and eggplant appetizer was inedible. Obviously tough spareribs received a rating of five out of ten from our new friend at the next table, while his wife said her Chinese chicken salad was so overseasoned and loaded with chunks of ginger as to be barely edible. My lamb chops were lamb chops, but Mary's liver and onions was very good. Raspberry sorbet and chocolate pistachio ice cream were both excellent.

As is so often the case with us and our hotels, we had not eaten at Meadowood but did decide on the spur of the moment to try its Sunday brunch before checking out. The elegant yet comfortable country-French-style dining room had indoor and outdoor tables overlooking the croquet lawns. Included in the excellent buffet were a large roasted corned beef, roast tenderloin of lamb, smoked salmon and sturgeon, perfectly prepared omelets, and much more. Service was perfect. We must assume that other meals here are also very good.

Spring Valley Road begins inconspicuously in a residential neighborhood on the north side of St. Helena, meanders past "Falcon

Crest" and up into the mountains separating Napa and Sonoma. At an elevation of two thousand feet, we turned onto even more remote Langley Road, which ended at Cain Cellars.

Cain Cellars, where we stayed Sunday night, has the most dramatic setting of any winery. A large swimming pool and a terrace with comfortable lounges and chairs is perched on the edge of a steep slope, providing awesome vistas of Napa Valley far below and the ridges of its distant eastern side where smoke billowed from forest fires. In our tasting, arranged by Manager Sandra Lovelace, we especially liked the platinum-prize-winning Merlot, Carneros Chardonnay, and the Sauvignon Blanc. Eagerly awaited is the release of Cain "5" utilizing all five Bordeaux grape varieties. Cain was founded by Michael Osborne of Palm Springs and Carmel after falling in love with winemaking in Bordeaux on a rest and relaxation vacation ordered by his doctor. He learned of the availability of the land now comprising Cain Cellars from conversation overheard at the next table in a local restaurant.

The talk of the town in Napa was Tra Vigne, then a new Italian restaurant in St. Helena by the conglomerate that owns Mustard's Grill and other eateries. The success of Tra Vigne is proof positive that ambience is more important than food or service to most diners. We joined fellow Michiganders Tom and Kris Thomas in this atmospheric brick structure Sunday evening for a dinner that featured poor service; underfried, unseasoned calamari; a "mixed green" salad that contained none of the listed ingredients except limp mache or lamb's tongue; a calzone of five cheeses, poorly seasoned and not as good as either Domino's or Little Caesar's pizza; a poorly seasoned veal chop stuffed with fontina (the waiter said it was stuffed with meringue); and seafood pasta so bad that it remained uneaten. Lest our foursome be thought grouches, fellow guests from Cain were equally unhappy with Tra Vigne. Like almost every restaurant in Napa and Sonoma, it has an admirable and diverse wine list.

Monday morning, accompanied by Tom and Kris, we took the meandering mountain road over the ridge into Sonoma County's Dry Creek Valley west of Healdsburg to Ferrari-Carano Vineyards and

Winery. If you didn't know it before, you heard it here first—Ferrari-Carano seems destined to become one of the most famous California wineries. Its first release, the 1986 Chardonnay, was a world-class wine selling for up to fifty dollars per bottle even in California restaurants. A 1987 Fumé Blanc was also released and joined in 1989 by the delayed release of the 1985 Cabernet and 1986 Merlot.

In addition to its original 250 acres acquired in 1981, Ferrari-Carano more recently purchased vast additional acreage, assuring itself of adequate future supplies of premium grapes for its ultra-ambitious program. This is important for two reasons. Napa and Sonoma grapes available for purchase are becoming scarce. Furthermore, the increasing emphasis on technique and control mandates total management of the vineyards and grapes, obviously impossible when grapes are purchased from others.

Ferrari-Carano competes with Sonoma-Cutrer in the drive for state-of-the-art winemaking with differing approaches. Just two examples are Sonoma-Cutrer's unique sorting table and Ferrari-Carano's vertical cooling strip on its metal initial-fermentation vats rather than the typical horizontal band. Also, Sonoma-Cutrer makes a separate wine from each of its vineyards while Ferrari-Carano blends in an attempt to achieve a consistent style.

We were greeted at Ferrari-Carano by Marketing Vice President Steve Meisner, about to leave for a boating honeymoon on Florida's west coast, and owner Don Carano, whose powerful personality drives this operation as well as his prominent Nevada law firm and Reno's Eldorado Hotel and Casino. Don and his wife, Rhonda, are second-generation Italian-Americans, strongly devoted to their cultural ancestry. The Ferrari in the winery's name is Don's grandmother, Amelia Ferrari of Genoa, Italy.

Ferrari-Carano is already an impressive facility, but will be enhanced by dramatic underground caves, Italian gardens, guest quarters, tennis courts, massive villa with reception and dining rooms, cooking school, and visiting celebrity chefs. Then, state-of-the-art show business will popularize state-of-the-art winemaking in the previously subdued Dry Creek Valley.

Steve Meisner hosted a lively lunch at Jacob Horn's, Healdsburg's finest restaurant, featuring zesty oysters in brocade and a Ferrari-Carano Chardonnay. Returning to St. Helena in Napa, we checked in at the famous Auberge de Soleil on the eastern rim of Napa Valley. The view from our suite and its terrace was over olive groves between forested slopes and then out over the valley where coveys of improbably huge hot-air balloons hovered. Tom and Kris, Mary and I all loved our Mediterranean country-style suites, by far the best public accommodations in either Napa or Sonoma. The living room, dining area, kitchen, bedroom, bath, and terrace were all spacious, well laid out, and lavishly furnished and decorated. Tiles similar to those in the lobby and bar of The Lark were used, not only on floors, but as countertops and baseboards. A large fireplace in the living room was laid and ready to light. Our doorway was guarded by guinea fowl who patrolled faithfully.

We had been told by patrons of The Lark that food at Auberge was mediocre and the service pompous. Some locals denied this, so we four Michiganders booked dinner. Shrimp fritters were not fritters but overcooked fried whole shrimp, though sautéed foie gras with black currants on a pancake was great. Roast chicken was very good, while sturgeon was overwhelmed with fennel. The service staff gave the impression they might well be pompous, but were not so with us, even producing an unlisted bottle of the great 1984 Spottswood Cabernet in lieu of the listed 1983.

Our Tuesday tour and tasting at Stag's Leap Wine Cellars proved a smashing finale to our trip. Warren and Barbara Winiarski's winery is located below the rocky Stag's Leap promontory east of Yountville on the Silverado Trail. Stag's Leap's search for perfection is exemplified by its work in "canopy management," controlling the amount of sunlight reaching grape clusters, and control of excess plant vigor through vine spacing and trellis design.

Warren Winiarski (justly famous and a leader in the industry), daughter Kasia, and their staff were charming hosts. We were fascinated to learn that Warren was leaving that day for Pakistan to join a viticulturist from the University of California at Davis and a biologist from Oregon State. There they searched the jungle for the primordial vine that still has separate male and female plants and is the progenitor of all contemporary forms of *Vitis vinifera,* from which all European-style wines are made. Acquisition of a female primordial plant could be the first step in controlling the excess vigor of modern vines, whose flowers combine both sexes. A plant was found and returned in quarantine, but unfortunately appears to be a male plant. Back to Pakistan?

If the wines of our trip were wonderful, so were the people, the scenery, and the weather. Only the food was lacking—rarely a meal where every course was good. Typically, breads, salads, and desserts excelled while first and main courses fell short. Small wonder that even mediocre Italian restaurants were swamped by locals fleeing their native cuisine. We did enjoy the restaurants of Domaine Chandon, and Meadowood Resort as well as The French Laundry, Jacob Horn's, and Garden Court Café.

We recalled that on our first trip to France, it had been comforting to come at last to a country where everyone was as interested in good food as Mary and I. In California, we experienced the same feeling of homecoming, but this time to a land of wine lovers. In fact, there was a much greater knowledge and appreciation of wine than in France.

Wine Lists and Wine Snobs

In 1995, The Lark's 18,474 guests ordered $300,010 of wine, compared with only $82,585 of cocktails, mixed drinks, brandy, and liqueurs. To say it is important for us to have a good wine list would be an understatement. Ours has grown to 100 selections listed on the back of the menu plus a separate reserve list of more than 430 additional wines. Selecting the best wines at fair and practical prices from the thousands available is a tremendous task that consumes at least as much time as menu research and planning.

Wines are stored at The Lark in natural redwood bins in an impressive wine cellar, air conditioned to fifty-five degrees. The cellar's floor is Mexican Saltillo tile. Walls are stuccoed, the ceiling textured. Special lighting enhances art works and a table for private dinners (never on Saturday). More than eight thousand bottles are on hand, an average of fifteen bottles for the 525 wines available. This compares with average bottles per wine as low as five at some restaurants whose lists have been made long for show rather than use.

Wine Spectator magazine, the arbiter in the field that presents annual awards to The Lark and a limited number of other restaurants, has three criteria for a great wine list: breadth, depth, and balance. But a list could meet those criteria and only serve the needs of dedicated oenologists, less than 5 percent of any restaurant's patrons. We believe a far better goal in developing a wine list is maximum enhancement of the dining experience of 100 percent of a restaurant's wine-drinking guests. Therefore, the list should:

1. Have at least the central core of the list on the menu. Many diners are intimidated by fine restaurants. Many only visit fine restaurants on special occasions such as an anniversary or birthday. It is the duty of every restaurateur to put them at ease so they will relax and enjoy the dining experience. A separate wine list is intimidating, not relaxing. Many diners are afraid to ask for such a list or will decline it when offered. They are afraid all the wines will be too expensive, or that they will not understand it, or that they will embarrass themselves in some way. If the list is on the back of the menu, all of these problems are solved. There is no reason to create such problems in the first place. A separate reserve list can list wines for which there is no room on the menu. Taillevent and many other great restaurants long ago reached this decision, and my experience as

maître d' and sommelier confirms it absolutely.

2. Be mistake proof. Since many patrons do not know wines well, some will choose mediocre or poor wines if they are present. Therefore, all wines should be superior. A restaurateur should not look down on his patrons as, for example, having a mediocre Mosel for those requesting "a Piesporter."

3. Have an adequate variety of good wines by the glass. Otherwise, the restaurant has not met the needs of those guests who wish only a glass or two of wine, or wish to match the wine to the dish it accompanies.

4. Have a reasonable number of good wines by the glass and bottle available at moderate cost to meet the needs of patrons of moderate means.

5. Have, for the typical patron, a good selection of wines most favored, especially California Chardonnays, Cabernets, and Merlots, champagne, white Burgundy, and red Bordeaux.

6. Have, for the classicist, a good selection of champagnes, red and white Bordeaux, red and white Burgundy, port, and so forth.

7. Have for the dedicated wine buff many of the talked about, hard to find wines, like Guigal's La Mouline, La Landonne and La Turque, A. Salon Le Mesnil, Ch. Petrus, Sassicaia, Vega-Sicilia, Penfold's Grange, Kistler Chardonnay, Spottswoode Cabernet, and Caymus Special Selection Cabernet, which are just a few of the many such wines on our list.

These are the criteria we have adopted. We believe that our list meets them better than any other list we have seen, and that we have met the needs of all our patrons and done the best job of enhancing their dining experience with fine wines. Other lists aimed at 5 percent not 100 percent of guests contribute to the public's image of wine snobs.

Le Bec Fin

This French term, literally "a fine mouth," identifies a gourmet, since a gourmet must, of necessity, have a superior sense of taste. In 1988, Mary and I visited Spottswoode Winery, which produces one of the finest Cabernet Sauvignon wines in the world, and enjoyed a glass of the 1985 vintage with proprietors Mary and Beth Novak. Eighteen months later, I borrowed a partial glass of the identical wine from a devotee who had ordered it at The Lark, saying he would save his own hoard of Spottswoode and drink ours instead. Mary knew none of this, nor that anyone had ordered this rarity, when I took the sample to her at the bar and asked her to taste it. She said it was "wonderful." I then asked her what it was, and she said "Spottswoode." A chill ran up my spine; she had previously tasted Spottswoode only at the winery and one California restaurant.

More recently, I made Mary a toasted cheese sandwich with Mucky Duck mustard, and she called it the best cheese sandwich she had ever tasted. I asked her what cheese I had used. She hesitated, and then said, "Cheddar, Gruyere, and Swiss." As I am the buyer and keeper of the cheese in our household, Mary had no idea what varieties were on hand, hence this was another astounding performance by *le bec fin*. You can probably guess who makes the difficult decisions among wines competing for a place on our list.

Fishing Where Eagles Soar

*W*e six fishermen gathered in Vancouver, British Columbia, from our homes in Britain, Michigan, Ohio, and the state of Washington. Before overnighting in the fine and well-managed Four Seasons Hotel, we dined at The Cannery Seafood House. One of Vancouver's best and most popular restaurants, it is not only awash in the freshest seafood, but has an appealing rustic ambience and fine views of the harbor and sea. I savored yellow scallops with steamed vegetables Provençale followed by fine Pacific halibut, while fellow diners also enjoyed halibut and British Columbia salmon, available grilled, pan fried, or poached.

The next morning, a twelve-seat plane winged us north to the Queen Charlotte Islands, an archipelago off the B.C. coast just south of Alaska. Switching there to a smaller float plane, we hopped to Langara Island, the northernmost island in the group, its name a reminder that Spanish explorers reached this far north. We settled into North Island Lodge, a floating fish camp of twelve twin rooms with private baths, dining room, and spacious, well-appointed lounge.

Despite the amenities of our lodge and two others around a point up the coast, we were in a wilderness area of sea and sky, rocks and trees, and distant mountain vistas. Other than fishermen and their prey, the only creatures noticeably present were a few ducks, many bald eagles, seals, otter, dolphin, orca (killer whales), and humpbacked whales. We were privileged to see them all. It was exhilarating to be where eagles were the most common bird and giant humpbacked whales broached the surface and spouted.

If camaraderie and nature were the true rewards of the trip, the purported goal was to angle for large Pacific salmon, hopefully chinook salmon over thirty pounds called *tyee,* their Native American name. Lest readers who have caught salmon that large in the Great Lakes consider it no great feat, let me assure you, as one who has landed thirty-pound-plus salmon in both locales, that the fight put up by a Great Lakes salmon is nothing compared with that of an ocean-cruising wild Pacific salmon.

Our craft were Boston Whalers ranging from seventeen to twenty-one feet in length, each manned by a captain/guide and two fishermen. Our fishing rigs resembled very large fly rods. That is, they had large fly-rod-type reels, although they were actually used for trolling herring chunks, brought down to depths of about thirty to forty feet by golf-ball-sized lead weights. We trolled four rigs, one forward and one aft on each side of the boat.

Each day began with an early breakfast so as to be on the dock by 7 A.M. clad in waterproof boots and bulky, but warm, foul-weather suits. We fished three and one-half days, switching fishing partners and guides so that I was able to fish with each of my five companions, active and retired executives Trevor Jones, Al Aitken, Ben Cosgrove, Clint Lauer, and Bob Marshall. My roommate Clint and I tied for the largest *tyee* at forty-one pounds. Trevor landed a huge halibut. Halibut and large ling cod were caught by jigging, as a break from salmon fishing.

The fishing was superb, with everyone landing salmon each day. The limit was four fish. The four I kept weighed twenty-five, thirty-one, thirty-eight, and forty-one pounds, and were smoked, canned, and shipped home. My halibut and ling cod, filleted and frozen in two-pound vacuum packs, arrived still frozen, a wonder of modern transportation.

Certainly, landing the forty-one-pound chinook salmon was the highlight of my trip. I had barely lowered my rig to the proper depth when it hit. Unlike most very large salmon, it jumped clear of the water a number of times between long runs and dogged dives. The fly-rod-type reel had no useful drag, so I applied drag by holding my palm against the bottom of the reel. Line was retrieved by raising the rod and reeling while lowering it back down. After forty-five minutes, I began to regret hooking the monster, which seemed especially strong, even for its size. Our young guide, who could be a twin of my number-four son James, finally slipped a net under the fish after sixty-five minutes. The hook fell out while the salmon was still in the net, having been bent to an almost useless shape by its efforts.

The many other memorable moments included watching another boat, not of our group, speeding after a seal that had grabbed their hard-fought and about-to-be-landed *tyee.* Overtaking the seal in a bed of giant kelp, they whacked it over the head with a paddle. That had no apparent effect as he withdrew, still clutching his giant prize. Dolphin and orcas frolicked nearby at various times. The pod of huge humpbacked whales put on its show on the morning we jigged for halibut and ling cod.

House-Smoked or Marinated Salmon

Experienced diners learn to avoid certain types of dishes, such as any special that the chef dreamt up that afternoon. One preparation that should be shunned at any restaurant is house-smoked or marinated salmon or other fish. Even at *Michelin*-starred restaurants in France, I have never had an acceptable version. Smoked offerings are either undersmoked and fishy or overcooked and dry, and the flavor and seasoning are never right. Marinated salmon invariably has an off, fishy taste and odor. The best commercial purveyors, be they Scottish, Irish, or American, have been in business for years, often generations, and have obviously refined their seasonings and techniques. It is the height of conceit for the young chef to "reinvent the wheel," especially as he cannot obtain fish of the same freshness or quality as the long-established commercial producer with its vast experience and superior contacts.

A Restaurant's Long-Term Welfare

The long-term welfare of a restaurant and its staff is identical with the welfare of its patrons. For example, if a patron is sold an unnecessarily expensive wine to boost the restaurant's profit and the waiter's gratuity, the restaurant and waiter achieve a short-term gain, but may well lose the guest's future business—a continuing long-term loss. It may seem obvious that it would be better for both the waiter and restaurant in the long term to recommend a more sensible wine choice and gain repeat business, but a high percentage of restaurant staff think only of today.

Curried Duck Salad

Dinner at the Lark begins with a carte blanche selection from an hors d'oeuvre trolley, which is rolled to each table. Choices include Maine oysters on the half shell, large chilled gulf shrimp, curried duck salad, and two other items that change daily. The Curried Duck Salad is especially popular and like the Rack of Lamb Genghis Khan, has received national attention.

2 roasted ducks, cooled and boned, the meat diced
2 large ribs celery, peeled and finely chopped
1 small onion, finely chopped
2 apples, diced
¼ cup toasted sliced almonds
1 cup good mayonnaise
⅔ cup Major Grey's chutney, puréed
8 teaspoons good curry powder
2 ½ teaspoons fresh lemon juice
8 teaspoons honey
1 teaspoon white vinegar
salt and pepper

In a mixing bowl combine the mayonnaise, chutney, curry powder, lemon juice, honey, and white vinegar. Blend well. Toss with remaining ingredients and season with salt and pepper to taste.

Chill and let marinate for at least 2 hours before serving.

Yields 8 servings as an appetizer.

New Orleans

*M*ary Lark, another couple and I spent three and a half fun-and-food-filled days in New Orleans in mid-February. Even though we had been to the Big Easy before, such a brief visit is obviously too short to be a basis for an up-to-date, definitive report. Each of us gained three to four pounds, however, so we do have some credibility.

Citizens of New Orleans were helpful, friendly, and proud of their new hotels, office buildings, and shops. The French Quarter, which had always seemed rather tacky and touristy, appeared to have improved since our last visit. Despite the many new hotels added in recent years, our favorite remained the Pontchartrain Hotel in the Garden District, away from the crowds of the French Quarter and downtown. Each of its one hundred rooms and suites is individually decorated, and some contain more than one-hundred-thousand-dollars worth of antiques and decorative art. The hotel until recently was owned and managed by "Mr. Albert" Aschaffenburg, son of the hotel's founder. Many of the staff have served guests for more than twenty-five years, and guests are treated like family. Although considered one of the finest small hotels in the world, wonderful suites cost no more than a small room in one of New York's famous hostelries.

Arriving at midday Sunday, we checked in and headed for the nearby Commander's Palace restaurant to experience its widely imitated jazz brunch. Commander's is owned by a branch of the noted Brennan family. We were greeted by Dick and Lauren Brennan and led to a corner window table in the famous Garden Room. We began with its fabled two-two-two course consisting of a small serving of three soups: turtle, oyster, and artichoke. The turtle soup with sherry from the original 1883 menu and recipe was superb and is considered the classic of its kind. Main courses of redfish with crab, oysters with artichokes, veal with fettuccine, accompanied by a house Sancerre, were all very good. Desserts included a hot-buttered-rum pecan pie and lemon mousse with kiwi. Accompanied by the charming jazz musicians, it was a memorable brunch. Commander's does an excellent job of maintaining quality in a large establishment seating about four hundred.

We were in New Orleans the week before Mardi Gras, which is ideal as the parades and other festivities are in full swing without the mob scene of Mardi Gras week. Early Monday evening we ordered a cocktail in the traditional plastic cup and strolled across the boulevard in front of the Pontchartrain to view one of the traditional parades. The floats and costumes were fabulous and the crowd friendly. Of course, we enjoyed catching the trinkets thrown from the floats.

The best item at dinner that evening at our hotel's well-known Caribbean Room was the Mile High Pie dessert, a ten-inch-tall creation of peppermint, vanilla, and chocolate ice creams with meringue in a good crust, topped with chocolate sauce.

Arising early Monday, we took the trolley on St. Charles Boulevard in front of the hotel to the edge of the French Quarter, and walked to Café du Monde for the indispensable café au lait with beignets—hot, crisp, doughnut-like fried buns dusted with confectioner's sugar.

Strolling through the Quarter afterwards we shopped at various stores, the best being Gentlemen's Quarter on Royal Street, which had good values in fine men's and women's apparel, and a nearby brass emporium with items ranging from weather vanes to candlesticks at giveaway prices. In fact, the proprietor did give Mary a brass horn. A wonderful bonus to our morning was supplied by the elderly proprietor of Stern's Antique Shop, who gave us a fascinating talk on antiques even though it was obvious we were only browsing. The Quarter was clean and free of crowds. Sales people were attentive and polite.

Arnaud's restaurant on Bienville off Bourbon Street was founded in 1918 by a Basque named Leon Betrand Arnaud Cazenave. By the 1930s its inventive local cuisine had made it the place to dine, and its founder had earned the honorary title of "Count." After his death in 1948, Arnaud's declined rapidly under his daughter's management, and by 1978 it had become a travesty with sales of only $150,000 and most of its rooms closed and devastated. At that point it was purchased by Archie Casbarian, an Armenian from Alexandria, Egypt, who was educated in hotel and restaurant management at Cornell and in Switzerland and was previously manager of the Royal Sonesta Hotel in New Orleans. Faced with a terrible image problem, Casbarian spent $2.5 million renovating the huge establishment room by room, revised the cumbersome original menu, and hired good chefs. Today it is once again a highly respected New Orleans institution, one of only two restaurants to be awarded four stars by the *Insiders' Guide to New Orleans Restaurants*.

Having written in advance, we were greeted on arrival at Arnaud's for lunch by Archie Casbarian, who proved a most gracious host. As with so many fine restaurants, there were tiled walls and floors in abundance and coat hooks on the walls. It was not crowded as most visitors save this important restaurant for dinner, lunch being reserved mostly for locals. For example, Roy Guste Jr., fifth-generation member of the Alciatore family and co-proprietor of Antoine's, was with a group at the next table. Archie introduced us, and all hands enjoyed restaurant banter at lunch, with Roy Guste insisting that Mary taste his main course of tripe. Very good! Roy described his new restaurant, Guste's, serving contemporary Louisiana cuisine in the renovated Jax Brewery complex.

A stop after lunch at Jax Brewery revealed not only Guste's but a host of other restaurants, food stalls, food stores, and boutiques spread over the six floors of the former brewery. Naturally, thoughts of Stroh's and Trappers' Alley in Detroit came to mind. The old Italian cab driver who returned us to our hotel pointed out that New Orleans had almost no French left and was mostly Italian and Spanish.

We looked forward to Monday night as the culinary high point of our visit—dinner at K-Paul's Louisiana Kitchen! and the cooking of Paul Prudhomme, America's most famous Cajun chef. Since reservations are not accepted, we arrived at 5 P.M., as instructed, to wait in line outside for the 5:30 opening. At 5:20, an SS-type woman appeared to harangue us with the house rules. No one would be seated unless the entire party was present. Waitees would wait outside. Smaller parties would be seated together—every seat must be filled. And so on. We trooped in at 5:30 and were seated in the seedy establishment with holes in the linoleum floor, paper napkins, and cheap, cheap tableware. We ordered a Cajun martini (with jalapeño peppers). All the other tables obtained their drinks, had orders taken, and began to be served food. When I asked the SS lady and our waitress why we had not received our cocktails, I was given the idiotic answer that the waitresses worked in teams. I finally prevailed on the bartender to get our martinis. A first course of Cajun popcorn (small fried shrimp) with sherry sauce was very good as was Cajun jambalaya. Main courses included blackened redfish, very good, and blackened boneless rib steak, which was literally coated with black garlic and too overpowering for even a devoted garlic fan.

Other main courses—an eggplant pirogue with scallops Diane, and garlic seafood—appeared to have identical sauces with too much butter and uncooked garlic and were essentially inedible. A variety of excellent rolls accompanied dinner, with the jalapeño roll and Louisiana black bread with molasses and nuts being especially good. Pecan pie was excellent, and the bread pudding stuffed with nuts was the best ever.

Dinner over, our waitress affixed silver stars to our cheek to reward us for eating well or not so well. Three of us received only one star.

Our friend Tom, who had been fortunate enough to order the jambalaya, redfish, and bread pudding, received three stars. Tom, who had looked so forward to K-Paul's that he originally planned to eat there three nights running, dined at the Old Nawlins Cookery after Mary and I returned to Michigan. He ordered most of the same dishes as at K-Paul's for comparison sake and declared them all superior. He also reported that Old Nawlins, founded by a former sous chef at K-Paul's, treated its customers with respect. *The Insiders' Guide,* referred to previously, awards K-Paul's only two stars and states, "Diners ... should not have to wait on the sidewalk at the mercy of a domineering service person who uses a walkie-talkie and police escort like a whip.... A great restaurant shows more consideration for its patrons.... The policies of this restaurant pull it down from greatness." These sentiments were echoed by every local when K-Paul's was discussed.

After Tuesday breakfast from room service, featuring freshly squeezed grapefruit juice and fantastic southern biscuits that appeared to weigh a half-pound each, we picked up our rental car for a tour of some of the plantation area and Cajun countryside west of New Orleans. *Frommer's Guide to New Orleans,* describing a day trip from the city, states, "I'll start with the plantation nearest New Orleans and describe each, for ready reference, in the alphabetical order in which it appears on the map, although that is not necessarily the order in which you will view them." I still can't figure out that sentence, which may explain why we never did discover a plantation worth viewing.

By late morning, our by-now-expanded stomachs demanded food and forced us to stop at an unimposing eatery in Thibodaux named Boudreux's. Crawfish-stuffed jalapeño peppers were ninety-five cents and crawfish pie a dollar and a half. Fried shrimp and crawfish were very good and the hush puppies world class. The man at the next table eating crawfish stew naturally offered Mary a bite (what is it with her?) and told us he came to eat at Boudreux's whenever he was within fifty miles of it. What a lucky fluke that we stumbled upon it.

Back in Nawlins by midafternoon, and now in a feeding frenzy, we drove past a very neat little neighborhood restaurant, Mid-City

Seafood, which also had an "oyster bar" sign. Another meal seemed ridiculous, but Tom asked, "Should we stop?" I said, "Damn right!" What a winner it was! Simple, charming, clean, gracious, and great drinks. Three dozen big-fat freshly opened oysters were $4.25 per dozen. Very large soft-shelled crabs were excellent at $4 each. My platter of over sixty boiled crawfish was $7.95. When we commented how many there were, the waitress said, "They crawl around like ants down here."

Tom, an idiosyncratic chili cook, had for some reason appeared in New Orleans with a wardrobe of tropical exercise outfits. As the temperature was generally in the forties, his touching suffering in the cold (as in line at K-Paul's) had reached a point where he had to purchase a coat. This was accomplished at our next stop, Brooks Brothers, in magnificent Canal Place, another excellent shopping complex. Incidentally, none of the restaurants visited appeared to even notice his bizarre attire, which is one more example of the friendliness encountered everywhere.

Mother's restaurant is home to what many New Orleanians consider their most typical dish. Not gumbo or crawfish, but a "Po' Boy," from the French word *pourboire,* slang for a tip. Many restaurants serve Po' Boys, but simple Mother's does it best. A Po' Boy is a sandwich of crusty French bread filled with a choice of oysters, friend fish, roast beef, or roast beef and ham. The beef and ham, called a Ferdi, is considered the best. Bread is spread with roast beef pan juices, and the meat is topped with Creole mustard, mayonnaise, pickles, and shredded lettuce. It drips all over the place. You can imagine how we felt Tuesday night when, mouths watering, we pulled up to Mother's and found it closed.

Being in no condition for a "serious" dinner after our day, we taxied on to Ralph and Kacoo's, a nearby seafood restaurant that our driver claimed was even better than Mid-City Seafood. Large and bustling with young singles and convention types, its seafood platter was mostly catfish fingers. Soft-shelled crab had the apron still attached, and a shrimp cocktail was made with small shrimp. Fried shrimp and stuffed shrimp were quite good, but both food and atmosphere were commercial and, to our taste, not comparable to Mid-City Seafood.

Many friends had recommended the Rib Room of the Royal Orleans Hotel. We were turned off by the restaurant's name but intrigued that its chef, Andre Appuzzo, was from northern Italy. We were excited, therefore, when informed that Appuzzo had just opened his own restaurant, Andrea's, serving strictly Italian food in the suburb of Metairie. Off we went for lunch and a restaurant scoop!

Andrea's is moderate in size with an elegant atmosphere inherited from the French restaurant that formerly occupied the well-designed building. Service was flawless and most of our food excellent. Pasta with mushrooms, salads, roast leg of lamb, and *cioppino* of mixed seafood were all very good. The osso buco and sautéed calf's liver with caramelized onions were outstanding. Brunello di Montalcino, one of Italy's finest red wines, was bargain priced. It was an enjoyable and appropriate final meal of a trip to a city whose largest ethnic group is Italian.

So, simply a fantastic time—fine restaurants, friendly people, good shopping, superb hotel, and unexpected adventures—all of it shared with and made the more delicious because of the enthusiastic and fun-loving couple who shared these experiences with us.

Soft-Shell Crab Every Wednesday

For many years our Classic Cuisine special each Wednesday was abalone. After a lot of soul searching and considerable regret, abalone was dropped from our menu because of difficulty obtaining the correct, less tough, species. Intense brain-storming ensued to select a worthy Wednesday replacement. The eventual winner was deep-fried soft-shell crab, one of Mary's and my favorite foods and the most requested dish at The Lark.

My first exposure to soft-shell crab was in Washington, D.C., while attending Georgetown Law School in the mid-1950s. A simple downtown restaurant featured a sandwich with a fried crab so big that it overflowed the large bread that sought to contain it. Later, soft-shell crab became one of our favorite dishes at Joe Muer's in Detroit. Oddly enough, Muer's is the only restaurant we know of, other than The Lark, that both knows and uses the techniques necessary for proper preparation of this superb crustacean.

Although most authorities, including Craig Claiborne, aver that these critters should be deep fried, many restaurants persist in sautéing them. They do this because it is more convenient for them. The public thinks it is healthier, and it sounds more "fancy." Actually, it is less healthy, as much less fat is absorbed deep frying at the correct temperature than when sautéing, which produces a soggy, grease-laden crab. Another trick or secret involves proper cleaning and preparation. The French accent added by our Chef Marcus's sauce and presentation are the last ingredients resulting in the best soft-shell crab anywhere.

"Come with Me and We'll Choose a Table"

One of our chili cooks at the annual Michigan Chili Cookoff, whose money I take at poker, was waiting for a table at a very popular Italian restaurant in Ann Arbor, Michigan. Excusing himself to visit the restroom, he cautioned his wife and the other couple with them, "Whatever you do, don't accept that table under the stairway next to the kitchen door." Sure enough, that's where they were sitting when he returned.

A very long article or short book could be written on restaurant tables and seating. Anytime there is an apparent difference in the location, configuration or any other aspect of restaurant tables, some of the dining public will perceive some tables as more desirable than others. Such perceptions are well spread by word of mouth and become self-fulfilling, sometimes with ridiculous results.

One of the editors of *Food & Wine* magazine once made reservations for Mary and me at the Russian Tea Room in Manhattan. Naturally, we were given the most sought-after table, which turned out to be one of the two booths actually located in the lobby! Other diners, arriving and departing, stared at us—obviously trying to identify the "celebrities" who had been so honored. For our part, we would have much preferred a quiet table in the main dining room.

Of course, the Russian Tea Room (now being totally revamped) also had a "Siberia"—the second-floor dining room. It is almost inevitable that if a restaurant has more than one room, one will be considered the place to be. All of which can, to say the least, be a major pain for a restaurant's reservation staff and its maître d'. In laying out the dining area of The Lark, care was taken to avoid creating undesirable tables. Nevertheless, there were initially tables "near the kitchen door." This was solved by the design and placement of an elaborate, upholstered, oak-backed banquette. Overnight these two tables for two became most requested instead of most rejected.

With regard to two rooms, The Lark, of course, has two booths in the bar-café in addition to tables and booths in the main dining room. Patrons are of at least four minds on the booths in the bar: some will not consider a booth in the bar; some will not sit anywhere else; some may have a slight preference for one room or the other, but are happy in either; and some don't care in which room they are seated. Not surprisingly, the more successful and notable the patron, the more secure they are and unconcerned over table selection. Given that, we are here to please and an oft-heard phrase from me or whomever is hosting is: "Come with me, and we'll choose a table." This is heresy to other restaurant hosts and is so unusual that many guests cannot believe what they have heard. It is our policy to offer a choice of tables when practical, although there are many reasons it may not be possible on some evenings.

One rather humorous aspect of seating concerns tables for two, which are so located that one person faces the dining room and the other does not, such as the banquette tables near the kitchen door previously described. In the most common situation where the party of two is a man and woman, I will seat the woman on the banquette "with a view of the room" and the man on the chair facing the oak divider "with a view of the lady." When stated that way, it's pretty hard to dispute, but many men do hate to have their backs to the room, and some do insist on the seat with a view of the room. I wonder whether they fear a stab in the back.

Come see us soon, and "we'll choose a table."

Tourtière

My mother was French-Canadian and left a legacy of French-Canadian recipes, The most loved is tourtière, literally a "pie tin," but in Quebec meaning a covered pie made with pork and potatoes. It is traditionally eaten at New Year's. The recipe, that of my grandmother Zoe Joly Gignac, calls for cutting the pork into cubes. Every printed recipe I have seen prescribes ground pork, a modern adaptation which changes the end product for the worse.

> *1 pork butt*
> *2 cups water*
> *1 onion*
> *2 potatoes*
> *salt, pepper and flour*

Cook the pork butt (or other pork) in a covered pot with 2 cups of water until tender and falling away from the bone (about 3 hours).

Cut pork into cubes.

Combine pork, ½ cup of liquid (from cooking) and 2 diced half-cooked potatoes, one diced onion, salt and pepper to taste with a little flour.

Bring to a boil and transfer to a pie plate lined with pastry. Top with pastry and bake at 450 degrees for 15 minutes. Reduce to 350 degrees and bake ½ hour.

Doe's Eat Place

In the good old days, some hunting buddies and I often attended Ducks Unlimited fund-raising dinners and purchased auctioned duck-hunting trips that had been organized and donated by DU members in other states. Most memorable were the two years we hunted near Stuttgart, Arkansas, an area of mixed rice fields, woods, and brush. Our local good-old-boy hosts took us to dinner one night. Like most hunters, they were serious about food and wanted the restaurant chosen to be very good. That ruled out Arkansas, at least in the 1970s, and prompted a drive to the closest acceptable spot, Doe's Eat Place in a creepy area of Greenville, Mississippi. You have to be serious about food to drive to another state for a good meal.

Doe's ambience consisted of old oilcloth-covered kitchen tables and rickety chairs. No wine list here, as it was strictly BYOB. Entrance to the small dining area was through the kitchen where piles of huge steaks, the house specialty, were visible. We began with Doe's famous appetizer—spicy finger-sized tamales—and then proceeded to steak. Having seen the size of them, I asked for the smallest one they had and was served a porterhouse of over two pounds. I should have split a steak with a fellow hunter.

All this was brought to mind by an article on Doe's in *People* magazine. Doe's popularity led the owners to open two additional Eat Places, one of which is on the outskirts of Little Rock, Arkansas. *People*'s interest resulted from that branch's patronage by then President-elect Bill Clinton and his staff. This surprised the hell out of me, as I would have assumed that crowd too yuppy for Doe's, more the fern bar type. Maybe there's hope for the country yet.

Great Britain and Ireland

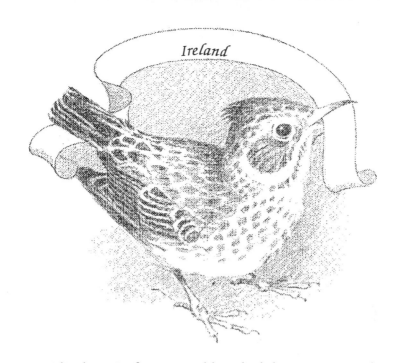

Ireland

*I*t was ridiculous. In fact, it was like a bad dream. Mary and I were seated at lunch in an elegant French restaurant, one of the nation's finest, dressed in jogging suits. Mary's outfit was at least subdued; my flashy Italian number was partly sky blue. The country was Ireland, the city Dublin, the time late November, the place Restaurant Patrick Guilbaud. We were spending a few days in Dublin before driving to western Ireland to join friends for driven-pheasant shooting at Dromoland Castle. Unfortunately, our luggage (including shotguns) did not arrive with us on the Aer Lingus flight from New York. Not their fault; the flight from Detroit was late arriving in New York for the Aer Lingus connection. Our only clothing, therefore, was the comfortable attire worn on the overnight trans-Atlantic flight.

The staff at Patrick Guilbaud were understanding and gracious, and our lunch was superb. A complimentary *amuse-gueule* (cocktail snack) of poached seafood mousse with chive sauce was served with our wine, a 1989 Côte Rôtie Côtes Blonde et Brune of Guigal. In *The Wine Advocate*, Robert Parker describes it as "the best (of recent vin-

277

tages) ... a deeper, more saturated color, fabulously rich fruit, a big perfume of black raspberries and roasted nuts and a rich, corpulent, long finish." Hot appetizers of sautéed king scallops with cèpes, and fresh crabmeat between crispy potato *galettes* were rich enough to stand up to the wine. Main courses were sea bass with trumpets of death (black chanterelles) and truffles for Mary, and wild Wicklow venison with a Hermitage wine sauce for me. A "pain perdue" dessert of crêpes filled with caramelized apple slices with a caramel-vanilla sauce proved a mellow finale to our first meal in Ireland—a hard act to follow. Guilbaud's prominence as a leading restaurant is illustrated by its selection by the House of Roederer Champagne as the site of its "Three Emperors' Dinner" in Ireland, just as The Lark was selected to host that dinner in Michigan.

We had never been to Dublin, our previous visit to Ireland some seventeen years earlier having been confined to the west and south. Based on readings over the years, we had intended to book at Dublin's grand hotel, The Shelbourne, centrally located at one corner of St. Stephen's Green and the subject of a recent $10 million refurbishment. But our long-time travel agent, Jeff Slatkin of Royal International Travel, strongly recommended the Hibernian Hotel. That hostelry was also the choice of travel writer G. Y. Dryansky. Unhappy with value received at The Shelbourne, he "checked out of its Victorian loveliness to move into a converted nurses' dormitory where *le tout* Dublin sends friends these days ... the women at the desk are worthy of a grand hotel and the prices fair." Our suite was one illustrated in the hotel's color brochure, always a good sign, and cost $135 compared with $250 for similar accommodations at The Shelbourne.

The Hibernian is not in the city's center, but this was largely made up for by a convenient, complimentary shuttle service, which took eight or ten minutes to drop us off at St. Stephen's Green. We had been forwarded to lunch at Restaurant Patrick Guilbaud by the Commons Restaurant, which was unable to accommodate us when we arrived without a reservation. You'd think we'd know better, but we were jet-lagged. Having introduced ourselves as proprietors of a small, good restaurant, we were accepted as confrères and passed along from one Dublin fine restaurant to the next. Thus, dinner that evening found us under the wing of Chef-Proprietor Colin O'Daly of Roly's Bistro, Roly being Colin's absent partner Roly Saul. Roly's Bistro was large, lively, and fun. Chef Colin O'Daly, who joined us for a glass of Muscat de Beaumes de Venise and a chat, proved a charming and gracious host. A gratin of penne pasta with smoked salmon and cockles was rich and satisfying. Main courses of black sole and pan-fried Dublin Bay prawns were followed by equally fine desserts—a chilled Irish Mist soufflé in a cookie shell with pineapple ice cream, and a chocolate yule log with a nut bark. It was now obvious that Irish cuisine, at least in the capital city, has taken giant strides forward and justifies a new and better reputation.

As usual on a first visit to a foreign city, we hired a car and driver for an orientation tour. Highlights included Trinity College with its dramatic two-story, long-room library, sixty-five meters long. Built in 1712, it houses more than two hundred thousand of the oldest books. Many fine manuscripts are on display, including the world-famous Book of Kells, a magnificently illuminated Bible dating from around 800 A.D., begun on the Island of Iona and completed at the Monastery of Kells, west of Dublin. We saw much in our drive, too much to report here. Readers planning to visit Dublin are urged to obtain the *Dublin Holiday Guide* from a Tourist Information Office.

The Commons Restaurant, where we had arrived without reservations the previous day, was our choice for lunch. Located in an old building where James Joyce studied on St. Stephen's Green, its fifty seats are much in demand by "serious business lunchers." Our lunch was rather serious—first courses of wild salmon with black trumpet mushrooms and sautéed sea trout with parsley *buerre blanc*. Dessert was a confection of chocolate, warm berries, and sabayon. A postprandial walk in order, we strolled past St. Stephen's Green to Dublin's premier shopping mecca of Grafton Street.

Still happily enmeshed in the Dublin chefs' old-boy network, we proceeded as suggested by Colin O'Daly to dinner at Le Coq Hardi

(The Brave Cock), set in its own imposing building. Inside, patrons are surrounded by an elegant and sophisticated atmosphere of deep carpeting, rich furnishing, and beautiful place settings. We were greeted warmly by Chef-Patron John Howard and his wife, Catherine Howard. John is a founding member of Les Euro Toques, the chefs' organization of Europe, and is past president of the Restaurant Association of Ireland. Like the other fine Dublin restaurants visited, his kitchen is essentially French. Following an *amuse-gueule* of sautéed duck liver, my first course was Coq Hardi Smokies of smoked haddock marbled with tomato, Irish farmhouse cheese and double cream, baked *en cocotte*. Mary's equally toothsome choice was warm Galway oysters with Irish bacon. Her main course of *Le Millefeuille de Saumon Cressonnière*, was a melt-in-your-mouth creation of fresh Irish salmon interleaved with light crispy pastry with a watercress butter sauce. My Le Coq Hardi was a breast of corn-fed chicken filled with potato, wild mushrooms, and special herbs, wrapped in bacon, oven roasted and finished with Irish Whisky sauce. The bacon formed a deliciously thin and crisp crust for the tender chicken and tasty filling. Throwing common sense to the wind (in for a penny, in for a pound), we opted for the dessert Assortment Le Coq Hardi of caramel ice cream, brown bread ice cream, *marquis au chocolat*, champagne torte, and fresh fruit. By now, we were thoroughly in love with Dublin and its fine restaurants.

Irish newspapers, and even those in the United States, had reported a crisis in the Irish government concerning a delay in prosecution of alleged misconduct by a priest and the inappropriate appointment to the Irish Supreme Court of the delaying bureaucrat. The prime minister finally resigned. We were intrigued to see his by-now familiar face in a party ascending the stairs to a private, second-floor room, where he could dine unseen.

Following the advice of the "women at the desk worthy of a grand hotel," we booked a car and driver to explore the Wicklow country south of Dublin on our last day in the area. Assuming we'd be picked up by a nice but unexceptional car, we were surprised to find a Mercedes stretch limo awaiting our departure. "Historic houses and gardens, spectacular scenery, golf, horse riding, drag hunting, rough shooting, and wonderful walks are some of the delights Wicklow has to offer," according to the brochure of Tinakilly Country House & Restaurant, of which more later. Our route took us through Eniskerry, reputed to be one of the most charming villages in Ireland. From there it was only a short drive to the "must see" Powerscourt Estate and Gardens, which has the highest waterfall in the country as well as extensive gardens. My notes describe the nearby residential village of Dalkey and its surrounding area as "like the best parts of Bloomfield Hills, only better," gently rolling and wooded with rustic roads meandering past walled estates. Glendalough is "one of the most picturesque glens of County Wicklow" with ruins of the sixth-century monastery of St. Kevin's, a twelfth-century Reffert Church whose graveyard was the burial place of the O'Toole clan, and the 1600-A.D. Glendalough Abbey, erected for Catholics when the English confiscated the ecclesiastical institutions in Ireland's cities.

Far be it for us to miss a meal, so we now repaired to the Victorian elegance of Tinakilly Country House & Restaurant, which has twenty-nine *en suite* bedrooms filled with antiques in addition to its acclaimed restaurant and wood-paneled, period-furnished public rooms. Tinakilly was built in the 1870s for a Captain Halpin who commanded the ship Great Eastern, which laid the trans-Atlantic telegraph cable. The estate is fittingly nestled in seven acres of grounds that front the Irish Sea. It would be an excellent choice for a few days' stay after a visit to Dublin. Our simple (for us) luncheon began with venison sausage accompanied by green lentils, followed by a fine loin of Irish lamb, and concluded with a Bailey's white chocolate mousse.

Dinner that evening was our last meal in the Dublin area and was (as directed by the Howards of Le Coq Hardi) at King Sitric, "the fish restaurant" located at the East Pier of the nearby fishing village of Howth. We had been charmed by the Irish warmth seventeen years previously. Now, being fellow restaurateurs, we were positively enveloped with hospitality at every eatery, and nowhere more so than by Joan MacManus at King Sitric, where husband Aidan MacManus is chef-proprietor.

The restaurant, which has views of Balscadden Bay, is named after King Sitric III, a Norse king of Dublin who had associations with Howth and was a son-in-law of the famous Irish king, Brian Boru. Seafood is the thing here. Their brochure enticingly recites, "Lobster, sole (as large as you like), salmon, trout, John Dory, bass, turbot, brill, crab...." Our very generous cold appetizer was shaped like a crab with a smoked salmon body covering a mound of lump crabmeat. The creation's claws were large shelled crab claws, and the legs were shelled and chilled Dublin Bay prawns—almost a meal itself. Main courses of lobster thermidor and grilled turbot were accompanied by a very light and flavorful puréed carrots and turnips—much better than it sounds to Americans. The house specialty dessert, Meringue Sitric, combined crisp meringue with ice cream, chocolate sauce, and almonds. The excellent wine accompanying our ultrafresh local seafood was a Pinot d'Alsace from the finest Alsace vintner, Zind Humbrecht. This wine is also featured at The Lark.

Having sacrificed ourselves to two and one-half days of feasting (someone has to do it) in order to furnish this report, Mary and I had failed to frolic at even one of Dublin's famous pubs. Upon hearing this, the cab driver returning us to the Hibernian Hotel from King Sitric volunteered to cease cabbing for the night and accompany us to "the locals'" favorite, The Royal Oak in Donnybrook. He called this a "real pub," as contrasted with tourist pubs, and promised much singing and high times. We would have snapped up this offer in an instant, but that we were driving across Ireland the next morning. Just the fact that the pub was in Donnybrook seemed reason enough to go (or not go?). We hope the next patron to visit Dublin will bend an elbow at The Royal Oak and give us a report.

By now accustomed to travel by Mercedes, I cleverly used a rental car upgrade coupon in the morning and was delivered a Mercedes for the price of a Mercury. A pleasant and surprisingly short two-hour drive brought us across the width of Ireland to Dromoland Castle near Newmarket-on-Fegus. The only recommended stop on the cross-country journey was The National Stud, Ireland being famous for its thoroughbred horses, hunters, jumpers, and so forth.

Dromoland was the seat of the O'Brien clan. In 1543, Morrough Prince of Thomond, Chief of the O'Briens, surrendered his royalty to King Henry VIII and was created by him, Baron of Inchiquin and Earl of Thomond. In 1962, Lord Inchiquin sold the castle to an American, Bernard McDonagh, who renovated the castle and opened it as a resort hotel. In 1987, the same consortium that took over Ashford Castle from the Guinness family purchased Dromoland Castle and built a new wing in harmony with the existing architecture. Dromoland now has seventy-three rooms including six deluxe suites. It is only eight miles (twenty minutes) from Shannon Airport, from which we were to fly home. Activities include its own golf course and tennis courts; hunting for snipe, pheasant and duck; fishing on the property or on the River Shannon for salmon and trout; deep-sea angling one hour away on Ireland's west coast; and horseback riding.

We had requested the same room we had many years ago, number 306, a huge bay-windowed beauty on the right front corner of the second floor. On our previous stay we awoke in the morning to see a large bat outlined by the morning sun behind the draperies. A gillie (fishing guide) arrived with his salmon net and swooped up the errant critter. When we asked what he planned to do with it, he replied, "Oh, sure and I'll let the little darling go outside." Irene Schneider, writing in *Condé Nast Traveler,* apparently had the same room: "We had late afternoon tea in our vast corner room. 'The Beatles once stayed in that room,' we were told. 'All four in two beds?' we asked."

Nostalgia is expensive; our room was about U.S.$375 per day, off-season. Head porter Eeamon Gardiner led us to our room. Eeamon is still fondly remembered by our children from their stay at Dromoland in the 1970s, when he took them under his wing, setting up croquet wickets and otherwise keeping the then youngsters occupied.

We reunited with our annual shooting group at a simple lunch in Dromoland's paneled bar. Present were David E. Davis Jr. of *Automobile* magazine and his wife, Jeannie; writer Jim Ramsey and his wife, Marnie; University of Michigan English professor Charles Eisendrath and his wife, Julia; banker Fred Schroeder of First of Michigan; and P. J. O'Rourke, former editor of *The National Lampoon,* writer for *Rolling Stone* magazine, and best-selling author of *A Parliament of Whores* and other conservative and humorous works. *The New York Times* calls him the "Hunter Thompson of the right."

This group, whose membership is somewhat fluid, has met yearly to shoot in such diverse locales as Wales, Hampshire, South Africa, Botswana, Argentina, and Hungary, as well as Michigan and other parts of the United States. That evening, we motored *en masse* through the fog to MacCloskey's Restaurant, which was rustic, but not a pub. The fixed-price dinner was about forty dollars per person plus drinks, tax, and gratuity. Starters included oak smoked salmon, mussels in a Chablis and cream sauce, and baked vineyard snails with garlic butter. Main courses were grilled salmon or black sole, fillet steak with peppercorn cream sauce, or noisettes of lamb with minted pan jus. Dark chocolate mousse in a Bailey's cream sauce with hazelnut praline and hot blueberries and raspberries with vanilla ice cream were two of the desserts offered.

We awoke the next morning for the first of two days of driven-pheasant shooting plus duck shooting on the grounds of Dromoland Castle. Our booking agent and head huntsman was genial Donald Walshe of Dromoland Game Sports Ltd. Our group had eight guns, seven men plus Jeannie Davis. The other three wives present accompanied their husbands. So other than David and Jeannie Davis, Fred Schroeder, P. J. O'Rourke, and Don Walshe, each "stand" consisted of a gun (husband), his wife, and a loader.

We traveled to the stands for the first drive sitting on bales of hay atop a flat-bed trailer pulled by a tractor. This being Ireland, we were dressed for possible inclement weather in Wellies (Wellington rubber boots) and Barbour or other brands of waxed rainproof outerclothes.

All shotguns were, of course, either side-by-side doubles or over-and-under doubles. I'd brought two over-and-unders—a Beretta Silver Snipe and Browning Citori.

The grounds of Dromoland, mixed rolling fields and woodland with a sizable lake, were reward enough for being outdoors, and the shooting was excellent. There is always plenty of action in driven shooting, but the quality varies tremendously. For example, in a poorly managed shoot, most of the pheasants might flush at the same moment on some drives, or there would be no drives with high birds, or the shooting in general might be too easy. Here, many of the drives were challenging, such as in woods where the pheasants appeared overhead for an instant and were then gone, blocked from sight by trees before and after their brief appearance. Highlights included Fred Schroeder shooting a white pheasant, "a fifty-pound bird," referring to the traditional fine levied on the gun who brought bad luck by shooting a white bird.

285

Both lunch and dinner at Dromoland were a set menu due to the size of our group, with Irish salmon featured that evening. Dromoland has a French chef and a fine kitchen.

We were honored the next day when Lord Inchiquin joined us to shoot. The second day also included a duck shoot in a marshy, lightly timbered part of the estate. We were served a nip of cherry brandy on both days, since as usual in Europe, there was no thought of alcohol and gunpowder not mixing. Shooting accidents are extremely rare in Europe. My personal bag for the two days totaled 101 pheasant and seven duck at an expenditure of 269 shells, or 2 shells per bird.

On our earlier trip to Ireland we lunched one day at Moran's Oyster Cottage, then known as Moran's on the Weir. Two hundred years old and run by the seventh generation of the Moran family, it is ideally situated near Galway Bay for a steady supply of the freshest and best Galway oysters and other bounty from the sea. Moran's appealing ambience is in fact cottagelike, small, and rustic with a thatched roof. On our last visit, we struck up an acquaintance with fellow lunchers, a Texas couple who had purchased ancient Knappogue Castle. As a result, we were surprised to be named the day's lord and lady of the castle at a medieval feast we later attended at Knappogue. Our privileges included control of the wine supply and the opportunity to address a speech to our fellow revelers. We were, therefore, pleased when our last dinner of our current visit in Ireland brought us again to Moran's with all of our group plus Don Walshe. As anticipated, this was one of the simpler yet most enjoyable meals of our trip, featuring excellent mussels with garlic and bread crumbs, Irish smoked salmon, fresh crabmeat, many Galway Bay oysters, and generous pints of lager. Don Walshe bested we Yanks, slurping five dozen oysters, with Davis and O'Rourke tied for second place at four dozen each.

Our seafood feast at Moran's was a perfect tasty and festive finale to a fine time in Ireland. In only six days, Mary and I had surveyed the prime sights of Dublin, looted the shops on Grafton Street, dined at Dublin's best four restaurants, toured the lovely countryside of

Wicklow, unwound at lunch at Tinakilly House, feasted at the best seafood restaurant in the port of Howth, traversed the country from east to west, luxuriated for three nights in one of the finest castle hotels in Ireland, enjoyed some of the best shooting in the world, had the pleasure of meeting Irishmen such as Lord Inchiquin, Don Walshe, and top restaurateurs, and spent quality time with old and new friends of our shooting party. We planned to do this again, perhaps spending part of our time at Mary's ancestral home at Enniskillen.

St. Patrick's Day

St. Patrick's Day is celebrated at The Lark with flair since we have Irish friends and because Mary's mother's family is from Enniskillen. Corned beef and cabbage is absent as this is a German dish, not Irish, introduced to Irish-Americans in New York by both Jewish and gentile German immigrants. We have never seen it offered in Ireland. Instead, the hors d'oeuvre trolley includes smoked Irish salmon, curried duck, and fresh oysters. Dublin Bay prawns (prawns are lobster, not shrimp) is one second-course choice, while such authentic Irish fare as fresh Atlantic salmon, lobster, lamb, and duck are among our main courses. Desserts are also in tune, while Harp Lager, Guinness Stout, and Old Bushmill's flow from the bar. We fly the Irish flag, deck the place in green, have hats for those in the mood, and Irish music for the CD player.

Looking Back

I was exposed to the concept of a man in the kitchen at an early age. My mother, whose French ancestors reached these shores more than three hundred years ago, was a highly proficient cook. Many of her recipes are still followed hungrily by various of her descendants to this day. However, regardless of her obvious skills, she did surrender her stove to my father at least once a month.

Predominantly of German ancestry, he would take all of a late Saturday afternoon to prepare potato pancakes for the whole family. A lot of strenuous grating preceded the main even. As early evening approached, he was ready for all seven of us. Using two large cast-iron skillets, he prepared as many pan-size pancakes as each customer desired.

Much later, when all other appetites had been satisfied, he would prepare his own dinner. The whole family was of one accord as he sat down to enjoy—he had earned it.

*L*arry Hagman, Mary Lark, and I were in the Wallops one late November on driven-pheasant shoots. Hagman, alias J. R. Ewing of *Dallas* fame, enjoyed it so much that he quickly booked to shoot again the next year.

Our well-acquainted group of seven couples, who gathered in London to drive in convoy to the country, were a high-powered mixed bag led by publisher-editor David E. Davis Jr. and included a retired CEO, top ad agency executives, a stock broker, and an ophthalmologist. The required minimum of eight "guns" or shooters was made up of the seven men in the party plus Jeannie Davis, a fine shot. While in London before and after our country sojourn, most stayed at Brown's, while Mary and I were at our favorite, The Connaught, which one authority named the world's best hotel.

Saturday in London included a stop at Holland & Holland purchasing last-minute shooting gear and admiring twenty-thousand-dollar-plus shotguns. Six of our guns used side-by-side shotguns, while I and one other had over-and-unders, all of us having brought our own shotguns from the United States.

The Connaught has a decent but expensive restaurant where I lunched well on partridge and Mary had blood-rare grouse, although she had ordered it medium. It became apparent during the trip that certain game birds, including grouse, woodcock, and snipe, are often cooked rare, no matter how ordered. The young French sommelier of The Connaught was an ignorant, pompous fool. Reception personnel, waiters, valets, maids, and doormen were exceptional. Porters (concierges) were competent, but greedy and needed watching.

A lively group dinner at the Belvedere restaurant Saturday evening was preceded by Sheep Dip brand Scotch, which cleansed us for our Sunday morning departure for the Welsh Marches in a Range Rover, Land Rover, and Mercedes G Wagon, all of which had four-wheel drive.

We broke our journey at the Hare and Hounds for a fine pub lunch of items such as very tasty steak and a mixed grill that included gammon, similar to country ham. The bill for our party of fourteen was less than half the cost of lunch the day before for Mary and me at The Connaught.

Midafternoon found us near Shrewsbury in Shropshire at Whitton Hall, a ridiculously atmospheric country manor in the Georgian style—our base for the next three nights and two days. We were pampered and spoiled by Chris and Gill Halliday, owners of the manor and farm, and by their chef, Sue. All meals were taken in the paneled dining room at the single tables set for fourteen, two at each end and six per side. Breakfast was at 8 A.M., departure for the shoot at 9, and cocktails in the lounge at 7 P.M. before dinner at 8.

Meals at Whitton Hall were excellent—the best of our trip to the west and better than all but a few spots in London. Full English breakfasts included superior bacon, bangers, eggs, cold ham, cereals, fruit, juice, toast, scones, coffee, and tea. Main dinner courses were roast pork, partridge, and roast beef, preceded by a hot appetizer, soup and salad, Blue Cheddar, Blue Shropshire, and other cheeses, and desserts such as *crème caramel* and lemon tart.

While we lodged at Whitton Hall, actual shooting was some

twenty-five minutes away across the border in Wales on the estate of the Earl of Powis. The owner and operator of the shoot is John Ransford, one of the most efficient people I have ever met, who leases ten thousand acres from the Earl and raises eighty thousand pheasant for the shoots he manages from the end of October until February 1.

The required number of guns for most shoots is eight, with each gun having a man assigned as loader. Birds are driven from cover by beaters. After gathering in front of Powis Castle, John Ransford assigned a loader to each gun. Since I had never done this before, I requested a loader with a sense of humor and was laughingly assigned twenty-three-year-old Neal Wainwright, himself a head gamekeeper on a much smaller nearby estate. There were six drives each day, four before lunch and two after. Initial shooting positions or "pegs" were assigned by drawing numbers from one to eight. Shooters moved up two numbers for each subsequent drive—the obvious origin of the phrase "to move up a peg." The English would consider the average shooting opportunity at pheasant in America as very easy. There, the goal is to have the birds flying over the shooters at the greatest possible height and speed. We later estimated that an average of four or five shells were expended for each bird bagged.

After a nervous start, I settled into my normal pattern—mediocre to quite good and average on the average, but did bag the first woodcock, greatly appreciated in Britain.

A simple but good lunch at Powis Castle was preceded by a drinks table offering sherry, table wines, beer, whisky, gin, and soft drinks—quite a contrast to the United States, where "alcohol and gunpowder don't mix." The obvious assumption was that shooters were adults and would behave as such. In fact, at a later shoot in Hampshire, sloe gin was offered between drives.

Our bag for the first day was 307. One of my pegs on the second day, when 327 birds and one hare were shot, was immediately adjacent to Offa's Dyke, the ancient demarcation between England and Wales. Lunch was at the Cottage Inn in Montgomery. We learned that all game shot, which belonged to John Ransford, not the shooters, was shipped in refrigerated trucks each Sunday to Runliss Market outside Paris, chilled to thirty-four degrees, not gutted, and in full plumage in boxes of twelve cocks or twelve hens.

Wednesday was a travel day for our move from Wales to our second shooting area in Hampshire in southern England, and it was fortunate we were not shooting since the day produced driving rain in a force-nine gale. Nevertheless, we made the obligatory stop on the Salisbury Plains to view Stonehenge—quite appropriate in the gloom, wind, and rain.

Our lodgings for the next three nights and two days were at Lainston House at Sparsholt near Winchester, a hotel in a very grand former manor, but less charming and with not as good cuisine as Whitton Hall. This is the area of Nether Wallop, a village, and the other Wallops, the setting for the rabbit-peopled book *Watership Down*. It is also the location of the finest chalk trout streams—the Test and Itchen. John and Anthea Russell, our guides in Hampshire and the local Orvis dealers, lived in a former mill on Wallop Brook, a tributary of the Test.

Thursday's shoot at Lockerly Hall Estate resulted in a bag of 293 birds and a fine lunch in their manor house featuring the very best shepherd's pie. Eric Trigg, my charming loader, said I had dropped a couple clankers, or missed a few easy shots, but made up for the remark by giving Mary a horseshoe from the "fourteen-eighteen war."

Our last day's shooting on Friday was at Cholderton Estate, which had a fine period gun room and where we enjoyed game pie at lunch. My own shooting ended on a high note this day. Our group's day total of 352 birds made a four-day bag of 1,279. These last two estates were those shot by Larry Hagman.

London was a short hour-and-one-quarter drive Saturday morning. Mary and I had a lunch of pheasant and snipe at The Marquis near The Connaught and rejoined our shooting party that evening for a farewell dinner at the St. James Club, highlighted by superb prawns and the excellent company to which we had become accustomed, as our group included world-class raconteurs and men who were more amusing than any professional comedian. For the payment on my part of eleven pounds, the CEO sang a touching version of the "Hawaiian Wedding Song," while an award was made on behalf of a chief operating officer who had bagged a pheasant that smashed into a car, dropped another that fell on his wife, and finally shot me in the ear with a stray but weak pellet.

Mary and I remained in London for four more days. Dining high-lights were the reputed best Chinese restaurant, Zen, not as good as our best; Bombay Brasserie, which some say is the best Indian, although Raj may have better food albeit less glitz; La Gavroche, which competes with Le Tante Claire for best French restaurant; Le Suquet, a French seafood restaurant where we were taken by Robert and Sandy Lacey, he being the author of *Ford: The Men and the Machine.* Le Suquet was not only very "in" (we waited to 10:30 for a table), but had excellent food—especially a stunning, fresh, and delicious *plateau de fruits de mer* of prawns, sea urchins, oysters, crab, whelks, snails, mus-sels, cockles, periwinkles, and more—even better than La Coupole's similar presentation in Paris.

Harrod's with its awesome food halls remains the top London department store, far outpacing faded Fortnum and Masons. Antique fairs are held at various locales each Sunday. There were excellent buys at the Park Lane Hotel's three-level event. Other worthwhile London activities were the Hogarth and Turner shows at the Tate Museum and general exploration in what many consider the best of cities. While anyone would enjoy London, our lasting memory will be of our unmatched country experience.

On Hunting

Ernest Hemingway said driven-pheasant shooting (which we've done in England, Wales, Ireland, and Hungary) is worth whatever it costs. There is, of course, much anti-hunting sentiment about these days, reinforced by the boorish behavior of many deer hunters whose activities resemble true hunting about as much as a shopping list does Shakespeare. Almost everything worthwhile pro- and anti-hunting was written by the Spanish existentialist philosopher Ortega y Gasset in his book *On Hunting.* He convincingly asserts that all the glory of civilization initially derives from the associations and rituals of hunting.

In *Zen and the Art of Hunting,* author Randall L. Eaton muses, "The people who most love roses, who spend hours pruning them, kill them; the people who most love vegetables are those who grow, kill and eat them; the men who most love waterfowl, who adorn their den walls with paintings of ducks and geese, who study and observe them for decades, who invest in their habitat and protection, also kill and eat them. Not much different than the hunting peoples whose myths, songs, art, adornments, dance and language imitate and celebrate the sacred animals they kill. This is paradoxical only to the men and women who live from the head, suffering from centuries of separation from Nature and thus their true nature."

Euell Gibbons said it a little differently in *Stalking the Wild Asparagus:* "Man simply must feel that he is more than a mere mechanical part in this intricately interdependent industrial system. We enjoy the comfort and plenty which this highly organized production and distribution has brought us, but don't we sometimes feel that we are living in a secondhand sort of existence, and that we are in danger of losing all contact with the origins of life and the nature which nourishes it?"

What is the effect of hunting on the individual? Statistics show significantly fewer crimes of violence by hunters than nonhunters. Relatively few homicides are the work of hunters. Consider Michigan's most noted authors. Non-hunters Elmore Leonard, Loren Estelman, and William Kienzle are obsessed with violence, while hunters Tom McGuane, Robert Traver, and Jim Harrison are philosophical. Man has been a hunter for millennia, but has relied on others to provide his meat only in the last few "seconds" of human existence. Ortega y Gasset blames most of the ills of mankind on this frustration of our essential nature. The Roman Colosseum did not prove an adequate substitute. Neither are the Silverdome nor Joe Louis Arena.

I wasn't happy about President Clinton in any event, and now he'd stolen my suite at Dromoland Castle. Mary and I were booked to shoot driven pheasant and mallard duck on the castle's grounds and the adjoining land retained by Lord Inchiquin. We'd done this the year before, staying in the castle's best suite, where we had also lodged seventeen years previously on our first visit to Ireland. This same suite was assigned to the Beatles and lately to visiting travel writers. When I faxed a request to reserve this huge bay-windowed beauty on the front corner of the second floor, Dromoland informed us that the entire castle had been preempted by the Irish government. We subsequently learned that it was reserved for President Clinton and party. Presumably, he and the first lady would be honored with number 306—the "Inchiquin Stateroom," named for the castle's former noble residents. The irony is that our alternative booking was to stay with the present Lord Inchiquin at Thomond House, his present seat as the eighteenth Baron Inchiquin.

On our expedition a year earlier, Mary and I had flown to Dublin and savored that city's best restaurants and toured the Wicklow country south of Dublin before driving west across Ireland to Dromoland, a mere two-hour jaunt. On this trip, our plan was to again fly to Dublin, pick up a rental car at the airport, and drive to the lake area of Northern Ireland to search out Mary's maternal Irish roots before proceeding on to Dromoland. Three days before our departure, a disquieting thought came to me in the middle of the night—I was planning to bring my two shotguns across the border from the Irish Republic into Northern Ireland. I had accomplished the required red tape to bring my double-bore Browning and Beretta into the republic, but had no permission whatsoever to bring them across the border to the violent north. A call to the Northern Ireland Tourist Office in New York elicited the hope that maybe my permit from the Irish government would suffice. I decided to cross that border when I came to it.

After an uneventful flight, there were no Mercedes available for free upgrade, but we did receive a Volvo Estate Wagon at no surcharge over our midsize reservation. An hour-and-a-half drive brought us to the border on a deserted two-lane road, where a sign announced "Checkpoint Ahead." It was a chilling sight. A remote-controlled traffic signal could either direct a vehicle to continue on the road without stopping, or to pull off into a paved inspection area. This out-of-the-way scene was overlooked by an observation tower. It did not take much imagination to guess the origin and purpose of the layout. At the beginning of the current troubles, there was a great risk that the occupants of a car stopped for clearance at the border might shoot the British soldier on duty. The solution: Put the soldier some distance away in a tower where he could study the car with binoculars and decide whether to let it proceed or pull it over for investigation. All the while, of course, the car was at the mercy of weapons trained on it from the tower. Because of the truce in effect, the checkpoint was unmanned and the traffic light on permanent green. Throughout our time in the north, we crossed and recrossed the border at will, often not knowing whether we were in Northern Ireland or the Republic. Everyone in Northern Ireland was jubilant about "the truce" and looked forward to more American tourists, whom the Irish sincerely love.

Our destination was the ancient town of Enniskillen in County Fermanagh, from which Mary's mother's family migrated to the Upper Mississippi Valley. This was perhaps no coincidence, since both regions boast dramatic hills and cliffs overlooking wide expanses of water. The largest stretch of water in the Fermanagh lakeland is Lough Erne, separated into Upper and Lower Lough Erne by an island on which Enniskillen is situated.

Our lodgings on the Upper Lough, one click south of town, was the Killyhevlin Hotel, simple but adequate, and with three stars, the best in the area. We enjoyed fine views from our suite over the Lough. Typical in Ireland, the staff's attitude was great, with an earnest and sincere desire to be helpful. As in most of Europe, the choicest selection of Irish country hotels and inns are the members of Relais & Chateaux, such as Dromoland Castle, Ashford Castle, Newport House, and Cashel House Hotel. But probably because of the fear of violence and that fear's effect on tourism, there are as yet no Relais & Chateaux in the north.

Enniskillen is the best headquarters for touring or fishing Northern Ireland's lake region, arguably the most scenic inland area of Ireland. Enniskillen itself is notable as the home of the Royal Inniskilling Dragoons and Fusiliers, two famous regiments that originated during the Williamite wars, which finalized England's conquest of Ireland. After a simple lunch, we toured the fifteenth-century Enniskillen Castle and the regimental museum of the merged regiments, which fought at Waterloo, in India, both World Wars, and most other major conflicts of the British Empire before being disbanded a few years ago. It has a well-staged display of ceremonial silver, porcelain, medals, weapons, colors, and uniforms.

As in much of Ireland, the countryside is littered with things to do and places to see. Readily available sporting activities include fishing for brown trout in the many lakes and rivers; walk-up shooting for pheasant, partridge, and woodcock; horseback riding; golf and tennis. Some of the sights in the area (other than the beautiful rolling country-side of high hills, forests, fields, lakes, and streams) are the Irish Kitchen Museum; Florence Court, a Palladian mansion and one of their most important houses in Ulster; and Castle Coole, the finest neoclassical house in Ireland. Mary and I drove west of Enniskillen on a very personal pilgrimage to St. Patrick's Church in Derrydonnaly, where Mary's great-grandparents, Hugh Leonard and Catherine Boland, were married. Highlights of dinner that evening at Killyhevlin included a very generous serving of Irish smoked salmon, steamed mussels, and duckling with apple and apricot stuffing. We were amazed and pleased to be able to order the 1990 Brunello di Montalcino from Castello Banfi, *Wine Spectator*'s "Editor's Choice" for the best Italian wine of the year. And yes, you may order it at The Lark.

We drove next morning along the south shore of Lower Lough Erne, an object of constant beauty with 154 islands and scores of old manor houses and castles. But our goal was more important than sight-seeing—we were off to shop for "stuff." At its western end, Lough Erne becomes a river flowing west past the village of Belleek before entering Donegal Bay at Ballyshannon. (What a great collection of Irish names in one sentence!) Belleek is, obviously, the site of famous Belleek Pottery. The pottery and salesroom are located on the bank of the River Erne in Northern Ireland—the other bank across a small bridge is in the Irish Republic. Belleek fine Parian china has been made in this small village since 1857. Any piece that is not perfect is destroyed, and Belleek is treasured by collectors the world over. It being very off-season, we were treated to a private tour of the pottery works, chatting with the craftsmen who must serve a five-year apprenticeship. There is no production line. Each piece is pampered through its various stages by one proud workman. A museum houses some of the oldest pieces of Belleek, including a magnificent centerpiece that won the gold medal at the 1890 Paris Exhibition and helped make the pottery's reputation. The statues, boxes, bowls, and other pieces we purchased arrived some weeks later in perfect condition.

Driving to the remote and lightly populated beautiful Donegal coast, we were saddened to find our luncheon destination, the locally famous Smugglers Inn near Rossnowlagh, closed on Tuesday. Not to worry, we had a well-sauced smoked haddock and Irish stew at The

Embers Restaurant above Paddy Donagher's Bar in Ballyshannon.

Meandering back toward Enniskillen along the north shore of Lough Erne, we cut across Boa Island, one of the larger islands from which Mary's great-grandmother had come to America in the mid-1800s. We stopped to explore an ancient cemetery, hoping but failing to find tombstones to any Bolands, but did note several stone figures with two faces. They were famous stone-age Janus relics reproduced in many books and on post cards, sitting unguarded for anyone to vandalize or steal.

We had now heard the great news on the "telly"—that Irish peace talks were afoot and that President Clinton was actually coming to Ireland. This was a "scoop" that we had known for weeks because of the problem booking our suite at Dromoland Castle. The Irish love Americans and any American president is ranked right up there, just below God. We prayed that peace talks would finally succeed. Unfortunately, the truce was broken some months later and the Killyhevlin Hotel at which we were staying was bombed by the IRA.

With a couple more days free before our shoot at Dromoland, we motored off the next morning to the nearby Cliffs of Magho Viewpoint in the Lough Navar Forest, with views of Lower Lough Erne and the Blue Stack Mountains of Donegal in the distance. Our next stop was the Connemara Coast Hotel on the north shore of Galway Bay, west of Galway City.

Michelin says of this hotel, "Connemara is a wild and beautiful region of mountains, lakes, tumbling streams, undulating bog, sea-grit promontories, unspoiled beaches and panoramic views. It is a Gaelic-speaking region and has attracted many artisans."

The Connemara Coast is a four-star hotel with an ultrascenic setting on Galway Bay and fine views from our digs up and down the coast. One feature, unique to our suite, was a real peat-burning fireplace. Our dinner at the hotel was the finest of our trip to date. Mary's baked Galway oysters with garlic and bread crumbs were followed by mixed seafood in phyllo over a sea urchin sauce. I began with oak-smoked Irish salmon and then a main course of roast leg of lamb with lamb jus.

We headed west the next morning, exploring the coast before cutting across eerie uninhabited peat bogs to strike the coast again farther north at Cashel Bay. Cashel House Hotel, a Relais & Châteaux member, stands in a fifty-acre, award-winning garden at the head of Cashel Bay with its own private beach. Rooms and suites are tastefully decorated, and the bar and grill where we lunched was especially appealing with luxurious dark leather chairs and sofas, a fine wood bar, and deep-colored terra-cotta walls.

On calling to inquire if lunch were available in this off-season, we were warned to only expect sandwiches and the like. Wrong! Mary again ordered Galway oysters, this time with a shallot vinaigrette, followed by a very generous smoked salmon platter. I had house-made duck terrine and a grilled one-and-one-half-pound lobster. Our wine was the 1989 Ch. Trimoulet. Service and food were excellent; the wine serviceable. Dinner choices ranged from a casserole of rabbit with apples and artichokes to poached fresh turbot with Dugléré sauce. The house special is live Connemara lobster from their tank, grilled or poached. We were extremely impressed by Cashel House, which is actually an elegant country inn, not a hotel. We had chosen the Connemara Coast Hotel because of its central location, but if we had to do it again, we'd choose the isolated Cashel House. This would be a great spot for a honeymoon or for anyone who just wanted to get away from it all.

Just before our trip, I read *Irish Gold* by Andrew Greeley, a historical novel of the "Troubles" in Ireland from 1919 to 1922, much of the action being set in the Connemara area we covered this day, such as Maam Cross near the peat bogs we traversed. I had passed the book along to Mary, who read it during our trip to her immense pleasure and increased appreciation of our journey. For a great adventure, go to Ireland, stay at all the Relais & Châteaux, add Northern Ireland's most picturesque counties before the rush of tourists who are bound to come, and read *Irish Gold* while you're doing it.

This evening, we dined down the coast at the highly recommended Boluisce Seafood Restaurant in Au Spideal. Breaking tradition, we had the same starter, baked Galway Bay oysters with herb butter. Mary followed with the "West Coast Platter" of lobster, large crab claws, prawns, mussels, oysters, and Irish salmon over rice with a "thermidor" sauce. My platter boasted scallops with roe, mussels, and shrimp. This fine local seafood was impeccably fresh and well prepared. Our wine was a superb 1994 Chablis Premier Cru Fourchaume. Having, as usual, presented my card and thus been accepted as one "in the trade," we were lavished with attention. The Irish tend to lavish all Yanks with attention, and when that is added to professional courtesy because one also has a restaurant, the result is overwhelming. But then, as I often say, "I love to be fawned on." Here this included complimentary sloe poteen, homemade sloeberry brandy.

Following President Clinton's progress on the telly, he was in Belfast this day and had canceled his plan to relax and golf at Dromoland after solving the Irish problem. This news brought mixed emotions, mostly disappointment because we knew everyone in the area of the castle was looking forward to a visit of an American president. On the other hand, we would not be forbidden to have one of the best pheasant drives—the one with a long broad lawn facing a woods in front of Dromoland. Also, we'd have our favorite suite. Interestingly, the president's bodyguards had been required to obtain a permit to bring their firearms to Belfast, while I drove around Northern Ireland with two shotguns and no permit at all at all. The "at all at all" is deliberate. The Irish talk that way.

'Twas off to Dromoland the next morning, stopping to shop and lunch in Galway City on the way. Mary found some good old prints and maps at Kenny's Bookshop and Art Gallery. Lunch at DeBurgos was merely okay. While Mary frittered money away on prints and maps, I found the 1989 Ch. Lynch Bages (my favorite red Bordeaux) in a shop for a mere £29.50 (U.S.$47.50) per bottle and bought two. I pointed out to the proprietor his price was well below the wholesale price, and he replied the Irish hated to pay more than £10 for a bottle of wine.

Arriving at Dromoland we were reunited with our shooting group led by David E. Davis Jr. and his wife, Jeanne. Other members were Jim Ramsey and his wife, Marnie; professor Charles Eisendrath and his wife, Julia; Fred Schroeder; Ham Schirmer and his wife, Weezie; Joe Frey and his wife, Karen; Hunters Creek Club proprietor Preston Mann and his wife, Maryann; and P. J. O'Rourke and his new bride, Tina. P. J. was a commentator on *60 Minutes,* balancing another new *60 Minutes* participant, ultraliberal columnist Molly Ivins. Anyone who knows this strange cast of characters can imagine what a time was had by all.

Most of the group had driven all the way to Ashford Castle for lunch and were now determined to retrace a good portion of their journey to have dinner at Moran's Oyster Cottage, just south of Galway. Mary and I love Moran's and its local seafood—especially the Galway Bay oysters from its own oyster beds—but begged off what would also be a retracing of our day's journey. Instead we joined P. J. and Tina for dinner at Dromoland. Mary began with crab and avocado in pastry, while I savored a superb *feuilleton* of lamb kidneys and sweetbreads. Our main courses were rack of lamb for Mary and my pan-sautéed breast-of-duck and leg-and-thigh *confit.* We chose ice cream and sorbets for dessert as the only other choices in Ireland resemble mush in one form or another, either some form of cream or mousse.

As noted earlier, "the group" had shot driven pheasant and mallard duck the previous year at Dromoland, enjoying it so much we rebooked. Drives are conducted on the Dromoland Estate and the adjoining land of Lord Inchiquin, who had shot with us the prior year. Each of our two days of shooting consisted of five drives, three before lunch and two after. In two days, our ten guns (the men plus Jeannie Davis and Marnie Ramsey) bagged 1 woodcock, 1,010 pheasant, and 98 mallards. My totals were 80 pheasant and 30 duck.

Our farewell dinner Saturday evening was hosted by Lady Inchiquin at Thomond House, where most of our party were lodged. We are all looking forward to other European shooting adventures.

Sun-Dried Plums

First there were sun-dried tomatoes from Italy. Then sun-dried Michigan cherries and blueberries, and the sun-dried cranberries that are often included in one of our salad offerings.

A main course sometimes offered on our menu is Chinese-Oven Crisp-Roasted Honey-Glazed Duckling with Sun-Dried Plums in Armagnac. The description is so mouth-watering that it is one of our most-ordered dishes. Thank God it tastes as good as it sounds, being perhaps the finest duck preparation extant. Oddly enough, very few patrons have gotten the joke—that sun-dried plums are prunes. Prunes are extremely popular in French cuisine, especially in desserts and as an accompaniment to poultry. We have long wished to pair them with duck, but the word prune would be the kiss of death because of its geriatric connotation in this country. However, we can attest that sun-dried plums have tremendous appeal.

After-Dinner Wines

Appropriate after-dinner and dessert wines, long out of favor, have regained popularity as the perfect ending to a fine repast. One choice is late-bottled vintage Porto in convenient half-bottles. Until this development, it had not been practical to offer vintage Porto since there is little demand for full bottles at a restaurant. Porto has a short life after being opened, and sediment makes it impractical for use in a

Cruvinet wine system. Late-bottled vintage Porto is left to mature in the cask and is only bottled shortly before shipment, almost eliminating sediment in the bottle. This lack of sediment and the half-bottle size make it perfect for restaurant service.

Other after-dinner wines such as German Beerenauslese, Italian Torcalato Maculan, and French Sauternes have long been available in half-bottles—a convenient size for service to one table. Fine Madeira is just beginning its resurgence, and we predict that the first distributor to make it available in half-bottles will score a coup.

*M*ary and I and six other couples returned to Britain in November for our second annual country-house party and dri-ven-pheasant shoot. Proving you can go home again, it was even more fun than the previous year.

We gathered in London on a Saturday and shopped for miscella-neous shooting gear at both Holland & Holland and Purdy's. Although these are the world's two foremost shotgun makers, no guns were purchased as they cost as much as $115,000 each and delivery takes up to three years.

Our pub lunch at the Audley was highlighted by the ploughman's plate, which included excellent cheddar and Stilton cheese, fruit, sal-ads and bread. A set dinner that evening at Rowley's began with a choice of a mixed or "Mexican" salad and proceeded to sliced rump steak with garlic sauce, *frites,* and a dessert trolley.

Our new London hotel on this trip was The Capital near Harrod's department store. A Ralph Lauren-decorated suite of living room, bedroom, and bath and a half was about $375 per day compared with the $700 we had paid at The Connaught. In addition to being a relative bargain, the staff of The Capital were free of the pomposity found at The Connaught. Most of our fellow travelers stayed at Brown's where double rooms (none are the same) ran from about $250 to $325. We feel safe in recommending a suite at The Capital (simple double rooms were small) or a room or suite at Brown's. Once again, one of our favorite restaurants was the French seafood bistro Le Suquet, which has a wonderful *plateau de fruits de mer*, a cold seafood assortment of oysters, prawns, mussels, crab, peri-winkles, cockles, and much more.

On Sunday we motored to "The North" in a fleet corralled by our leader, David E. Davis Jr., which consisted of a Mitsubishi Montero, Land Rover, Volvo sedan, and Ford Scorpio, all of which performed faithfully. On our drive north the previous year, Jeannie Davis selected The Hare and Hounds near Shrewsbury as our lun-cheon stop because their parking lot was so full. Keeping in mind the old adage "If it ain't broke, don't fix it," we again stopped at The Hare and Hounds and were greeted like long-lost friends by the pub-lican who remembered us from our prior visit. Gammon (country ham steak) and porterhouse steak were both excellent.

As in the previous year, our lodgings were the atmospheric coun-try house, Whitton Hall at Westbury, between Shrewsbury and the Welsh border. Our hosts, Gill and Christopher Halliday, are both charming and efficient. Sue, their chef, provided some of the best food of our entire stay in Britain. John Ransford, who leases vast stretches of land from the Earl of Powis in nearby Wales, managed our shoot to perfection. Our bag for eight guns—the seven men plus Jeannie—totaled more than 350 birds per day, plus one red fox. Local foxes have killed as many as 500 pheasants for pleasure in one night.

All birds shot are shipped to the Paris market since "the French will eat anything." John Ransford also manages grouse moors in Northumberland in northern England and reported a tremendous resurgence in the number of grouse. This was apparently not so in

Scotland since the Scots, "a mean people," had overshot their moors and not hired enough keepers. The opinions quoted are not those of this writer.

The required number of guns for most shoots is seven or eight with each gun having a man assigned as loader. Birds are driven from cover by beaters. Everyone appears to be in costume, but actually the period clothing and gear are dictated by utility as much as custom and are perfectly suited to weather (often cold and rainy) and to each participant's activity. Shooters wear rubber Wellington boots, knickers or trousers stuffed into the boots, shirts, ties, Norfolk jackets, and Barbour brand rain gear when necessary. Loaders wear Wellingtons, knickers, and rain jackets. Beaters appear to be ragged escapees from a Tom Jones movie set. Picker-uppers with Labrador retrievers and spaniels may be additional employees or volunteer sportsmen seeking practice for their dogs.

The combination of unique characters, wonderful costumes, colorful game, working dogs, and the activity itself—all in an other-worldly country setting—combine to produce an experience that would be a highlight of the most jaded life and proves Hemingway correct in saying it is worth whatever it costs. We hope we can afford to return again.

Shooting in Britain is even better later in the season and continues for several months. In addition to driven shooting for pheasant, partridge or grouse, walk-up shoots with bags of up to sixty birds per day per gun can be arranged by John Ransford.

Rack of Lamb Genghis Khan

Time was when almost every good restaurant had a signature dish—a specialty for which it was known. Today in contrast, the specialty at some establishments is different at the end of the evening from at the beginning. The antithesis of this feverish approach must be the pressed duck served since at least 1890 at La Tour d'Argent in Paris. After the meal, guests are presented with a card showing the number of the duck they have eaten. By 1996 the count had passed 842,000. Many years ago we had pressed duck at Hector's, a French restaurant in Caracas, Venezuela, and were given a similar numbered card. The specialty of L'Oustau de Baumaniere, the Michelin-starred restaurant at Les-Baux-de-Provence, is *gigot d'agneau en croûte*, a tiny leg of lamb in pastry, and patrons ordering the dish are presented with a numbered card that includes the recipe.

Our house specialty, Rack of Lamb Genghis Khan, has appeared on every menu since we opened June 2, 1981. Partly for fun with tongue in cheek and partly out of respect for tradition, we researched the number of racks served since our opening and began presenting a numbered card, complete with recipe, to our guests who order this most popular main course. By mid 1996, more than thirty-five thousand racks had been served, having been ordered by more than one in six of the 220,000 patrons of The Lark to that date.

Rack of Lamb Genghis Khan

3 lamb racks (8 ribs each) trimmed and silverskin removed
1 cup hoisin sauce
Lamb marinade

Place the lamb and marinade in a plastic bag, tie, and place in refrigerator for 48 hours, turning occasionally. Remove lamb from marinade and let stand at room temperature 1 hour before cooking. Brush with hoisin sauce. Place lamb on rack in shallow roasting pan and roast in hot oven, 450 degrees, for 15 to 25 minutes for rare lamb, depending on the size of the racks, or longer for a greater degree of doneness. Let rest for 6-7 minutes before carving. Yields 6.

Lamb Marinade
> *1 cup onions, finely chopped*
> *2 tablespoons garlic, minced*
> *3 tablespoons lemon juice*
> *¼ cup honey*
> *3 tablespooons curry powder*
> *1¼ teaspoons cayenne pepper, ground*
> *2 teaspoons Coleman's mustard powder*
> *2 teaspoons black pepper, ground*
> *2 tablespoons salt*
> *1 cup water*
> *combine all ingredients*

It might be assumed that the great success of a restaurant would inspire feelings of contentment and peace in its proprietor. Not so, said Sirio Maccioni, owner of New York's top-rated Le Cirque, in a *Regent* magazine profile. He knows the envious wish him ill, and he views them as animals hoping he will fall. "Running this show ... is like being Daniel in the Lion's Den. And I'm determined not to be eaten." I couldn't have said it better.